To David
Best Wishes

Carl **Fogarty**

Other books by this author:

WORLD SUPERBIKES
The first ten years

HONDA'S V-FORCE
The four-stroke V4s on road and track

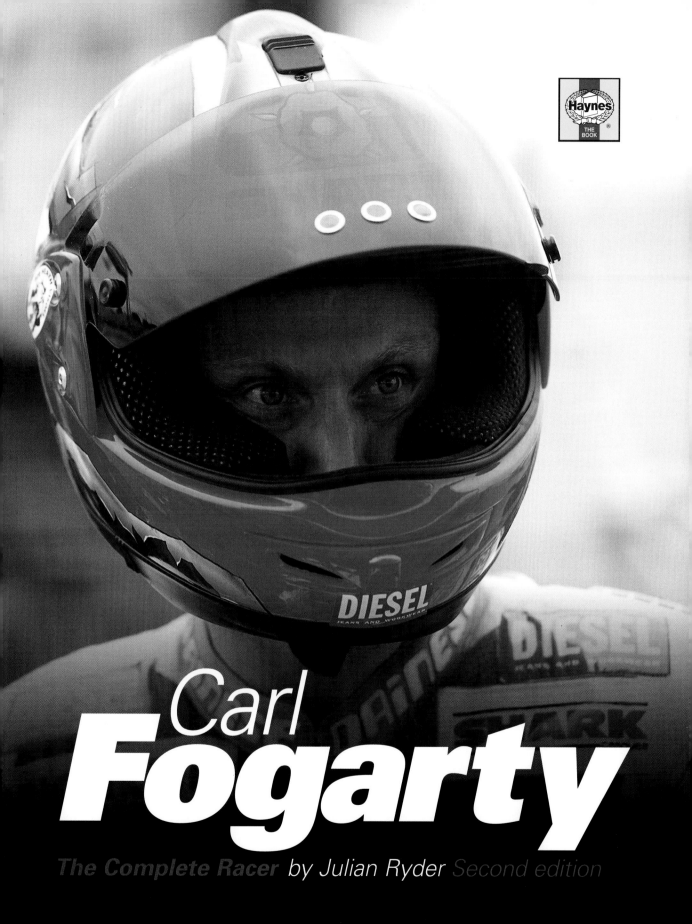

Carl
Fogarty

The Complete Racer by Julian Ryder *Second edition*

First published by Patrick Stephens Limited in 1996
Second edition published by Haynes Publishing in November 1999

British Library Cataloguing in Publication Data:
A catalogue record for this book is available from the British Library

ISBN 1 85960 641 5

Library of Congress catalog card no. 99-72049

Haynes Publishing, Sparkford, Nr Yeovil, Somerset, BA22 7JJ.
Tel: 01963 440635 Fax: 01963 440001
Int. tel: +44 1963 440635 Fax: +44 1963 440001
E-mail: sales@haynes-manuals.co.uk
Web site: www.haynes.co.uk

Haynes North America, Inc.
861 Lawrence Drive, Newbury Park,
California 91320, USA

Photograph previous page: Kel Edge

Typeset by J H Haynes & Co. Ltd.
Printed and bound by Imprimerie Pollina s.a., Luçon, France n° 78439

Contents

Introduction

Brands Hatch, August 1999: Michaela Fogarty is puzzled, she can't understand why anyone would want her autograph. On reflection, she decides that it's probably because she is usually the nearest anyone can get to Carl. She is right, in more than one way. With over 120,000 people crammed into the Kent track, Foggy is a prisoner in his motorhome; even getting to the hotel at the circuit entrance is impossible, so he sleeps in the paddock the night before the race. The biggest single-day crowd of the year at a UK sporting event is heaping expectation on Carl's shoulders, and on race day morning Michaela wonders aloud what would be a bad result. 'Two seconds,' is the instant response.

As usual, the whole Fogarty family has been working up to the event. Carl's mood always swings days before a race, but for home races the tension creeps in weeks earlier. Never a patient man, he becomes positively intolerant as he thinks ahead to the next start. Writing in *The Mail on Sunday*'s magazine, Steve Tooze noted that interviewing Carl the week before a race was a strange experience because most of his consciousness was already at the track running through the race that was yet to happen.

If he didn't win last time out he will also have been mulling over what went wrong, dwelling on every detail for the weeks that separate rounds of the World Superbike Championship. Those laser eyes transfix anyone who irritates him, although Michaela doesn't seem to be seriously affected and elder daughter Danielle is wonderfully, obliviously immune to the sort of stare that vaporises normal human beings. She is not immune to daddy losing, though. Carl's first victory during his troubled year with Honda came after Danielle told her dad that she didn't like him losing, and she was in tears after Brands – and not, you suspect, simply because Carl was going to be about as pleasant to live with as a bear with brainache for the foreseeable future. The will to win is obviously in the Fogarty genes.

The lot of a racer's wife is not an easy one, but Michaela knew exactly what she was getting into, that she would have to be selfless, take a lot of flak and rarely if ever hear the word 'sorry'. She's known Carl and his family since she was a school friend of Carl's sister and was only too well aware that motorcycle racing was his one and only ambition. What neither she nor Carl could have imagined even in their most optimistic dreams was exactly what motorcycle racing would bring them. Four World

Superbike Championships mean that Carl now commands a basic annual fee of well over £1 million and adds considerably to that basic salary with riding equipment endorsements and personal sponsorship. He is one of the highest-profile, highest-earning sportsmen in the UK, a hero in Italy where the media call him Lionheart, and now gets recognised even in countries like the USA where Superbike racing is nowhere near as popular. Suzuki had offered him over £2 million for 2000 well before the end of the 1999 season.

All the trimmings of success are in place: the beautiful house in a desirable part of the world complete with Porsche 911 – registration plate FOG 1E – in the drive, frequent travel by helicopter, and kids at prep school. But there's one crucial deviation from the celebrity norm: all this is in Blackburn. While his competitors reside in tax havens like Monte Carlo alongside the glitterati of Formula 1 and other high-profile sports, Carl still lives in the town in which he was born and brought up, and he always will. There is nothing flash about the Fogartys; sure, the house and the cars are paid for, but the rest of the money is safe in long-term investments. 'Put away,' as Michaela succinctly describes it. They still know the value of a pound; when they fly off on holiday it'll be on bargain tickets from a bucket shop just like most of his fans.

Carl has few close friends, none in the Superbike paddock now that James Whitham has left the class, and all of them have been close since school days. The parallels with multiple 500cc GP champion Mick Doohan are obvious; neither can be friends with the men they have to beat, as it might distract them from the only thing that matters – winning. Both champions also manage to look a lot older at the race track than they do away from it… And like those other demigods of motorcycling, Wayne Rainey and Eddie Lawson, both are completely different personalities back home away from the pressures of racing.

Michaela is glad that she and Carl got together before the big money started rolling in; his suspicion that people now want to be with him because of what he's done rather than what he is would have made getting close to him difficult, if not impossible. Today they are so close that Michaela is essentially part of the team, but it wasn't until the 1998 World Superbike Championship that, at Carl's insistence, she went to every race. The kids, Danielle and Claudia, go to many of the European races, but those other essential members of the Fogarty back-up squad, the grand-parents, look after them when that's not possible. Michaela's dad Alan and step-mum Pat look after the house, slipping out of the door as soon as possible after Carl, Michaela and the girls get home. The night after a race Carl will relive it, twitching in his sleep as his mind comes down from the hyper-level of concentration demanded by two stints of riding on the edge for 45 minutes. He might have had a few beers but he's not a drinker and has never been near a drug in his life, if you don't count a brief spell of sneaking a ciggy behind the bike sheds when dad George wasn't looking.

Carl Fogarty at home is a completely different person from Carl Fogarty at a race track, or to be more precise Carl Fogarty during the run-up to, running of, and aftermath of a race. When he's with family and friends he's more open, has a bright smile as opposed to the lupine snarl he exhibits on the winner's rostrum, and seems to be both smaller and younger. At the local party to celebrate his third world title, he publicly thanked Michaela – 'It's all down to her' – something he is highly unlikely to have done at a track or motorcycle-related occasion, before singing with Jim Whitham's band the Po'Boys.

Following pages: *Foggy leads at Brands, but unfortunately not for long.* (Kel Edge)

Inset: *Just a small portion of the 120,000 Foggy fans who packed Brands Hatch in 1999.* (Kel Edge)

WORLD CHAMPIONSHIP
GERMAN ROUND
HOCKENHEIM. 10-11-12 SEPTEMBER 1999

Jim, Carl's only close friend in the paddock, says the sense of humour that only surfaces occasionally in interviews and hardly ever in the paddock, is definitely there, but it's quite cruel. He illustrates this by saying that if he and Carl saw someone slip on a banana skin, Carl would laugh while Jim would rush over to see if the bloke was all right. When the two came together as racing rivals at Brands Hatch in 1998, Jim said that he didn't try and overtake Carl because he was thinking about what the crowd would do if he brought them both down. If the situation were reversed, it's impossible to imagine Carl Fogarty hesitating for a millisecond. No one got to be a World Champion as many times as Foggy without that ruthless streak.

It's that element of his personality that sometimes jars on the outside world, but not on Michaela. She sees the doting father, the husband who'll stand up for her when it matters, the guy who hasn't changed a bit as his circumstances have altered out of all recognition. The outside world has seen some changes, notably Carl's progress

Top, left: Under pressure at Brands. (Kel Edge)
Bottom, left: Michaela, Carl and Slick looking relieved at Hockenheim. (Kel Edge)

Hoisting his fourth World Championship trophy, as Paolo Flammini, Ducati MD Claudio Domenicali, Michaela and Akira Yanagawa look on. (Kel Edge)

from tongue-tied young man to the sort of self-confidence that only total self-belief can give. But those original contradictions are still there: he will take over a racetrack press conference with the force of his personality yet refuse to talk – as opposed to answer questions – in public because 'I wasn't brought up to do this sort of thing'.

Even when he seems relaxed, as through nearly all of the '99 season, there's still that undertow of tension. His first words on retaining his title at Hockenheim were 'Now I can get back to being a nice person again'. There was also the chance, he reckoned, of eating and sleeping again.

But the reason why Carl Fogarty attracts 100,000 motorcycle fans to a track is not just because he's a winner, but also because he is identifiably one of them, a man who is true to his roots, speaks his mind, and above all does his best every time he goes to the grid. The last word should go to Michaela, who has to deal with the down side of all those fans' expectations: 'He never bores me – I love him to bits.'

chapter one

A fast kid

Geoorge Fogarty and Neil Tuxworth were feeling quite pleased with themselves – they'd just finished second and third in the Southern 100 road races on the Isle of Man. Back in the paddock, George's 15-year-old son Carl wasn't impressed. He'd already made his mind up that he was going to be a road racer and couldn't understand why his dad and Tuxworth were so pleased when they hadn't won: 'When I race I'm going to beat them all.'

The comment was totally in character for the kid with the piercing, pale-blue eyes. He was bright but introverted and hated school with a passion; he was a good soccer player who hated losing

Carl's first bike – a Raleigh Chopper, with sister Georgina. (Fogarty family)

Christmas time with Georgina – and what looks suspiciously like a Manchester United strip. (Fogarty family)

even a playground kickabout. He had no doubts at all that when he left school he was going to be a motorcycle racer, and time spent in class until then was time wasted. Father George is a significantly different character, chatty and outgoing with a reputation as a nice guy. 'It's odd,' says Carl. 'Dad was always reckoned to be one of the nicest guys in the paddock – and I turned out to be a complete twat.' As he took his helmet off in the Southern 100 paddock, Neil Tuxworth was probably thinking something very similar.

That remark of Carl's is a useful indicator to some of the contradictions in the younger Fogarty's character. He was always a slightly retiring, even shy, character but also acutely self-aware. Very rarely does he drop his defences totally and let the outside world get a glimpse of the private man. Even after his World Championship victories, he still retains that essential isolation from everyone except his family and a couple of close friends. He sees his job as winning races and World Championships, and is not at all keen on the idea that he should also be a public relations man for motorcycle racing or the motorcycle industry,

Getting close to childhood hero Kenny Roberts at Silverstone. (Fogarty family)

although he does admit – cautiously – to enjoying his new-found celebrity.

Teenage Carl had already done time in schoolboy motocross and enjoyed himself, but he wasn't a winner on the dirt so saw no point in continuing. 'I was never going to be World Champion – but I won every race at my last meeting.' Oddly, the overwhelming will to win wasn't there in motocross as it was everywhere else, including the playground. 'It's like I was just filling time until I could go road racing.' School came even lower down his list of priorities. He knew absolutely that he was going to be a motorcycle racer and had no interest in anything that delayed the day he could compete on tarmac.

Mum Jean had already seen a change in her son's character. 'Up until he was about 17 he was happiest at home; he'd

rather lie in front of the fire and watch TV than go out.' A playmate of his sister, Michaela Bond, of whom much will be heard later, first met him when he was 11 and remembers a 'really horrible kid. He'd steal my shoes from the treehouse and sling them in the stream – he was *horrible*.' As a teenager he was painfully shy. 'It got so I used to worry about him not going out,' recalls Jean. His sister Georgina's main memory is of friends she brought home being appropriated as Carl's girlfriends. Michaela remembers a teenager who was so shy that he hardly emerged from his room, never mind left the house. But when he got his first motocross bike and started racing there was that change. Jean will now tell you that the kids were indulged – spoilt even – but their early childhood was the classic northern working class upbringing, strict without being hard. George and a couple of his brothers were busy building

Carl's first trophy, at Aintree in his first season, 1984. (Fogarty family)

up their haulage business into a force in the industry with not just a fleet of wagons (as we say north of Watford) but an innovative rail/road terminal in Blackburn that was impressive enough for the Chairman of British Rail to pay a visit. The brothers sold out to Galbraiths at the end of the 1980s.

George was a good road racer and more than handy around the Isle of Man; in fact he was good enough to be Mike Hailwood's team-mate when Mike the Bike made his comeback to the TT in 1978. So it was only natural that Carl would follow his dad on to the tarmac.

Carl's first season, 1984, was also George's last. Fittingly, George won his last race on a 500 and his son finished 11th on a 600cc Formula 2 Ducati, but Carl had already got his eye on the fearsomely combative 250cc class. The following season he embarked on his first full year of racing on a second-hand 250 Yamaha, and had broken his first lap record by the end of the year. He also broke his collarbone on his 18th

birthday, racing. In 1985 he got really serious.

The main aim of the 1985 season was to win the Marlboro Clubmans Championship, a well-organised, well-sponsored series for young riders. He ended up second but won the final tele-vised round at Silverstone after a dice with Darren Dixon – who went on to become a World Champion in sidecars. Carl also attacked the Isle of Man Mountain Circuit for the first time. Nowadays that would be a strange thing for an aspiring young racer to do, but in the mid-1980s it was a natural career progression. After all, the TT was still the best payday in the British season and Carl had grown up in a household where the closed-roads racing of the Isle of Man and Ireland was held in high regard.

George wasn't totally convinced about his son going to the Island: 'Maybe it'd be a good idea if we left it to next year...' Carl was having none of that. His first visit to the Island as a racer was for the Manx Grand Prix, the amateur's TT. He won the Newcomers' 250 race and finished third in the Junior (250cc) GP. He also met James Whitham for the first time. Out in practice on his 250 he came across this other red-jacketed Island novice, blasted past him on the straight, and was highly irritated when this lad came back past him in the corners on a converted production bike that was much better suited to the wet conditions.

They swapped places for a lap, neither of them having the slightest idea where they were going, touching bits of tarmac no other bike racer had touched for years. 'It could very easily have ended in tears,' James recalls. Back in the paddock they introduced themselves. After the race Carl couldn't find James's name in the results – he'd crashed and broken a collarbone.

In 1986 Carl stepped up to International level, taking on the estab-lished stars like Alan Carter and Donnie McLeod on a new Yamaha 250 with a little help from local sponsor Appleby Glade. To general astonishment he won his first ever International grade race – at Thruxton in the pouring rain. It was the opening race of the early-season three-round MotoPrix series. Carl ended up second overall after his gear lever broke in the final race. Despite this show-ing at 18 years of age, the weekly bike press didn't pick up on Carl, and he hardly got a mention. His first TT was nothing to write home about, though. He retired on lap two of the 250 race.

But on the short circuits, from July onwards, he could do little wrong. He broke the lap records at Scarborough, Snetterton and Aberdare Park on con-secutive weekends to close right up on the factory Armstrong riders Niall Mackenzie and Donnie McLeod in the British Champion-ship. The established fast men of the domestic 250 scene remember him bursting on to the stage and winning straight away. He was the young gun who got instant respect from the old hands. His bikes weren't the fastest but he rode them at, or usually over, the limit and made up on the brakes what he lost down the straights. Off the bike he was sociable enough but obviously still very shy and not a party animal, and there in the background was George providing the support. The opposition had already noticed one thing about Carl: his piercing blue eyes when framed by the aperture of a crash helmet turned into the scariest race face since Eddie Lawson. 'I glanced over my shoulder at the hairpin to see who was behind me and looked straight into Foggy's visor,' said one paddock comedian at the time. 'I screamed, jumped off and ran away.' Carl still has that laser stare but now it

Carl spent the next eight weeks in traction, his season over

comes with a brooding, dominating presence that can subdue a grid.

Such was Carl's impact on the British 250 scene that he began to try and get a start at the British GP at Silverstone. In the late 1980s the grids were full and entries over-subscribed. A lot of fast talking eventually procured an entry. Practice was a bit of a shock – Carl had never qualified on the back row before – but on race day it rained.

It was the perfect scenario for a young privateer on an under-powered machine; the track conditions negated some of the power advantage of the regular GP men, but Silverstone still had lots of long straights and fast corners. Carl finished 11th, Mackenzie was the only

Brit in front of him in tenth, McLeod was 15th. Fogarty now knew absolutely that he wanted to be a 250cc Grand Prix rider and started exploring the idea of achieving his ambition. It all looked so good.

A week later it looked very bad indeed. During a practice session at Oulton Park Carl crashed the Yamaha – maybe because he was running very old slicks – and suffered a compound fracture of the leg above the knee. It happened in a critical double right-hander where you really have to commit yourself, a double-apex corner you must get through as quickly as possible or the whole lap is ruined. Carl spent the next eight weeks in traction, his season over.

At the start of the 1987 season Carl found out that if you aren't around and winning races you cease to exist: he

Carl's first Grand Prix, the 1986 British 250cc at Silverstone. (Don Morley)

On his way to fourth in the 1987 Isle of Man Junior TT. (Phil Masters)

couldn't get a sponsor or a worthwhile deal. Worse still, he couldn't sit on a 250 comfortably. He decided to have a go at the European Championship with two new Hondas. The bikes turned out to be troublesome and Carl suffered the humiliation of failing to qualify for the first round in Spain. The doctors now decided that they wanted to rebreak the leg to set it properly, an offer Carl felt able to refuse. By the TT early in June things were better. He got fourth in the Junior TT and started going well again on the short circuits, winning the first round of the British Championship. In the second race he crashed again and rebroke the leg. It transpired that an infection had weakened the bone around the area where a traction pin had been inserted, and when he slid off in what looked like an innocuous incident the bone gave way.

For a 20-year-old racer on the verge of an international career it was a traumatic blow. Carl had already given up his job as a heavy goods vehicle mechanic – 'I wasn't learning anything' – and racing was his whole life.

This was the sort of incident that can stop a promising career in its tracks. It's not just motorcycle racers who fail to come back from that sort of injury. Any sports person puts their motivation to the ultimate test when they have to go through all the frustration and pain of weeks of inactivity followed by months of physiotherapy. And it's even worse the second time, knowing exactly the problems they're going to encounter.

Carl Fogarty is made of tough stuff. It may be his background, the father and

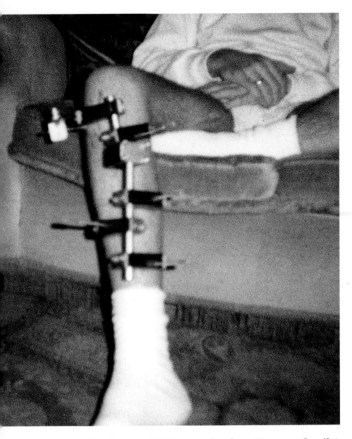

Medical scaffolding on that leg. (Fogarty family)

uncles who built up their business from nothing, or it may rub off from the town itself. Blackburn, where the Fogarty clan still lives, is a big place but it's self-contained and just far enough away from the big cities to feel a little isolated. Just because it's in Lancashire as are, ostensibly, Liverpool and Manchester, it would be easy to think it's the same sort of place. It isn't. Your street-wise Scouse Scally and cutting-edge Manchester clubber regard Blackburn as the sort of place where flares and kipper ties never went out of fashion. If you were looking for a stereotypical industrial town with dark Satanic mills and gritty, uncompromising inhabitants, then Blackburn would be high on your list. It's an area that produces more than its share of successful sports people, not just motorcycle racers but soccer players, athletes and others.

Carl would need all that in-bred resilience, plus the special element that only champions possess, to get over this latest setback.

chapter two

Because I could fit on it

It was George Fogarty's idea. In 1988 he bought a Honda RC30, a big 750cc four-stroke, a street bike but a machine as near a racer with lights on as anything yet made. Honda had designed and built it to enable them to go Superbike racing. This was a new formula in world racing – yet another attempt to come up with a successful series based on production machines – but that wasn't what George Fogarty had in mind.

He was thinking of the TT F1 World Championship, the series that was invented in 1977 to compensate the Isle of Man TT for the withdrawal of its

Getting to know the Honda RC30. (Fogarty family)

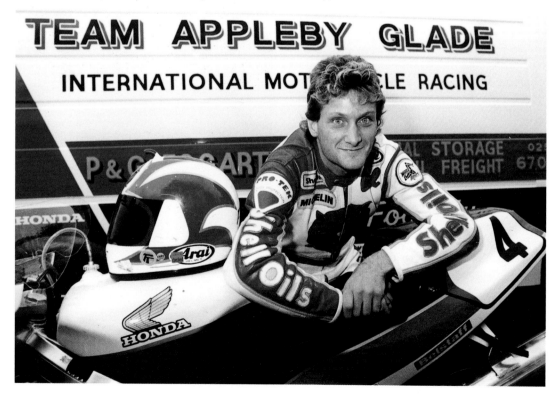

World Championship Grand Prix status earlier in the decade. It started as a one-race World Championship, which meant nothing outside the limited confines of the real-roads racing fundamentalists. However, it outlasted Formula 750 to grow into a hybrid Championship based on the road circuits of the Isle of Man and Ulster plus a few short-circuit venues and some backwaters that were too dangerous to host GP or World Superbike racing.

George also had in mind the fact that current British racers who were making money – as opposed to just getting by – were in the 750 class, not on 250s.

Carl was not at all keen on the idea. He was absolutely committed to the 250s, but when he sat on the RC30 he was comfortable on a racing motorcycle for the first time in nearly two years. It was simple. The 250 was too small for the movement Carl now had in his twice-broken leg. Even so, he wasn't really sure that going racing in 1988 was a good idea and seriously contemplated taking a year off, to get fit again.

Against all his instincts, Carl tried out the RC30. He found that although he was riding at 80 per cent – the consequences of another crash were too horrible to contemplate – he was enjoying himself and going quickly. Very quickly.

There was no game plan for the 1988 season. The TT seemed like a good idea, but the fact that Carl went to the Isle of Man without bothering to change the road suspension or wheels for proper racing equipment gives you an idea of just how unfocused he was. Almost unremarked, Carl wobbled and bounced his way to fourth place in the F1 TT, his problems multiplied by using Metzeler slicks for the first time. Given the self-imposed handicaps it was a fine result

Carl at the Gooseneck during the 1988 Isle of Man TT. (Phil Masters)

Getting away from a fuelling stop . . .

. . . winning . . .

. . . discussing, and . . .

. . . celebrating with Joey Dunlop at the World TT Formula 1 Championship, Pergusa, Italy, 1988. (All Fogarty family)

and encouraged him to have a go at a few more F1 rounds.

Carl ventured abroad for the first time – to Assen, the Dutch circuit that would play such a significant part in his future. Still riding what was really a street bike, he wore through his boots and large chunks of his fairing to finish ninth. Significantly, multiple F1 World Champ, works Honda rider, TT star and Irish working-class hero Joey Dunlop only finished one place in front of Carl after a troubled race.

The next round was at Vila Real in Portugal, a closed-roads street circuit that Championship leader Roger Burnett felt well able to miss in order to race in the World Superbikes in Austria. The race was stopped and restarted because of rain when Carl was leading. He led again in the wet second half. He'd always been an ace in the rain on the 250 and that talent appeared to have transferred across to the big four-stroke.

Carl Fogarty's first World Championship win was minutes away when his engine cut out. Water had found its way into the ignition. The bad luck continued in Finland, compounded by bad planning. Carl didn't take on enough fuel at his mid-race pit stop and had to make a second hurried stop, which put him back to fourth.

It was Ireland next, the Ulster Grand Prix in Joey Dunlop's back yard on the fast and fearsome 7.4-mile Dundrod circuit. The form book said unequivocally that the Championship leader and local hero Joey Dunlop, the King of the Roads, would demolish the opposition and go on to regain the title he had won five times in a row from 1982 to 1986.

It didn't look good for Carl. He missed the only dry qualifying session with engine problems and started well down the grid. Crucially, Joey's tyre choice was badly wrong. He started on slicks on a drying track but had to stop and fit intermediates; he managed only

seventh. Meanwhile Fogarty's form in the wet in Portugal had given him confidence. 'On race day it was just like the conditions I'd practised in, so I thought I could do well. At the start I just went flying through and picked them off on the first lap and won it.' In fact he won it by 16 seconds and closed to within 5.5 points of Joey in the Championship.

It was an emotional moment. The Fogarty clan's solidarity had been forged at tracks like Dundrod, and for Carl to get his first win there in a World Championship race was enough to reduce strong unemotional northern men to tears.

Italy was next, or rather Sicily and the bumpy, patched, mosquito-ridden Pergusa circuit. Dunlop's bad luck continued. He hurt an arm in a practice crash, then found that his bike wouldn't start on race day. Carl won after a fierce fight with works Bimota rider Gianluca Galasso and went to the top of the Championship. There was now one race between Carl Fogarty and a World Championship, and the final round was at Donington Park in the heart of England.

At this stage Carl was quite happy for his dad to be the front man

But what to do? Should Carl take it easy and keep an eye on Joey or should he go for it like normal? To get his title back Dunlop had to finish in the top three with Fogarty outside the top 10. Carl's view was that if he deliberately kept the speed down he would be less likely to concentrate. And when racers lose concentration they make mistakes. The only thing to do was go for it.

Nevertheless, Carl started the race a little more gingerly than usual and it wasn't until he got a signal telling him that Dunlop was way down the field that he speeded up to finish fifth and take the

title. He returned to the pit lane to be greeted by a small crowd of Lancastrians wearing 'Carl Fogarty World F1 Champion' T-shirts. To be a World Champion at 23 years of age is a major achievement, but being World TT F1 Champion was not going to catapult Carl into the Grands Prix.

F1 was a British ghetto (20 of the 26 finishers at Donington were British or Irish) and in 1988 the class had to cope with the new World Superbike Championship running in parallel. This forced F1 further away from the high-profile short circuits and on to obscure and dangerous places like Pergusa and Vila Real. There was the traditional British whiff of sour grapes as well, usually articulated along the lines of 'If Carl Fogarty can win then it can't be worth winning.' Of course if that national institution Joey Dunlop had won again the very same people would have been going on about 'the major achievement, King of the Roads', etc.

Carl, while under no illusions about the profile of the class, shrugged off the criticism with a typically brief 'I've seen it all before'. What he hadn't seen was the number of press who wanted to talk to him including, for the first time, regional TV. Before the Donington race he seemed tongue-tied and overawed by all the attention, and was little different after it, experiencing the usual 'it hasn't sunk in yet' syndrome. He was a little more chatty the following day. Realisation had come while he was sitting at home watching TV: a sports bulletin had announced that Carl Fogarty of

Wearing his World Championship medal at the FIM Congress in Brazil alongside sidecar champions Steve Webster and Tony Hewitt.
(Fogarty family)

Blackburn was the new World Formula 1 motorcycle racing champion.

Journalists now seeking out Carl Fogarty for the first time usually found when they played back their tapes that they had a few non-committal comments from Carl and a cassetteful of George's opinions on everything from Carl's health to the structure of the World Championship.

Some racers' dads fall into the classic trap of living out their own fantasies through their sons' careers. George Fogarty has never been one of them. Given the chance, though, he can talk for as long as you let him. At this stage in his career, Carl seemed quite happy for his dad to be the front man, and if you did get a comment out of him it was usually of the 'I dunno really' type. George said he would be happy to let go of Carl if the right team took him on – but it had to be the right team.

If Carl hadn't yet developed his media-friendly confidence, he most assuredly had an imposing presence. The British journalist Mac McDiarmid remembers meeting Carl for the first time: 'I was confronted with a quietly hostile, suspicious, ill-at-ease young man, already a destroyer of reputations on the track but unsure of his own off it.' Every journalist, British or foreign, can tell you

about suddenly getting Carl's attention and having that laser stare turned on you.

A dispassionate analysis of Fogarty's 1988 F1 season uncovers quite a few notable points. Remember that he was not fully fit, he'd never seen any of the tracks before apart from the Island and Donington, and he had to contend with a posse of fast locals at each of the foreign rounds. The Finnish, Dutch and Italian rounds were all hard races in which Carl had to fight for his points, and he certainly had no machinery advantage. Similarly, Metzeler worked hard on their slicks but didn't have the experience to give the back-up that Dunlop or Michelin would have provided. Far from being an advantage, his tyres were a handicap, and he could not afford to – and did not – fall off. Carl himself, with

As always, Carl's father George was there with advice and encouragement. (Phil Masters)

hindsight, says that the Championship was just 'a bonus, just being consistent. Okay, it wasn't all that competitive but you can only beat who's there. I think a lot of people didn't accept it because I hadn't won any races in England. But I knew that would change in 1989. I just knew I'd beat everybody in 1989.'

But before the next season came round another significant event would change Carl's life. On the evening of 17 December 1988 in a Blackburn pub he saw one Michaela Bond for the first time in over three years. She'd been living in Oxford and Carl greeted her with the romantic words 'I thought you were dead'. In her own words, Michaela was at the time living in a 'grotty bedsit' while working as a dental nurse. Carl took her out to lunch the next day and moved into the bedsit that same evening. 'It was meant to be,' says Michaela. 'Even when I was in Oxford I used to think about him and I'd watch any bike racing on TV

even though I didn't like it in case he was in it. We were destined to be together.'

The next move came one evening after Carl took Michaela to see a flat over a bookies' shop. Looking back, that was pretty grotty too, but by comparison with the bedsit it was sheer luxury.

From the next season onwards, Michaela was a permanent addition to the Fogarty pit. Anyone who made the assumption that Michaela's stunning looks meant that she was merely a blonde bimbo soon realised the error of their ways. She is just as strong a character as Carl, which is saying something. Many journalists have paused in the act of knocking on the Fogarty motorhome door when they've heard Michaela putting Carl right on some point, although the well-informed say that if you want to hear her in full force you need to be within earshot of her having a row with her dad Alan, a large and genial retired cop. Alan Bond knew of the Fogartys; he vividly remembers pedalling his push bike as 'a 19-year-old wet-behind-the-ears PC' and encountering George and his brothers 'all drape jackets and Brylcreem' hanging around on street corners. 'You can imagine how delighted I was the first time Michaela brought Carl home!'

Carl's first world F1 title had also given the RC30, Honda's flagship model, its first World Championship, which meant that he was in line for some factory help. For 1989 he got assistance from the UK importer to try and retain his title – head office regarded that as the priority – and fitted in some Superbike rounds.

Carl wasn't sure which of the two four-stroke series was going to survive, but wanted to defend his title, not just because everyone told him that defending a title is more difficult than winning it in the first place, but also, one sensed, because he thought a champion had a duty to defend his crown. Unfortunately,

not everyone was so committed to F1 and it looked as if the series would lose its status until the Assen organisers rescinded their decision to run a Superbike round at their Speedweek and reverted to F1, thus helping to provide the minimum number of rounds required for a World Championship.

As befitted his new status, Carl was able to go to Japan, with Honda's help, to contest the first round of the F1 Championship, something he hadn't done in 1988. He battled against the array of full works F1 machines – remember that his RC30 was more like a Superbike – in wet conditions to finish 13th and get a two-point start on the F1 regulars whom he wouldn't encounter until the Isle of Man TT. Joey Dunlop wasn't going to be one of them, though. A serious early-season crash had left him unable to get fit in time. This year Steve Hislop was to be the main competition.

When Carl got to the Island it was for more than the F1 race. He was also entered in the Supersports 600, Production 750, 125 and Senior TTs.

He didn't even give up the lead when stopping for fuel

It was one of the Isle of Man's worst years. Five riders died including Island stars Phil Mellor and Steve Henshaw in the big production class. Carl's friend Phil Hogg, a Manxman, died in practice for the Supersport 600 race, and Fogarty pulled out of the race. He did race in the F1 TT, qualifying sixth and finishing fourth on a bike he'd never got sorted in practice week, as winner Steve Hislop became the first man through the 120mph barrier.

Carl collided with a slower ride in Parliament Square, Ramsey, hit the kerb at Appledene, had an exhaust bracket break and still upped his best Island lap from 115.8mph to 119.5. 'I'm pleased I

rode, and to have 13 points towards the [World F1] Championship,' he told the press. 'I had a bit of trouble with the front brakes and had to pump them from time to time, and had a frightening moment at Ballacraine on the first lap when I hit the kerb.'

Two days later Carl had a very busy day indeed. In the morning he raced a 125 for the first time and finished third after a tremendous charge over the last half lap. In the afternoon he rode an RC30 in the 750cc Production TT – and won. He diced on the roads with TT specialist Dave Leach on a Yamaha right through the 150-mile race. It was a race decided by pit stops: Steve Hislop stopped every lap for a top-up, Dave Leach only stopped once on his Yamaha, and Fogarty decided at the last minute to gamble on just two stops and not rev the bike too hard on the first circuit. His winning margin after 1 hour 18 minutes and 57 seconds of racing was 1.8 seconds.

Just to underline his all-round Island abilities, Carl borrowed a 250 Honda from an Irish sponsor who came forward after a Manx Radio appeal, rode it once on the Thursday of practice week and finished fourth on it in the Junior TT. He rounded off the week with his only DNF in the Senior after an oil line split, but not that many people cared about that race after the events of the 1300cc Production TT.

Carl was more than a little thankful that Assen was next on the F1 calendar. He dominated proceedings. No one went faster than him in any practice session, and hardly anyone saw him in the race – he didn't even surrender the lead when he stopped for fuel.

In terms of the Championship, the most important factor was Steve Hislop's 11th place, which dropped him from joint leader to third. Carl now led the

A classic Isle of Man TT shot from 1989 – Carl at the Creg. (Phil Masters)

Championship with three races to go. Hislop won on the hilly streets of Vila Real, Carl returned the compliment at Kouvola, hard up against Finland's Russian border and a circuit he really liked. 'It's like racing around an industrial estate – every bend's a right-angle and you have to dodge the pot-holes. It's not too dangerous, though; if you fall off you slide into a ditch because the buildings are always on the inside of the track.'

So they went to Dundrod with Fogarty knowing that sixth place would be enough for him to retain the title and that Hislop was the only man who could take it from him.

Fogarty set an unofficial lap record in qualifying and led the early stages of the race in patchy conditions. He briefly surrendered the lead to local man Steve Cull on one of the very rapid (in a straight line) rotary-engined Nortons, and even took to the grass right in front of the main grandstand before retaking the Ulsterman and pulling out a big enough lead to enable him to keep it when pitting for fuel. Hislop, strangely subdued earlier on, charged in the closing stages to take victory from Carl by less than a tenth of a second, but Foggy was World Champion again.

There was also time for a first visit to the Suzuka 8 Hours as Steve Hislop's co-rider on a private Honda. It wasn't a good race – they spent nearly eight hours playing catch-up after an early crash – but Carl got to work with mechanic Anthony Bass, known to the paddock as 'Slick', for the first time.

The future was not, however, totally rosy. At least not for the F1 Championship, as Carl realised at the time: 'There just isn't room for two 750cc World Championships. They should put the F1 on good short circuits leaving the TT and Ulster as optional rounds,' he told the motorcycle racing annual *Motocourse*. 'Then standards would rise.'

It was a forlorn hope. Superbike was inexorably taking over, not just because it ran on good circuits but because after a politically rocky first two years the FIM (the sport's governing body) had signed a three-year deal for the Italian Flammini Organisation to run the series. There were also a good number of top-flight teams doing the whole Championship. In 1989, the only rider to race in every round of the F1 World Championship was Carl Fogarty.

Any doubts the home crowd had about his class were banished when he took on Niall Mackenzie, then unquestionably the UK's top rider, in the one-off King of Donington meeting. Admittedly Niall was getting off his 500 and on to a big four-stroke, but Carl still beat him handily. The slow-down lap celebrations were revealing – uninhibited, air-punching, foot-kicking joy. Not the usual Fogarty style, and an indication of the significance, to Carl if no one else, of the wins.

Carl worked on the bikes himself to keep the costs down

One major effect of the successes with Honda was that Carl and Michaela were able to move into a detached house on a smart new estate on the edge of Blackburn. 'We had a new house and a £12,000 cheque from Honda in the bank,' recalls Michaela fondly. 'We really thought we'd made it.' The new house was shared with a small, snappy cross-bred chihuahua dog called Arai adopted after Carl had come home to the flat babbling about this puppy for which one of his uncles was looking for a home. 'No way!' said Michaela, until she was introduced to this tiny creature that she could fit in the palm of her hand. For ten years this most unlikely pet for a world-champion motorcycle racer was the senior member of a large and varied Fogarty menagerie that Carl assembled over the years, often amusing visitors by attaching itself to the rear leg of the resident Great Dane. There's still a picture of Arai next to the Fogartys' back door.

It is important to grasp the differences between a Honda RC30 Superbike and a Honda RVF750 F1 bike in order to understand the battle between two formulae that superficially look so similar and which were vying for Carl's attention.

Both are based around road-going machines, but F1 only requires the retention of the basic engine castings – crankcases, cylinders, cylinder heads – from the base bike. The rest of it, all the cycle parts, the fuel delivery system, can be anything the team or manufacturer wants. The result is a four-stroke Grand Prix machine, a lightweight missile crammed with the highest technology and the newest, lightest materials.

The 1990 Honda Britain team – Carl Fogarty and Jamie Whitham. (Kel Edge)

Superbikes, on the other hand, have to retain the base bike's engine casings, chassis, swinging arm and, crucially, fuel delivery system. If the bike is sold with 34mm constant-velocity carbs then that's what it races with; you can't convert it to fuel injection. The best analogy is that a Superbike is a two-wheeled version of a Touring Car and, just as in four-wheeled motorsport recently, it was that formula that came to the fore.

The bad news for Carl at the start of the 1990 season was that F1 no longer had a World Championship. Only five tracks applied to run an F1 race, so the series was downgraded to the status of FIM Cup. The good news was that Carl would no longer be a privateer. Honda Britain's new team signed him and James Whitham to ride RC30s under the management of Neil Tuxworth.

Despite being outwardly very different characters, Carl and James became

Carl and Michaela soon after they met again – check out Arai the chihuahua. (Fogarty family)

The amazing comedy dogs – Arai and Bridget. (Fogarty family)

firm friends. Carl's introspection and intensity contrasted with Whitham's jokey persona. 'Sometimes I wish I could be more like James,' Carl said. 'He can bounce back from finishing second, laugh it off. I can't.'

The team was not, however, a big-budget operation. At the first Superbike round of the year, at Jerez, the team turned up without any paintwork on the fibreglass, just stickers, and Carl was working on the bikes himself to help keep costs down. The objective was to win the F1 title again and fit in as many Superbike events as possible around his domestic commitments, the most important of which was the TT. There was also an introduction to Daytona – the one-off event at the Daytona Speedbowl in Florida – and a first outing on a factory 500 Grand Prix machine.

On his way to winning the 1990 Senior TT – note the patchy road surface. (Don Morley)

The traditional season-opener at Daytona wasn't really attracting a top-line entry at the turn of the decade but was seen as a useful, high-profile warm-up. It wasn't a successful foray: Foggy crashed after 34 laps and Whitham followed suit while second with only 12 laps to go.

That was the start of a season of problems with the front end of the bikes, a season in which Whitham crashed over 15 times and nearly ruined his career. Carl didn't hit the deck so frequently but had other troubles. For some reason he'd developed an unfair reputation as a crasher, probably because his style was so aggressive. He always looked like he was going to crash but very rarely did – although the troublesome RC30 nearly changed that in 1990.

The F1 season again started with the Japanese round at Sugo, and again Carl was the only Championship contender to go. With his RC30 he faced up to a grid full of top-flight F1 machinery from the

On the rostrum for the 1990 Senior TT win, with Dave Leach and Trevor Nation.
(Don Morley)

Japanese Championship ridden by factory testers and hired guns from Australia and the States. He was fifth and the first RC30 home in a race dominated by the factory RVFs, further enhancing his standing with the factory.

It was a nice warm-up for the Isle of Man. Carl dominated the opposition, making up for what he considered a disappointing showing in 1989. In practice he became the third man to lap at over 120mph on his RC30, but he damaged forearm muscles when taking the jump at Ballaugh Bridge and had to load up with pain-killers to race. He was far from sure of his ability to go the distance – not that you'd have noticed. He was still having handling problems – the front end didn't behave any better on pure road courses than it did on smooth short circuits – and was still intensely dissatisfied. However, as usual he simply rode round any problems he encountered, a scary sight on short circuits but a downright terrifying one on the Island.

The only thing he seemed concerned about was getting his revenge on Steve

Hislop, and he told anybody who'd listen that that was exactly what he was going to do. The fact that Steve was his partner in the Honda Britain TT squad didn't concern him one jot. The fact that Hislop, the triple-victory hero of 1989, got all the attention obviously did.

Journalist John Cutts noted in *Motocourse*: 'He wouldn't concede the faintest possibility of anyone else winning. He acted like a man possessed, the fire raging in his eyes while he adopted a tough, swaggering demeanour. Was this just his ruthless race face or a psychological game?'

The F1 race turned out to be an anticlimax. Hislop ran out of brakes on lap one and overshot Ballacraine, while Carl had conserved his resources carefully and ran away to win, putting in a 121.29mph lap on the way. 'Apart from my rev counter falling off on the first lap and my running wide when Steve went up the slip-road, I had no moments and no problems at all,' he said afterwards with unconscious understatement.

The second Hislop-Fogarty showdown was due for the Senior TT, the traditional climax of race week, but Foggy found time to finish second and first Honda home in the Supersport 400 race and fourth in the 250cc Junior TT, which he realised he couldn't win so spent the time waving to the crowd and showing off over the Ballaugh Bridge jump.

Come Friday the weather was appalling. The Senior TT was put back, but when it was run not every rider was convinced it should have gone ahead. Steve Hislop pulled in at the end of the second lap saying that conditions were too dangerous. Carl didn't agree. He put in a 108mph lap from a standing start to lead by over 20 seconds, and won by over a minute.

It was a classic Foggy display of pure bloody-minded aggression in the worst conditions – streaming wet at the start and gradually drying to just patchy by the finish. Carl stayed with cut slick tyres right the way through. Despite the evidence of every spectator's eyes, he claimed that he was taking it easy and everything was nice and smooth – apart from the rev counter falling off again. It was Fogarty's third TT win and without doubt his most impressive, but Carl was determined that it would be his last. The place was, he said, just too dangerous. Significantly, he'd only finished behind Hislop once all week. He felt that he had made his point.

Carl's F1 TT victory put him to the head of the Championship – sorry, Cup – standings again. Honda wanted the title, so off went Carl in the van to Vila Real to win by a distance on his 24th birthday. Another lonely van journey to Kouvola – there wasn't the budget for Tuxworth as well – and the Cup was Carl's with a round to spare. This time he lapped the whole field.

Carl is often described as three-times World Formula 1 Champion, but in the pedantic interests of accuracy it should be pointed out that he is a two-times World F1 Champion and also an FIM F1 Cup winner.

He wouldn't race an F1 series again, but he would come back to the Isle of Man TT, and in 1990 he didn't even compete in the last race of the Cup at Dundrod. He was otherwise engaged racing a 500cc Honda in the Swedish Grand Prix.

chapter three

On the world stage

Between the Portuguese and Finnish rounds of the 1990 F1 Cup, Carl Fogarty had been offered a ride on the injured Pierfrancesco Chili's Grand Prix NSR500 Honda. Japan had only agreed after a prolonged bout of politicking and made their approval conditional on Carl retaining the F1 title. That long trip to Finland was worthwhile in more ways than one.

Jumping on a 500 GP bike mid-season after precious little testing is never an easy task, and the NSR500 Honda was reckoned to be even more of a brute to come to terms with than the rest of the evil breed. To add to the pressure, the first event in which Carl would race a 500 was the British GP at Donington Park.

He did get to ride the NSR500 before Donington – at Cadwell Park on the Wednesday – and therefore arrived at his home Grand Prix on Thursday having at

The first 500 GP ride, Donington 1990 on the injured Pierfrancesco Chili's Honda. (Kel Edge)

least sat on the bike. It wasn't a happy race. The Roc team weren't keen to alter things to suit Carl who felt isolated without his usual team and the family around him. He could ride it fast enough but reckoned that it felt like a different bike from Cadwell, and qualified 11th out of the 18 entrants, behind Jean-Philippe Ruggia's Yamaha and in front of Ron Haslam's Cagiva.

The problem was in sorting out the handling. Worryingly, he was having the same type of front-end problems that afflicted him on the RC30 at Donington and again couldn't seem to tune them out. Every other team there had the advantage of over half a season of racing experience, plus testing, to cure such problems. But there was no way Carl and the French-run team with its German race engineer were going to establish efficient lines of communication in one race.

When I saw those faces I realized they wanted a Brit to do well

Like most GP teams they also had two bikes. Carl, used to his lone RC30, found swapping between the two more confusing than useful. Almost inevitably, his race was a short one. He was up to seventh on lap three and thinking about overtaking Christian Sarron when he crashed going into McLeans. The culprit was the front-end chatter that had afflicted him all through qualifying. Despite the suspension problems, the front tyre hadn't slid in practice so Carl decided to ignore it. But, in Carl's words, this time 'it chattered, then jumped and went'.

As he got to his feet in the Donington sandpit, Carl's first thought was, 'Thank fuck that's over.' Then he looked at the crowd and saw a sea of faces, every one of them registering utter disappointment. It was a moment of revelation. 'I didn't think anyone knew or cared that I was there, but when I saw all those faces I realised they wanted a Brit to do well.'

Before this incident Carl had raced for himself. From Donington onwards he was acutely aware of the number of Union Jacks dotted around the circuits and of his fans' expectations. This damascene conversion is typical Fogarty: a subject either doesn't exist or it gets total commitment.

There wasn't a lot of time to dwell on it – the Swedish GP at Anderstorp was on the following weekend. Again practice was fraught and Carl only managed 13th on the grid out of 18, and was last of the factory machines. Again the main worry was the front end. Between qualifying and the race he came to the conclusion that his style, relying as it did on high corner speeds that load up the front end, must be a major part of the problem because no one else seemed to be having similar difficulties. Roc boss Serge Rossett reckoned he still hadn't adapted to the difference between four- and two-strokes.

This time, maybe because the pressure of a home race was lifted, Carl rode splendidly. He started well, repassing Mackenzie after the Scotsman had gone past, and spent most of the race embroiled in an at times hectic dice with the Yamahas of Ruggia and Juan Garriga. Foggy was delighted to find that he could blast past Ruggia on the long straight, even if the Frenchman could force his way past in corners, and finished up winning the three-way dice for an excellent sixth-place finish. The team was conspicuously delighted and Carl disappeared among much back-slapping when he got back to the pit lane. He looked genuinely happy and not a little relieved.

But that was the high spot of Carl's brief 500 sojourn. In Czechoslovakia he had a very mixed time, crashing in qualifying, then getting away with the top four in the race. Two near-fatal front wheel slides – yes, the front end again –

forced him to back off and settle for a few points. He ended up tenth.

In Hungary he again crashed in practice and was still more frustrated that the team wouldn't even move the footrests or handlebar position for him. Instead they taped some foam to the back of the tank to move him backwards. He qualified tenth and, after another excellent start, finished eighth. He then declined to go to the final Championship round in Australia.

The incident that sums up what was, for Carl, an unhappy interval happened in the Swedish paddock. A rather lonely Carl was sitting on a bench by the paddock cafe when the Suzuki team manager Garry Taylor saw him. Taylor gestured at the crowd around the cafe and asked Foggy why he didn't throw all these people out of his motorhome. The joke being, of course, that under-funded Foggy didn't have such a luxury.

Carl now reckons that all he was there for was to keep the sponsors' colours on the grid and in front of the TV cameras. It may not have been the entry on to the GP scene that Carl would have wished for, but plenty of people had noticed his talents. In each GP he finished he beat at least one of the regular works V4 riders, and in Hungary out-qualified four of them. He might not be able to set up a 500 but he didn't let that stop him racing with the usual Fogarty facility for riding round problems.

Brave but not yet the finished article was the general verdict.

The 500 Grands Prix were out of the question for 1991 but Carl was determined to do the full World Superbike Championship. Honda agreed, but there was a price to pay. He would have to do the TT again.

The season started with another visit to Daytona. Carl was pretty sure from his first visit that he didn't like the place. After this one he was certain. Carl had got to the front when an accident brought out that most American of institutions, the pace car. Fogarty couldn't see any good reason for this and, to add injury to insult, the field closed right up under its influence. After the pit stops Carl was relegated to third and was blazing mad when, on lap 40, he crashed at high speed on the banking. The only real bright spot at the start of the season was Carl and Michaela's wedding in March. Alan Bond's father-of-the-bride speech was a highlight; he opened by saying how nice it was to see so many people who should have arrows on their pyjamas…

On with the Superbike season. Carl had been promised equal machinery to ex-double champion Fred Merkel and honestly thought he could win the title. He got a shock, though. The RC30 wasn't competitive any more and was being abandoned by many teams in favour of the 888 Ducati.

The whole Superbike season was hard

Wedding day had to include a motorbike.
(Fogarty family)

work and, says Carl, a lot of people thought he had a bad year. He doesn't see it that way. He beat Merkel in the Championship, was top Honda rider, and finished every race bar one – and that was the first race at Donington when the gear-lever linkage broke. The best results were a brace of fourth places in Sweden. For a bloke who was supposed to be a crasher, that sort of reliability and mental toughness were a revelation. Hammering round, riding as hard as you can with the prospect of finishing in the top six if you're lucky, is not the sort of thing that inspires a racer. It was a thoroughly professional performance and got him seventh in the Championship.

One of the things that kept Carl going was the thought that Honda would recognise the good job he was doing. With that in mind, Neil Tuxworth faxed Honda's racing HQ after Sweden asking for some help at the next round, which happened to be in Japan. After all, Fogarty was well ahead of Merkel in the Championship and surely deserved a little extra assistance. A reply came quickly saying that yes, they would help, so Fogarty and Tuxworth arrived at Sugo with high hopes.

Carl's face fell like a kid's when he doesn't get the present he's expecting

Those hopes soared when they saw a brand new bike in Fred Merkel's pit, but then a Japanese engineer came into the Honda Britain pit and handed over a large cardboard box. The English asked what it was. 'It's your help,' came the reply. The box contained an exhaust system. Carl's face, Tuxworth recalls, fell like a kid's at Christmas when he doesn't get the present he's expecting – although the language after the Japanese engineer had left the pit was far from childlike. Typically, Carl was top Honda rider in

both races, but Tuxworth now thinks it was an incident that later helped Carl to choose a Ducati ride over Honda when he had the option.

Honda were kinder when it came to the TT. They wanted to clinch their tenth consecutive F1 TT and as a welcome by-product steal the headlines from Yamaha who were celebrating their 30th year in the Isle of Man. So they sent over two works RVF750s for Fogarty and Steve Hislop. To put it mildly, this was a mixed blessing. Sure the RVF was the fastest, highest-tech bike you could run on the Island, but would they be too fast? Hislop and others had already gone on record as saying that 750s were too fast for the Island – and they were talking about RC30s, not RVFs.

Carl himself had said the previous year that the place was too dangerous, and he now had an extra concern – Michaela was pregnant. They had already decided that they wanted children, and were a little concerned when nothing happened. They both went for tests – no macho posturing from Carl – and it was discovered that Michaela had a trivial problem that was simply sorted by a course of pills. She fell pregnant straight away.

In 1990 Carl had been blazingly intent on beating Steve Hislop. They hardly talked during race week. The inner Island demons that drove him to his two wins had been satisfied; he really didn't want to ride the RVF and get in another lap-record-pace duel with Hislop. The 1990 TT had given Carl a few inklings of his own mortality. On a short circuit the penalty for a mistake or mechanical failure can be a broken bone; on the Isle of Man capital punishment hasn't been abolished. Of course it is quite possible to have a very serious accident on a moped around the Isle of Man Mountain Circuit, but the awe that the RVF inspired highlighted the inherent risks of the place.

Back at home Michaela was worrying. The Isle of Man TT, she says, was the only time she wondered if Carl would come home safely – or indeed come home at all. As is the lot of every racer's wife, she couldn't let her husband know the way she felt. That would only have distracted Carl and made things worse.

There was one moment of light relief, a pure piece of Foggy lore, when Carl and Steve were taken into Honda's Island HQ for the first time to choose their bikes, then go out for their first rides. They were riding over 10 minutes apart and didn't see one another. Hislop was the first to come into the pits, and in response to Tuxworth's 'What's it like?' said that it was the best bike he'd ever ridden. When asked the same question a few minutes later, Carl came up with a catalogue of complaints: 'It bloody hops about, it doesn't have any…' A surprised Tuxworth butted in to tell Carl what Steve had said. 'Fucking typical! I got the shit bike again.' It was a prize example of Carl's conviction that he was usually not just racing the other guys on the grid but fighting most of the outside world as well.

It wasn't a description anyone else would recognise. The RVF was 20-30kg lighter than a race-ready RC30 and was reckoned to make a genuine 145bhp. Just the magnesium-bodied carburettors would cost an estimated £15,000.

First time out, Hislop went round at over 121mph and admitted that he was going too fast too soon. In other words, even he was in over his head. Carl wasn't so ambitious but was having the traditional front-end problems. It was, he said, skipping so badly that he was backing off the throttle when he should have been gassing it.

The following day, Tuesday, Hislop went round at 121mph in comfort, and Carl, still having front-end problems – 'it's awful' – went round at 122mph and just five seconds slower than the lap record. On Wednesday Hislop went round at 122.8mph, an unofficial lap record (records have to be set in racing rather than in qualifying). Carl's prob-

Steve Hislop and Carl show the strain of riding a Honda RVF750 around the Isle of Man. (Mac McDiarmid)

lems were magnified by the fact that he was sharing the bike with Joey Dunlop, who would take over the RVF for the Senior race.

Both riders were now talking openly of the problems of riding a guided missile – and of their fears. Basically, the RVF was too light for the Isle of Man; it skipped from bump to bump. The look on Carl's and Steve's faces after a qualifying session said it all – after they'd yet again traded fastest laps and gone faster than any human had ever done around the world's most dangerous race circuit.

By Thursday, Koichi Oguma, the head of HRC (Honda Racing Corporation) was getting worried. He watched that day's practice session at the bottom of Bray Hill, the flat-out plunge between suburban semis that starts the lap, with Neil Tuxworth. The public

They look more relaxed with a 125mph sign for an MCN *photocall. Note Arai in Carl's right hand.* (Phil Masters)

Above: *Blast off on the RVF.* (Mac McDiarmid)

Following pages: *The story of the '91 F1 TT: Hislop leads on the road and on corrected time.* (Mac McDiarmid)

address announced that Fogarty had lapped at 123.6mph, then Hislop took more than 14 seconds off his mark of the previous day at 124.3mph. Oguma-san had seen and heard enough. He slapped Tuxworth on the leg. 'Must have plan,' he announced.

Back at the team's hotel the two riders, Oguma, Tuxworth and Honda Britain boss Bob McMillan came up with a plan of action. Oguma – an ex-racer himself – pointed out that if either of them crashed Honda would win nothing, so it was decided that Carl and Steve would go for it on the opening lap, but if they got together on the road they would not race each other. Hislop had asked for a later start number than Foggy. Carl had number 8, and as TT riders start in

pairs at 15-second intervals, he set off 30 seconds ahead of number 11 Hislop.

On the first lap Hislop went round in an astonishing 122.8mph from a standing start, taking a 10-second lead over Foggy. On the second lap Carl's bike started cutting out and he seriously contemplated pulling in. When he did the bike chimed back in, but Hislop's 18min 20sec lap at 123.48mph was a new record and had put him right with Carl on the road. Carl had those machinery problems and the team orders, and many observers think that they saw a unique event at the 1991 F1 TT – they think they saw Carl Fogarty give best to another rider.

Even Carl's mental toughness couldn't withstand the shock of Hislop taking so much time out of him so quickly, and he settled for second place for what most people think is the only time in his life. Carl does not see it that way. He admits to being scared from time to time and totally lost after practice. 'It took all week to get it half-right; nothing went right and I didn't enjoy it.'

He is still irritated by that misfire, which, he is sure, cost him the lap record on the last lap – team orders or not. 'I thought "This is it" and didn't shut off down Bray Hill. People watching there and at Union Mills told me afterwards I went through so quick, much faster than anyone else. Then it cut out again at Ballacraine – I almost came to a stop, it cost me at least five seconds, it would have been at least 124mph for sure – absolutely definitely – and probably 125.' The fact that the team never told him the source of the misfire still rankles.

After the F1 TT Carl flew out to the American round of the World Superbike Championship, leaving Joey Dunlop to take over the RVF for the Senior race.

He said he wouldn't be back, but he'd said that before.

Both Carl and Steve got to ride the RVF again, but in very different circumstances at the Suzuka 8 Hours. This is the most important single race in the international calendar, an event run in front of every decision-maker in the Japanese industry, an event described by Oguma-san as the examination that every aspiring works rider must pass. It's nominally part of the World Endurance Championship, but in reality is a race apart from anything else. All the Japanese factories fly in their top Grand Prix and Superbike riders for one-off endurance rides and build bikes especially for the event, which attracts massive crowds.

As Suzuka is owned by Honda, their defeat the previous year at the hands of Yamaha had to be avenged. They handed a new RVF to Aussie superstars Wayne Gardner and Mick Doohan and flew in the finest pit crew in the world, the Honda France squad that runs the factory's endurance and Paris-Dakar Rally bikes, to make sure they spent the minimum time possible in the pits.

He settled for second place for probably the only time in his life

Carl and Steve got the same 1989-model RVF they'd ridden in the Island, while at least 15 other teams turned out on bikes with two year's further development. Qualifying 11th was in itself an achievement. Neil Tuxworth understood the basic truth of endurance racing, which is that it is fatal for a team's morale, and therefore its chances, to lose the time you make on the track with sloppy work in the pits. He drilled the pit crew for a whole day, doing wheel

Following page: *Carl rode the UK short circuits too. This is Cadwell Park.* (Phil Masters)

Carl on his way to third in the 1991 Suzuka 8 Hours. (Honda Racing Corporation)

change after wheel change, brake-pad change after brake-pad change, until mechanics and riders knew their roles by heart.

Another common failure in endurance is to have a team's riders racing each other – trying to better each other's times. Tuxworth countered this simply by refusing to let Carl and Steve see any lap times and ordering them not to take any chances in the race, and above all not to crash.

It worked perfectly. They circulated quickly, regularly and safely, the crew did their part with total efficiency, and Carl and Steve brought a two-year-old motorcycle home to third place only one lap behind the factory Yamaha of GP man Chandler and Kevin Magee, and one lap ahead of a factory Kawasaki.

On the rostrum at the Suzuka 8 Hours. (Honda Racing Corporation)

Carl meets his one-day-old daughter for the first time . . .

The factory were delighted. Their top team had won, but third place as well was a bonus. It was also a good payday for Carl, although he says that Tuxworth had 'destroyed him mentally' before the race. Carl had fallen off in the previous two 8 Hours and Neil had drummed into him the importance of not doing it again. He had also told Carl that there was no way he was going to start the race. The previous year he had been pushing an uncompetitive RC30 so hard that he was running in eighth in the first hour, up with the RVFs and other factory F1 bikes, when he crashed simply because he was trying too hard. 'In 1991 I just rode around, I didn't ride well at all.'

It wasn't all bad news, though. Michaela gave birth to a daughter in September. The plan had been for Carl to be present at the birth, but this needed some planning as he ended the season by racing in Malaysia. Michaela's blood pressure meant that she had to be induced, a process started at 6.30 one evening and timed to allow Carl to get home. The baby had other ideas, and by 10pm Michaela had to summon Jean Fogarty

. . . and a little later feeds her for the first time.
(Fogarty family)

for moral support. Next day Carl rang from Heathrow Airport to be told by his mum 'You're a dad!' So there was the new father bursting with pride and wanting to tell the world – something you can't do in Terminal 1's baggage reclaim hall. Michaela remembers Carl arriving in the maternity ward carrying a giant bouquet in one hand and a bottle of champagne in the other and still wearing his yellow team shirt – he'd come direct from the airport. The new arrival was christened Danielle and, as children do, would change Carl's life for ever.

Enzo Ferrari used to say that his drivers slowed down when they got married and had children. Michaela is adamant that fatherhood didn't change Carl's attitude to racing one little bit. The only issue was the TT; Michaela had stipulated that Carl should not return to the Isle of Man. There wasn't an argument; Carl had come to the same conclusion, although he would return one more time. He had some unfinished business to attend to.

chapter four

Annus mirabilis

Honda's British importers did not run their World Superbike team in 1992. The RC30 was growing increasingly uncompetitive, Carl had no intention of riding one, and Neil Tuxworth told Honda that there was no point in going World Superbike racing with it again.

It would have been very easy for Carl to fade back into the usual round of British Championship and TT racing that has been the fate of many promising British riders. Instead, he embarked on the most remarkable year of his career, racing three different makes of motor-cycle in three World Championships and returning in record-breaking form to the TT.

Carl's top priority was still World Superbike, but the only way to stay in the series was as a privateer. With no deals from big teams available, Carl had to use all the money he'd won over the past couple of years with Honda and borrow from the family to buy and run a Ducati 888. To help finance the Superbike year, Carl signed to ride for Kawasaki in the World Endurance Championship with fellow Brit and Superbike contender Terry Rymer as his co-rider. The endurance commitments, as well as

financial considerations, would preclude Fogarty from competing in every round of the Superbike season.

Endurance is very much a French sport and the works teams are French run. Kawasaki were no exception: the factory team was run by Kawasaki France with ex-racer Christian Bourgeois as team manager. As usual the team's lead rider was French, reigning World Champion Alex Vieira, teamed with Scottish TT hero Steve Hislop, who had been building up a nice sideline in endurance. Bourgeois was subjected to heavy criticism in the French press for signing three Britons, but countered by saying that British riders didn't make unrealistic demands. 'If they have no works contract,' he said, 'they buy a van and drive themselves to the track.' What he could not have foreseen is just how comprehensively his B-team would dominate the Championship.

Carl also returned to the Isle of Man TT. At short notice and without any big money deal from the Tourist Board he agreed to ride a Loctite-sponsored Yamaha for the British importer in the F1 and Senior races. Then there was the small matter of the British 500cc Grand Prix.

A winter revolution in the GP world

had installed a new system that contracted teams to do the full season, rather than entering each race individually, thus excluding privateers from doing the odd race. Instead, two local riders would be allowed to enter their local GP. Carl and James Whitham were selected as the British wild cards in the 500cc class.

And in between all the World Championship racing, there was the important matter of fitting in televised British Supercup meetings to keep the sponsors happy and trying yet again to win the North West 200 in Ulster in a one-off ride for Honda.

It is impossible to overstate just how precarious was the state of Carl's career at the start of 1992. Equally, it is impossible to overstate how brilliantly he rode in the course of an impossibly crowded season.

A race-by-race diary of Carl's international season makes startling reading.

5 April
World Superbike Championship Round 1, Albacete, Spain
Twelfth in streaming rain in the first race, tenth in the second after running with the leaders and being fourth at half distance.

19 April
World Superbike Championship Round 2, Donington Park, UK
The meeting where it all started to go right after looking like it would all go wrong. One of the good things about the World Superbike Championship has always been the two-race format. Fans get to see two races for their money and riders get the chance to make up for any mistakes or breakdowns in the first race. No rider was ever more grateful for that

The first winning Superbike ride, Donington 1992. (Phil Masters)

On the rostrum at Donington with Michaela and Danielle after Carl's first World Superbike win. (Kel Edge)

chance than Carl Fogarty at Donington Park.

In the first race he was leading comfortably, pulling away from the works Ducatis and Pirovano's Yamaha, when he tipped off at Goddards, the left-hand hairpin that leads on to the start/finish straight. The cynics sniggered: Fogarty was a crasher, Fogarty couldn't set a bike up, Fogarty couldn't take the pressure. His typically candid admission that he didn't know why he'd crashed only gave the snipers more ammunition.

In Kawasaki leathers and contemplating his first 24-hour race. (Kel Edge)

Behind that frighteningly frank admission was the fact that Carl was ready to give up on the Ducati and stick with the Kawasaki endurance ride to try and pay the bills.

In the second race he answered all the critics, and any doubts he himself might have had. Carl ran away from the factory Ducati of Raymond Roche and Scott Russell's works Kawasaki to win unchallenged, breaking the lap record on the way. The post-victory celebrations were more a release of tension than an outbreak of joy. To Carl, it was a justification of his confidence in himself and of his family's trust and backing. It was, he now says, the most emotional weekend of his life. To the outside world it was his first win in a Championship that really mattered. Raymond Roche, 1990 Superbike World Champion, understood exactly the implications of what he'd just seen: 'You will be World Champion,' he told Carl, before adding with a grin, 'but not this year.'

The general public were equally impressed. A businessman who heard about Carl's financial situation over the track PA system gave him a cheque for £5,000 with a promise of more. A van driver who told Carl the race had reduced him to tears handed over £20.

25–26 April
World Endurance Championship Round 1, Le Mans, France
The script said Vieira would win and progress to another title while the young Brits would qualify on pole and then either blow the bike up or – more likely – crash. To no one's surprise the Vieira/Hislop bike pulled away from the field, but to everyone's surprise Rymer and Fogarty, with third rider Michel Simul, stayed with them, but only after Carl had fluffed the start from pole position and been last away. Hislop broke the

On the way to the first British Bol d'Or for 21 years. (Kel Edge)

lap record in darkness as the race turned into a Kawasaki benefit. Then the Vieira/Hislop bike broke its camchain, leaving Fogarty's bike five laps ahead of the field. The bike was coaxed to the finish in front of the factory Suzuki, one of whose riders was Michel Graziano of whom more would be heard at the end of the Championship.

3 May
Dash For Cash, Donington Park, UK
A novel idea that Carl couldn't afford to resist. He won the £5,000 feature race.

10 May
World Superbike Championship Round 3, Hockenheim, Germany
DNF and 11th.

17 May
North West 200
A one-off outing on Simon Crafar's Honda. DNF in F1, 4th in the Superbike race.

24 May
World Superbike Championship Round 4, Spa-Francorchamps, Belgium
Carl didn't make the first corner in the first race as the rear wheel cush drive sheared on the start line. Eighth in the second race for tenth overall in the Championship.

1–12 June
Isle of Man TT, UK
He'd said he wouldn't go there again, but Carl helped to make it the fastest and maybe the greatest TT of all. The sport's governing body was still making sure that the TT didn't clash with their four-

Looking strangely pleased with second place. (Don Morley)

stroke World Championships in 1992, and British motorcycle importers still attached much importance to a win on the Mountain Circuit. So Carl found time to accept an offer to ride Yamahas in the F1 and Senior TTs that opened and closed the week's racing. Honda's decision not to send factory RVFs to the Island opened the way for a three-way fight between the rotary-engined Nortons, Irishman Phil McCallen on a Honda, and the theoretically out-gunned Foggy. Carl, however, wanted to finish his TT career on a high note. What he perceived as the disaster of the RVF year was a wrong that he desperately wanted to right.

As with so many of Carl's most famous victories, he first disappointed both his fans and himself. The F1 event opened race week in glorious weather after a wet practice week, thus putting Foggy and Hislop at a disadvantage. Both of them were new to their bikes and were short of vital testing time in race conditions. Typically, while Hislop arm-wrestled the brutal Norton, Carl wrung the neck of the Yamaha.

It was vintage Foggy. All the old stories about him were coming true in front of 40,000 fans: he just wound the throttle wide open and rode around any problems that manifested themselves. He led from the first checkpoint, by 10 seconds after the first lap, and by 23 seconds when they stopped for fuel. Hislop lost nearly a minute in the pits removing the front mudguard to get more air to the radiator but still Carl didn't relent. He rode with the pure aggression that you are supposed to save for short circuits, not unleash on a 37-mile circuit lined with stone walls, telegraph poles and a lethal reputation.

At the end of the fourth lap he was over 40 seconds ahead and was no longer looking to increase his lead at every signalling post. But the unrestrained Fogarty style had taken its toll on his bike. Going up Snaefell mountain for the fifth time the gearbox cried enough as he rode over the railway lines at The Bungalow. 'I changed down and there was this horrible noise,' he said. It signalled the end of his race.

Yamaha staff, devastated that they'd come so near to breaking Honda's stranglehold on the F1 TT, were amazed by Carl's reaction. Instead of slagging the bike off as a piece of uncompetitive junk as works riders are prone to do, he said how sorry he felt for Yamaha after all the work they'd put in. Carl is fundamentally a shy man who doesn't like to parade his emotions in public, but the Yamaha crew were touched by his obvious sincerity.

On the Friday of race week came the Senior TT and it was crystal clear that if mechanical failure didn't rear its ugly head again the fans were in for a showdown between Hislop, the lap record holder, and Carl, who predicted that if he had to chase the Scot in the closing stages that record would be broken.

What no-one had foreseen was the epic scale of the encounter

He was right – but what no one could have foreseen was the epic scale of the encounter. Eight times the Yamaha and the Norton swapped the lead in the fastest TT ever, with the gap between them never exceeding eight seconds over the 226-mile race. As predicted the lap record was broken, but first by Hislop before Carl's final charge took him round even faster, in 18min 18.8sec, which equates to 123.61mph. Hislop won by four seconds and the race is remembered primarily as the first Norton win in the Isle of Man since 1961, and in all probability the historic marque's last, rather than for Foggy's lap record.

Jeff Turner, the UK Yamaha importer's race co-ordinator, who spent the race in conversation with a very, very worried Michaela, is absolutely convinced that that motorcycle could not have been ridden round that race track one iota faster. The record stood until 1999, an astonishing length of time, and it took Scots hardman and closed-roads specialist Jim Moodie on a full works Honda RC45 to beat it.

28 June
World Superbike Championship Round 5, Zeltweg, Austria
6th and 7th.

4–5 July
World Endurance Championship Round 2, Spa-Francorchamps, Belgium
One of the greatest 24-hour races ever. Fogarty's Kawasaki diced with the factory Suzuki for 22 hours at Superbike rather than Endurance pace, the lead changing hands eight times as the Suzuki squad made up in the pits what they lost on the track.

Fogarty, Terry Rymer and Jehan d'Orgeix were fastest, but were delayed by silly mistakes during routine pit stops, like the chain being knocked off the gearbox sprocket, necessitating the removal of the fairing. The crew also managed to spray petrol in Fogarty's eyes at one rider change.

On the track Foggy broke the little finger of his right hand when he smacked it into a track marker at 6am, and thought it was all over as he hit the slick left by the Suzuki when it finally exploded under four-times World Endurance Champion Hervé Moineau as he strove to fend off the faster green machine. Carl was flat on the tank in the fast and dangerous Blanchimont corner when he hit the oil and slid. Warning flags weren't out but the ambulance was parked at the side of the track. Carl saw it the instant the bike started sliding and knew that if the bike fell he would slide straight into the ambulance at over 100mph. Out of control, he missed it by inches. It is, he says, the nearest he has come to death.

After surviving injury, a rain storm and near disaster, Foggy and Tel ran out winners by eight laps from their team-mates to give them a maximum 80 points in the Championship. Significantly, Graziano's fourth place put him second on 60.

19 July
World Superbike Championship Round 6, Mugello, Italy
7th and 4th.

26 July
World Endurance Championship Round 3, Suzuka, Japan
There is no race like the Suzuka 8 Hours. To the Japanese factories it is the single most important race of the year and winning it is as important as a world title. Although it is part of the World Endurance Championship, the Japanese factories call up their top Grand Prix riders and build them special bikes just for the 8 Hours, which makes it difficult for the endurance regulars to get on the rostrum, although it is possible for them to score valuable points for lower leader board finishes.

Carl's and Terry's status was under-lined by the provision of a trick new bike with which they qualified ahead of the other European visitors. Such is the pace at which the 8 Hours is run that if a team hits a problem they stand no chance of getting in the points. In a 24-hour event, bikes are regularly rebuilt after massive crashes and work their way back on to the leader board. Before the start Carl told Terry not to bother bringing the bike back if he crashed, so when Terry slid off after a quarter of an hour he took Carl at his word. Their World Championship points lead wasn't affec-ted as none of the endurance regulars

who'd made the journey finished in the top 15.

2 August
British 500cc Grand Prix, Donington Park, UK
More pressure. British riders were regarded as under-achievers by team managers and factories. It was important for Carl to prove that he could ride a 500 if a Grand Prix career was ever to become reality. The signs were not good. He had a Harris Yamaha – standard privateer tackle – provided by the Medd brothers, long-time loyal sponsors of British racers. It was not regarded as the sort of bike on which even the most talented of wild cards could make an impression in a one-off ride. After all, popular wisdom had it that you needed months of testing to master a 500, and the best privateer in the Championship, Australian Peter Goddard, was 18th in the Championship going into Donington with just 10 points to his credit.

Nevertheless, Carl found the Harris Yamaha much easier to come to terms with than the Honda he rode in 1990. After a minor spill on the first day, Carl qualified seventh and top Briton ahead of Niall Mackenzie on a factory Yamaha, Doug Chandler on a works Suzuki and Alex Criville on a works Honda. Wild cards were not supposed to be that quick, especially when they didn't have the benefit of the new 'big-bang' close-firing-order motors that made the works 500s more user-friendly than they'd ever been.

Neither were they supposed to get stuck in on the first corner and come out of it sixth, then pass John Kocinski to go fifth. Juan Garriga, on another factory Yamaha, got past but Foggy was running with the big boys; a hack privateer machine was racing with the thorough-bred works mounts.

Two-thirds of the way through the

race, with the home crowd working itself into mild hysteria, John Kocinski's Yamaha blew its 'big-bang' motor at the start of the 25th lap. That started a chain of events that ended in one of racing's enduring images – Kevin Schwantz snatching an oil flag from a stunned marshal and running down the track to warn oncoming riders of the treacherous surface at Redgate Corner. Doug Chandler had been the first victim, crashing on the oil while running eighth. Next time round he was joined in the Redgate sand-trap by Schwantz and, to a groan that could be heard in Blackburn, Fogarty, who planed the skin off a couple of toes.

Wayne Gardner won, his 18th and last GP victory in the country that took him to its heart back in the mid-1980s. In a prize example of the pot calling the kettle black, he took a verbal swing at Fogarty for over-aggressive riding in the first corner. Carl retaliated on live TV. Having said that he was glad Gardner had won because he was one of his racing heroes, Carl added waspishly, 'Pity he's so obnoxious off track.' This caustic comment was picked up in the august weekly *Autosport* by F1 journalist Nigel Roebuck, who devoted his whole column to the GP and lamented the lack of such outspokenness in the F1 car paddock. The vibes from the bike GP establishment, however, did not suggest that they would welcome such honesty.

13 September
World Superbike Championship Round 9, Assen, Holland
Fourth and second with only factory Ducatis in front of him. The second race was stopped and restarted due to rain. Carl got a good hole shot and, with the weather negating the works bikes' power

Going into battle as a wild-card in the British 500cc GP, 1993, Donington.
(Don Morley)

advantages, scored his first World Superbike rostrum place since Donington.

19–20 September
World Endurance Championship Round 4, the Bol d'Or, Circuit Paul Ricard, France

No team of British riders had won the Bol d'Or since Ray Pickerell and Percy Tait on a Triumph Trident in 1971. But this wasn't the foremost thought in the team's mind. It was probable rather than possible that they would win the title if they won the Bol, so team manager Bourgeois shuffled the pack, moving Steve Hislop across to be the third man to Rymer and Foggy.

With the absence of other works bikes from the full Championship, the Kawasaki team only had to keep an eye on a couple of privateers and keep going through a day and a night to take the title and avoid the expense of going to Australia and Malaysia for the final two rounds.

Carl's attacking style had already made him a star in the eyes of French endurance fans. At the end of the first of two warm-up laps he saluted them with a massive wheelie the length of the start/finish straight. The fans, thousands of them packed in the stands opposite the pits, went mad. So did Christian Bourgeois, who had expressly forbidden such flamboyant behaviour before the start of a 24-hour race.

Carl led the early stages, televised live in France, and as the Suzuki and Yamaha works bikes crashed out early, the race turned into a Kawasaki benefit. The all-British squad pulled out a comfortable lead over their team-mates and held it throughout to win by four laps. Carl's only unsettling moment came when he found out that Hislop was faster at night than he (Hislop) had been in daylight. He retired to the team truck shaking his head in disbelief as Hislop talked animatedly of the concentration necessary to keep lap times down at night.

The usual track invasion signalled the start of what the team management seemed convinced were celebrations of a world title for Fogarty and Rymer. It wasn't until British journalists pointed out that Michel Graziano's fourth place made it mathematically possible for him to be champion by four points if he won the remaining two rounds that the truth sank in.

Bourgeois said that he would stick with the team's schedule not to go to Australia and Malaysia. Meanwhile Suzuki tried to work out their best option for helping Graziano to the title. In the end, after a prolonged bout of politicking, Kawasaki decided it was worthwhile ensuring that they retained their crown.

17 October
World Endurance Championship Round 5, Phillip Island, Australia

Carl and Terry didn't want to go in the first place, and once the race had started they would happily have been anywhere else. At first it looked like it was going to be a routine demolition of substandard opponents. Carl led off pole but during his first session it started to rain and it didn't stop, it just got heavier.

The six-hour race was run half in daylight and half in the dark as a curtain-raiser to the World Superbike Championship the next day. It quickly turned into a survival test. The Phillip Island circuit is 135km south of Sydney on the coast and can be windswept at the best of times. On this occasion the weather was enough to put more than a few unlucky marshals in hospital with hypothermia and the riders didn't fare much better.

Apart from the physical discomfort and inability to see through the rain on the high-speed circuit, there was the problem of avoiding the legion of falling riders, one of whom nearly took out Carl early in proceedings. The winning margin was three

And Danielle came too . . . (Fogarty family)

laps, with the other factory Kawasaki second, but most importantly Michel Graziano could only manage third, four laps further back. Fogarty and Rymer were World Endurance Champions.

18 October
World Superbike Championship Round 11, Phillip Island, Australia
Carl rode the endurance Kawasaki in the Superbike event, seventh in the first race and a DNF in the second.

25 October
World Endurance Championship Round 6, Johor, Malaysia
The last race of the Championship really was an anti-climax. The Kawasaki team dutifully went through the motions for the requisite six hours. Carl took the lead on lap two and the World Champions were never headed. A truly anti-climactic end to the endurance year.

21 November
Macau Grand Prix
Back on a 500 with Jim Whitham as his team-mate for the annual non-Championship race on the fearsome port-side closed-roads circuit in the old Portuguese enclave on the coast of China. After opining with masterful understatement that the place looked a bit dangerous, Carl took a win and a third for overall victory in front of Japanese ace Toshihiko Honma, on the latest works Yamaha, and Whitham.

Any one of the key races – the Donington Superbike win, the British Grand Prix, the TT, the Bol d'Or – would have been a major achievement on its own. Mix in the World Endurance title, ninth overall in the World Superbike Championship without doing all the rounds, and that lap record in the Isle of Man, and you have a picture of versatility unparalleled in the modern era.

Back in the days of pudding-basin hel-

mets and all-black leathers, it was common for riders to compete in more than one class at each meeting on different makes of motorcycle, even at GP level, but in the last 20 years crossover has been limited to the 80 to 125cc and 250 to 350cc classes. Since rationalisation reduced the GPs to the 125, 250 and 500cc triptych, only Freddie Spencer in 1985 has raced in two classes. The widely differing demands and techniques required, as well as the increased levels of fitness demanded by modern machinery, simply made it impossible.

Similarly, if a rider was competitive on the short circuits used for GPs and World Superbikes, he wasn't quick on the pure road circuits like the Isle of Man and Ulster. Not only would his bike have to be set up vastly differently for the bumps of public roads compared to smooth purpose-built circuits, but its rider would also have to find a completely different mental approach. He doesn't race against opponents he can see – Carl never saw Hislop in that TT, they started too far apart – and he cannot throw caution to the winds as he might on a short circuit.

The vast majority find it difficult to readjust to short circuits after two weeks in the Island, unable to step as close to the edge as they could a month before and unused to the close-quarters combat of short-circuit racing. The resulting re-acclimatisation period has often ruined the Championship ambitions of British riders at home and abroad.

Carl Fogarty is one of the very few men who can switch instantly, although those who saw the way he treated that Yamaha in the Senior TT are willing to swear that he was on the limit – and usually over it – for the entire 1 hour, 54 minutes and 4 seconds he was in the saddle.

And Carl, of course, had gone faster on the Yamaha than on the RVF Honda. It shouldn't be physically possible to dominate a 750cc motorcycle and force the thing to do your will, but that's what Foggy did. And even though he didn't win, for once he was satisfied because he'd done his best and put the record straight.

Yet none of this catalogue of achievements convinced the GP team bosses that he was worth recruiting. Carl was to a large extent a victim of the recent history of British riders in the 500 class, a succession of whom had failed to win a race or make a significant impact on the world scene. GP teams and their Japanese bosses assumed that only Americans or Australians were capable of winning on a 500. Carl was also naive enough to assume that his talent would get him a ride. He wasn't and never will be a political animal, he doesn't trust anyone enough to be his agent, and he pointedly fails to accept that someone's nationality or a sponsor's preferences should dictate who gets a ride.

During 1992 Carl found himself out on his own, often without the family and without the familiar protective cloak of a British team around him. The Swedish journalist Jan Leek encountered him for the first time in the paddock at the Hockenheim World Superbike round at the start of the season.

'Fogarty was spending his own money and as we now know was so far into the red he was over the border of financial disaster. He seemed to have attached himself to Mac McDiarmid who he travelled two steps behind. The highlight of this performance came in the press room – on race day! This was the World Championship and between the two races there was Foggy, already a multiple World Champion and TT winner, seated in the middle of a group of English journalists drinking coffee.

'I saw he was trying to show his face in public, possibly to help attract sponsors. If it was his idea or someone else's I don't know, but it looked very strange. One big table of German journalists, another table with the British and me, Mac talking incessantly, and a strangely silent and stone-faced Carl Fogarty.

'When Mac, in an attempt to ... I don't know ... to ease ... whatever, asked me how one would translate Foggy into Swedish and what it would sound like, I answered "dimmig", pronounced "dimmi". Mac laughed and repeated the answer two or three times to himself, to Carl, to the table in general. Carl's eyes bored his dark sunglasses, small oval ones, into me. He was flat broke and trying to cut a colourful figure. I don't think it suited him.'

Another journalist, Ken Wootton of *Australian Motorcycle News*, summed up Carl Fogarty's 1992 perfectly: 'He proved he could go very fast on any motorcycle in any kind of conditions and on any kind of circuit – without anybody noticing!'

What neither Wootton nor Fogarty knew was that Alan Cathcart, the British writer, racer and fan of all things Italian, had been called by Massimo Bordi of Ducati. He wondered if by any chance Alan could provide Carl Fogarty's telephone number?

chapter five

Works rider

Ducati's first call came from ex-racer Davide Tardozzi who was starting a new career as a team manager. He wanted Carl to ride for him. The next day Raymond Roche rang; the ex-champ had also stopped riding and was going to manage the works Ducati team. Showing faith in the prediction he made at Donington the previous year, he also wanted Carl. If you're interested, said the Frenchman, get on a plane today. Carl did. The meeting was short. How much did Carl want for the year? Foggy thought of a number: '£50,000'. Afterwards, Roche laughed at Carl: 'You could have got £100,000!' He also told Carl that he must wear Shark crash helmets, a French make with which Roche had connections. That relationship still stands. Carl did bring up the question of expenses, though. Here's an extra £5,000, said Ducati – sort out your own flights. Tardozzi, incidentally, was given Spanish GP hero Juan Garriga as his rider. Although he quit after less than half the season, Garriga was seen as a vital signing for Ducati specifically and Superbike generally, so the Castiglionis obviously had faith in Tardozzi.

The history of production-related four-stroke and 750cc World Champion-ships is a troubled one. Formula 750 lasted three years and F1 never achieved any significance outside the UK, for whom it was invented as a one-race Championship in 1977 as compensation for the Isle of Man TT losing its World Championship status.

Superbike, by now five years old, was at the point where it had to make the jump to international significance or face the probability of fading to, at best, second-division status or, at worst, extinction. The prospects weren't wonderful. The Championship lost its three top riders of 1992 – champion Doug Polen to a season of domestic racing back home in the States, ex-champion Raymond Roche to team management, and Aussie tough guy Rob Phillis, who retired from international racing.

Thankfully for the Championship, the 1993 season developed into an epic confrontation between Carl and Kawasaki's latest hotshot, Scott Russell. It quickly became apparent that the two disliked each other intensely; by mid-season hatred would not have been too strong a word. The reason was simple, as Carl

Pushing off as a works Superbike rider on the Ducati 888. (Kel Edge)

later explained: for the first time he had met somebody who wanted to win as badly as he did. The main plot was underpinned by subplots of the little Italian Ducati factory taking on the might of Japan, the taciturn Lancastrian against the typically media-friendly sound-bite-conscious American.

The two leading characters enjoyed, if that's the right word, support from a strong cast of bit-part players. Most notable were Russell's team-mate Aaron Slight of New Zealand, and two Italians – Carl's team-mate, the fearsome Giancarlo Falappa, and the equally intense but physically tiny Fabrizio Pirovano on a Yamaha.

Two significant events shaped the future of the World Superbike Championship in 1993. First, Raymond Roche retired from riding and took over as manager of the factory Ducati team. Second, the British satellite TV station Sky Sports abandoned Grand Prix coverage to the pan-European station Eurosport and decided to show the Superbikes live (the author was hired by Sky Sports TV as one of the commentators). For the first time the UK audience had the prospect of watching a Briton challenge for a world motorcycling championship – race by race, as it was happening.

Carl's move wasn't as prestigious as it now sounds and was definitely second-best to a Grand Prix ride. Superbike had yet to establish itself as a significant world series and no one would have dreamed of comparing it with the GPs. Foggy only took the ride when he saw any realistic prospect of a 500 GP ride disappear, and that would only have been on a Harris as a privateer. He comforted himself with the thought that signing for Ducati might lead to a ride on the 500 Cagiva,

Signing for Ducati might lead to a ride on the 500 Cagiva

even wondering aloud with typical candour, 'Who knows what might happen if one of the regular riders gets hurt?'

A major plus for Carl was that he finally got to work with 'Slick'. Anthony Bass wasn't just the token English mechanic in the team; he became a vital component of Carl's inner circle. Roche's laid-back style of team management was also good for Carl, although he didn't always see it. His favourite memory is of Roche practising his golf swing in the pit garage. He used an apple. 'There were tiny bits of it everywhere, in my leathers, in my helmet . . .'

Slick remembers a happy team and is full of admiration for the way Raymond dealt with Carl. If they had a disaster, Roche might grin 'Fucking Englishman!' at them, but that was the end of it. Roche also had the ability to gee Carl up, to snap him out of the depression he can slump into if he doesn't win or if the bike breaks. Michaela thinks the relationship worked so well because Raymond and Carl are very similar characters.

The team wasn't as large as you'd expect – it looked more like an experienced privateer set-up than a full factory effort. Catering, for example, was by one of Raymond's mates who cooked pasta in the back of the van, and that was on a good day. Slick swears that they lived on salad for the whole season. Roche was very much a hands-on manager who got involved in the detail of bike set-up, and he and Carl communicated well in what seemed to most observers like basic Anglo-Saxon. Unfortunately for Raymond, he also managed to spend a good deal more than the budget allowed and suffered the usual mid-season fallout with the Italian management.

However, it was Carl's – and Superbike's – good fortune that Sky Sports appointed Martin Turner as producer for the series. One of the relatively new channel's radical young producers with a background in music videos, Turner turned the series into real television, not just pictures of motorcycles going round in circles. Programmes included studio guests in well-designed sets, slow-motion pieces cut to music, up-to-date graphics, the whole armoury of modern TV. When Turner moved on from Superbikes it was to produce Sky's coverage of rugby union, for which he won satellite TV's first Bafta award.

This coverage was an integral part of the appeal of Superbikes in the UK, helping to attract big crowds to the British rounds of the Championship over the following years. For the first race of the season – the Irish round, even though it was held at Brands Hatch in the south-east of England – Sky Sports showed the climax of final practice live on Saturday afternoon plus both races on Sunday, despite which a crowd of 12,000 braved the elements to see the action in person.

Race day was wet. Miniature rivers were running across the track and the start was delayed by half an hour. According to the form book this should have suited Carl perfectly, his record in the wet being impeccable: 'I used to laugh at the rest of them if it was raining.'

No one was laughing when Carl led the field trailing a great plume of spray down towards Clearways, the last bend, on the first lap. The instant he hit the brakes the front wheel locked. The red bike dropped on to its right-hand side and slid down the track, on to the grass, over the sandpit and into the tyre barrier. Carl followed close behind, aquaplaning on his back and spinning through 360 degrees several times as he appeared to pick up rather than lose speed, then smacked into his bike, flipped over the fairing and into the tyre wall. There were no broken bones but he damaged shoulder muscles badly enough to prevent him from going to the line for the second race.

It was the worst possible start to the season. World Championship contenders can rarely afford the luxury of giving their main contenders a head start if they are to make a serious title challenge. The second round in Germany offered some consolation with a third place in the first race, followed by a disappointing seventh in the second. Worse still, team-mate Falappa now had three wins, and Russell had a win and two second places.

Team morale got a major boost when they took time off from World Superbikes to take the Ducati to Ulster for yet another go at the North West 200. After years of disappointment it all came right with two crushing wins and an outright lap record, which an emotional Carl described as making him feel as good as anything he'd done.

With his personal Irish question answered, Carl found more consolation and a hint of things to come back with the Superbikes in Spain at Albacete, which would turn into one of his favourite circuits. This time luck was firmly on Carl's side, but it had nothing to do with him taking the lead early on and quickly pulling out a big lead, by Superbike standards, of over four seconds. Slight chased forlornly, followed by Falappa and the slow-starting Russell. It took Russell 10 laps to get past the Italian, who promptly tried to get back past on the brakes at the end of the start/finish straight, lost control and crashed. His bike scooped up the Kawasaki and moments later both men were getting to their feet in a cloud of settling dust. They did not exchange words.

To general amazement Foggy repeated the dose in the second race, clearing off from the start to win from Russell. Falappa had to retire and didn't just lose his Championship lead, but also dropped to third behind the Kawasaki duo of Russell and Slight. Fogarty's double win, his first in World Superbike,

took him from eighth to fifth in the standings, but more significantly he was only 17 points adrift of the leader now, not 51. Maybe a Championship challenge was possible after all.

The picture came into sharp focus at Brno, then still in the united state of Czechoslovakia. All through race weekend Russell and Fogarty battled. They fought for pole position, then they spent large chunks of both races nose-to-tail or side-by-side on one of the most spectacular tracks in Europe.

Carl won the battle for pole and the first race, but only after spending half the race in the first head-to-head confrontation of the season between the two men who would dominate the rest of this year and all of 1994. He made the decisive break and set the fastest lap, leaving the American short of grip as his tyre gave up the unequal struggle.

Race 2 was a replay of the first, further simplified when both Falappa and Slight crashed. This time Carl's gearbox started making disturbing noises and despite again setting the fastest lap he couldn't find an answer to Russell's inspired form. As if to prove that its rider wasn't shamming, the Ducati locked up solid on the slow-down lap. Carl and Scott ended the meeting with a win and a second place apiece and went to first and second in the Championship table with 21 points between them. The scene was set for a dramatic second half to the Superbike season.

When he signed on Ducati's dotted line Carl had wondered aloud about the prospects of a 500 ride. He got his wish at the British GP with a one-off wild-card ride on a spare Cagiva. Given his position in the World Superbike Championship, quite a few people

Fogarty leads the first race of the 1993 Superbike Championship – the Irish round, at Brands Hatch – but he crashed out half a lap later. (Don Morley)

Barry Sheene was there to give advice at the British 500 GP, Donington in 1993.
(Phil Masters)

doubted if this was a good idea – including some top men at Ducati and the Castiglioni brothers, who own the Cagiva Group of which Ducati is part. The regular Cagiva 500 riders – Mat Mladin and Doug Chandler, both carrying injuries that would prevent them from starting – were conspicuously unimpressed to see him there.

After one test session at Mugello, he fronted at Donington Park on Friday and went second fastest in the morning's untimed practice. He was fast enough in the timed afternoon session for a front-row grid position despite a minor crash and spending more time in the pits than out on the track. More problems saw him unable to go faster on Saturday, and in the closing stages of qualifying he was knocked back to fifth fastest and a

Previous pages: A very wild wild-card at the British GP. (Don Morley)

second-row start. Inquisitive British journalists – and Michaela Fogarty – observing the progress, or rather the lack of it, were seen to move further down the pit lane every time Carl came back in. He wasn't happy.

Come race day only 23,000 fans were willing to pay what was seen as the exorbitant entry price demanded by the new GP regime, despite Carl's qualifying performance. Those that did were treated to an extraordinary race. Unable to find neutral after the warm-up lap, Carl botched the start and got a grandstand view of an astounding crash at the Esses first time round. From sixth place, Carl saw Mick Doohan smack into Alexandre Barros's Suzuki and complete his demolition of the Suzuki team by tailgating Kevin Schwantz. The dust had just about settled when the Yamaha team of Wayne Rainey and Cadalora led over the line at the end of the third lap with, in third place and heralded by the crowd rising to its feet in an unplanned and almost hysterical Mexican wave, the red Cagiva of Carl Fogarty.

The next time round Foggy was in second and thinking about winning, as was the crowd if the noise they made was anything to go by. It wasn't to be, however. The front brake lever was soon coming back to the handlebar and Carl had to back off to adjust it, thus giving Cadalora the chance to repass him. Then British fans realised that Niall Mackenzie was blasting up through the field after an awful start – one rostrum place left and two Brits in contention. It was decided on the run to the very last corner. The Cagiva faltered – it was running low on petrol – and the Scot was through to get third by one-fiftieth of a second.

Carl was, of course, bitterly disappointed, but he had equalled the team's best finish of the year after minimal practice on the bike and done more than any other wild card with the exception of Japanese test riders at home in Suzuka. It was another demonstration of Fogarty's talent for riding an imperfectly set-up bike faster than was thought possible. All great racers have to ride around problems and Carl had demonstrated yet again that he could do this, but like his British contemporaries he had still to prove he could set a bike up.

Back at the Superbikes a growing audience of increasingly excited British fans now saw an increasingly confident Fogarty closing the gap on Russell and patently starting to get up the American's nose.

For the past three years the alleged superiority of the V-twin Ducati over the four-cylinder Japanese bikes like the Kawasaki had been a sore point with the riders who had chased Roche and especially Polen to their runaway title wins. The regulations gave V-twins a lower minimum weight limit and a higher capacity limit to compensate for the greater efficiency of the multicylinder motors.

The effect of this was to make the Ducatis stop quicker on the brakes and fire out of slow and medium speed corners better. Ultimate top speeds were comparable and on a race track irrelevant, but the overall effect was to make the Ducatis more user-friendly on most tracks. Certainly you only had to listen to Russell's Kawasaki motor screaming to realise that its power was packed at the top of its five-figure rev range.

The Fogarty-Russell clash brought this old argument back into sharp focus during the season and was exacerbated by the growing personal animosity between the two men. The public caught on when Russell appeared to ignore Carl on the rostrum.

British fans and media went to town in a fit of moral outrage at this offence against sportsmanship. What they were seeing was two men for whom the cliché 'he who finishes second is the first loser' isn't just a truism, it's a basic article of faith. At their level of commitment the universe is collapsing if they see another motorcycle in front of them on a race track. This is of course true of all sports people operating at the very peak of world competition, but some are better at hiding the fact than others. Americans, as Scott Russell himself pointed out when challenged, are only interested in first place. But even Fogarty's will to win couldn't overcome his Englishness: he did manage to do the decent thing and shake hands when he was beaten.

Not that he was beaten often in the middle third of the season. He scored back-to-back doubles in Sweden and Malaysia, with Russell second three times and fourth once, and was within five points of the American as the Championship went to Japan. It was apparent that the Ducati team were starting to give Carl the tools to do the job.

He's usually alone, head down, in a world of total concentration

He still wasn't particularly good at communicating with the Ducati factory technicians or setting up the bike, but Slick and Ohlins suspension technician Anders Andersson were starting to read him and relate his observations to the bike's behaviour.

Down the other end of the pit lane it looked as if the Muzzy Kawasaki team hadn't made any progress since Daytona when Russell was only beaten by Eddie Lawson, an impression reinforced in Japan when Russell qualified third behind local Kawasaki man Keiichi Kitagawa. He could only finish eighth in the first race on a bike that was patently off the pace; worse still Kitagawa and his team-mate Shoichi Tsukamoto finished second and third; and to put the tin hat on it Foggy won to take the lead in the Championship for the first time.

It all looked so good for the Englishman. Four pole positions in a

row, obvious signs of discontent in the Kawasaki camp with the Championship leader unleashing his considerable temper on anyone in a green jacket behind a locked pit garage door. Carl had even got over the niggling worry of not crashing since Brands by tipping off going into the chicane in practice. Back at home the fans were already getting worked up about the British round at Donington in three races time. It did indeed look good. Until five laps from the end of Race 2.

The Muzzy Kawasakis had new motors in, courtesy of Kawasaki Japan, after the debacle of Race 1. Russell started repaying the debt as soon as the lights turned green by leading into the first turn. It took Carl three laps to get up to him and another to pass him, but there was to be no repeat of Race 1. It was like Brno all over again, a confrontation between the best two riders in the Championship, but this time only one of them made it to the flag.

Twenty laps into the 25-lap race Carl made the first significant break, pulling

Raymond Roche, manager of the factory Ducati team, looks over Carl and Michaela at Donington, 1993. (Phil Masters)

out a lead of over a second. Then he came on a local rider in the first corner. The backmarker did not give way, trying instead, as Carl was to say later, to race him. At the next corner, another right-hander, Carl again made a move to pass. Maybe he was over-anxious because of the looming Russell or just plain angry, but he wasn't going to wait to pass him on a straight. Again the backmarker blocked him and this time Carl got on the gas too hard and too early, lost traction and was flipped over the highside. He had led the World Superbike Championship for fractionally under three and a half hours. Conspiracy theorists were disappointed to note that the guilty backmarker was on a Honda.

Fortunately for Fogarty, his second go at playing catch-up started in Holland on the Assen circuit he describes as 'built for the way I ride a motorcycle'. He made it five pole positions in a row, then proceeded to destroy the rest of the field on what is usually thought of as a rider's circuit. Like the sublime Phillip Island in Australia, it was designed specifically for motorcycles and is only used by the bikes. It's almost chicane free with sweeping corners that put a premium on corner speed rather than outright power, and it has an atmosphere that can only be generated by decades of world-class racing in front of millions of spectators.

To see Carl at Assen is to be reminded of his Isle of Man triumphs. He's usually alone, head down behind the Perspex bubble of the fairing, alone in a world of total concentration, racing the track not his opponents and travelling at lap-record pace. The layout of Assen, following the path of old public roads in places and with cambers and crowns reminiscent of the street not the track, adds to the impression.

Scott Russell did manage to lead as far as the first corner, then hang on to Carl's wheel for half of the first race, but in the second race we saw the first total destruc-tion of the field by Fogarty. He led off the line, had a comfortable lead half way round the first lap, a big lead at the end of it, and a massive lead next time round. He won by over six seconds despite spending much of the last lap waving at the Union Jacks liberally dotted around the spectator banking.

In spite of his two second places Russell looked a picture of dejection on the rostrum. He still led the title chase but only by seven points. Fogarty had won eight of the last 10 races, crashed once and crucially been beaten just once by Russell. He looked as if he had acquired the vital weapon that all champions need – total self-belief.

And so to Donington. Ducati, conscious of the lack of support Fogarty had received recently from their other riders, supplied a bike for Niall Mackenzie. Ostensibly he was there as back-up, but no one told Carl if there were any team orders. Eventually he brought up the subject with the Scotsman, who later wryly reported, 'He asked what I was going to do and then said, "Not that I care, mind".'

I just pushed too hard – I can't believe Russell's luck this year

Lots of people did care, though. The crowd was on a par with the numbers the GP attracted, and most of them were disconcerted when both Russell and Slight went faster than Fogarty in qualifying. Towards the end of the final qualifying session on Saturday afternoon, Russell rushed into the pits to make adjustments and give his team's eardrums a severe blast. He was incandescent with anger when he left the pit lane.

On the next, plummeting rush down

Following pages: *This is what the whole 1993 season was all about: Fogarty versus Russell, both on the track – and off (Donington).*
(Both Phil Masters)

Craner Curves, Russell asked too much of a new cold rear tyre and was flung through the air at well over 100mph. The beating he received was severe enough for him to be pushed back to his motorhome in a wheelchair and carried inside. His back, a knee and an ankle were severely bruised and his team had to raise the seat on his bike and lower the right footrest to enable him to race.

Sunday's first race started with more drama when a blow-up at the Melbourne Loop spread oil over the racing line. Slight was the first to crash on it and was followed by five others; the race was stopped. The first five laps counted and at that point Russell had been leading from Slight and Fogarty. As the race would now be decided on the aggregate times, the 1.23-second gap between Russell and Fogarty would be crucial to how the restarted second half of the race would be run. Fogarty was first to the chequered flag but Russell was

In action on the 888. (Kel Edge)

only half a second behind him and won overall.

Round one to the American, who said it didn't hurt when he was on the bike but it sure as hell did when he was off it.

Now the pressure was really on Fogarty. He led from the green light but Russell was in front the fourth time round. Carl hammered straight back into the lead and kept the pace up to try and make a break, but he was trying too hard. On lap eight, with a lead of about a second and gambling all, he too fell victim to Craner Curves. 'I just pushed too hard,' he said. 'I can't believe Russell's luck this year.'

Fogarty's lack of charity was typical – and understandable. He'd won many more races than the Kawasaki rider yet he had to concede that Russell's 32-point lead meant that the Championship was effectively lost. The British crowd, while disappointed with the result, were in awe of Russell's mental toughness in beating Foggy twice in front of his own fans and

Foggy's bike is taken away after the Donington crash. (Phil Masters)

on a circuit he rides as well as anyone, and especially after a fall that would have put most men out for a fortnight.

The end of the season was strangely subdued, but with surreal tinges. In Portugal, on the strangely modified Estoril circuit, a long hold on the red light resulted in Russell retiring with a burned-out clutch, but Carl was in no position to take advantage, having slung the Ducati into a sand-trap after hitting a damp patch on lap three.

Carl's mood went from desolation to elation when he realised that the Championship was still alive. In the second race he stormed away to an emphatic win, and then treated the crowd and TV viewers to some explicit hand signals to the effect that Foggy was number one and Russell was not a very nice person. It wasn't the most sporting gesture of the season, but it was an indication of just how intense the rivalry had become, and with the gap at 29 points the title chase was still alive.

In Britain the fans at last had a winner to cheer

Unfortunately the last round in Mexico never happened. During qualifying, footballs and dogs were seen on the track, then Scott Russell, flat out down the fast straight, saw a pick-up truck cross in front of him. As there was no way the riders' safety could be guaranteed, racing was cancelled and Scott Russell was confirmed as World Superbike Champion.

Fogarty's mood was not helped by the statistics: he'd won 11 races, Russell had won five, but after the Brands Hatch crash he'd been chasing Russell all year and taking risks that resulted in crashes at Donington and Estoril. 'Every time I won,' he said later, 'Scott seemed to be second.'

It is difficult for any racer to accept that they aren't champion when they've won over twice as many races as anyone

else in the season, but titles aren't always won by the fastest man. The rest of the statistics fill in the picture: Carl finished second just twice, whereas Scott was runner-up 12 times; Carl was third twice, Scott just once; Carl was on pole six times, Scott four times; and, perhaps most significantly, Carl fell off four times and Scott just once – and that was when Falappa torpedoed him.

Both men were totally convinced that they were the best and fastest racer out there. The Englishman was convinced that the scoring system must be crazy to put him second, the American was convinced that he'd won despite the handicap the regulations imposed on his bike. The outside world saw two evenly matched racers of very different character on motorcycles of very different character.

In Britain the fans at last had a winner to cheer, their first since Barry Sheene in the late 1970s. Not that Carl was comparable with Sheene and his cheeky-chappie media persona, but British bikers had found a new hero. Some of the paddock inhabitants weren't too sure about Carl. He could still be a difficult specimen to deal with, hypersensitive to what he perceived as paddock politics or bullshit of any form. He could welcome you like a long-lost brother or be crude and offensive. If Foggy was feeling good you knew about it, and if he wasn't happy you knew about that too.

James Whitham – his friendship with Carl now cemented by the fact that his long-time girlfriend Andrea Cooke and Michaela had also become close friends – has an interesting view on the Fogarty character. When the two couples went on holiday together Carl spent the first two days talking about how good he was until he was firmly shut up by the others. From then on, says James, Carl was perfect, exhibiting a sense of humour that is the best. On the grounds that Whitham is himself one of the quickest-witted guys in the paddock, that is some compliment. A clue to this may be that they don't talk about motorcycle racing. There are precedents for this type of single-mindedness. Great champions like Wayne Rainey, and especially Eddie Lawson, rarely exhibited a spark of humour at a race track – they were after all at work – but were quite different off duty at home. Very few people at race tracks get to see the private Carl Fogarty.

British industry was now well aware of his value too. Neil Tuxworth, nowadays an employee of Honda UK, was going to be manager of the factory's Superbike team in 1994 and wanted Carl as his lead rider. He and Honda MD Bob McMillan secretly met Fogarty at a motorway service station on the M62 to discuss terms, but Carl was wary of the Honda after his experiences on the RC30 and felt no need to move from Ducati – especially as they had a new bike for 1994, the mighty Ducati 916.

chapter six

World Superbike Champion

Ducati gave Carl not just a new bike but a new team for 1994. Virginio Ferrari took over as works team manager with an all-Italian crew plus the omnipresent 'Slick'. The old 888 was replaced by the stunning new 916, as stylish as it was effective. It was, though, a brand new chassis, and the usual lack of pre-season testing meant that Carl and the crew would have problems in the early races getting the thing to work. Ferrari brought a more professional approach to the team and a lot more hardware. Ducati's paddock encampment now looked every inch as impressive as that of a top GP team with its massive transporters and a full complement of staff, including a chef.

Elsewhere, of the top men in the Superbikes, only Aaron Slight moved camps. He was supposed to be the second rider in the brand new Honda team with double ex-World Champ Doug Polen as lead man. The significance of an official works team in World Superbike put out by the world's biggest bike-makers cannot be over-estimated; it was another big step forward for the Championship.

In 1993 the racing had been entertaining, but the farce in Mexico, the unsatisfactory state of the track in Portugal, and the total lack of promotion in Czechoslovakia had tarnished the image of the series. And as Carl Fogarty was now an integral part of the World Superbike scene, it diminished his reputation too.

The new season needed to be free from off-track politics and problems if it was to progress further and if the credibility of its top riders as world-class racers was to be sustained. There had always been some sniping between the GP and Superbike paddocks – usually from team managers and organisers rather than riders – but this year it would escalate as the superbikes elbowed their way to centre stage. Carl, never a diplomat, opined that the 500s would be dead in a couple of years once Schwantz and Doohan retired because 'no one's going to watch Capirossi smacking into the straw bales'.

Well over 25,000 fans turned up to Donington Park for the first race of the year. It was yet another indication of the gathering momentum of Superbike in the UK, and put further pressure on Carl. They saw Fogarty and Russell take a win each with Slight second both times, so it was a mighty relieved Foggy who

Conferring with new Ducati team manager,
Virginio Ferrari, 1994. (Kel Edge)

took a one-point lead to Germany for the second round.

But his habit of giving the rest of the field a start had not been cured. In qualifying he hit a patch of oil on the Sachs Curve, ironically one of the slowest corners on a very fast track, was flung in the air and broke two bones in his left wrist when he landed. Scott Russell promptly rubbed metaphorical salt into Carl's all too real wounds by winning both races in fine style. The only positive aspect of the situation was that there was a three-week break before the Italian round, just about time to give Carl a chance of recovering enough to race at the front rather than circulating at the back and hoping to pick up a few points. However, that turned out to be rather optimistic.

The paddock's attention was diverted from Fogarty's health when the FIM announced that a fuel sample taken from Slight's bike after the second race at Donington had been found to be illegal and the Kiwi would be stripped of the points he scored in both British races. The Castrol Honda team announced

that they would appeal. It was exactly the sort of thing the Championship didn't need, appeal and counter-appeal dragging on through the season with riders' points totals changing between races.

Back on track in Italy, Carl's wrist was still in plaster to the elbow but hadn't given any problems for two weeks. As soon as he got back on a bike, however, it hurt badly and hampered his riding. Carl's gearbox then blew in the first race when he was seventh, and to make matters worse Russell won again. In the second race Carl was obviously having difficulty in sections requiring a rapid change of direction, but under the circumstances his fifth place was heroic. He didn't see it that way. 'Any time I'm not on the rostrum I'm not happy.' But even then of

Following pages: *The Hockenheim crash that so nearly ruined the season and the title challenge.* (Kel Edge)

course if he's second or third he's not happy because he hasn't won.

Russell's second place meant that he'd won four races, been second once and fourth once; Slight had three seconds, a third, a fourth and a crash. Carl was now fourth in the Championship with 46 points, while Russell led with 110. Not a promising situation for Carl with over a quarter of the season already run.

Spain was next – Albacete. If his title hopes were to be kept alive, nothing less than a win, preferably two, would do on a track where he'd dominated last year. In untimed practice the Ducati team suffered a near tragic blow when Giancarlo Falappa crashed and suffered severe head injuries. For a while he teetered on the edge, but although he did hold on to life it left the Italian team in a profoundly depressed state.

He could not afford the luxury of another crash or breakdown

Carl's wrist was still strapped but didn't give any problems. He took pole. Then he got the holeshot in Race 1. Russell fought through to second after four laps but Fogarty simply increased his lead, seemingly at will. And then came the incident that turned the season: Russell crashed on oil at the end of the main straight. To complete Foggy's joy, best mate James Whitham got on the rostrum in third. The second race was a startlingly precise carbon copy of the first – in every detail apart from Foggy taking two laps to get to the front. This time Russell crashed when his front wheel tucked under on a slow corner. The points gap was down to 24. It was the start of an epic Fogarty charge.

Russell, for so long the totally focused professional, suddenly had a crisis of confidence. Two big testing crashes before the Austrian round, on top of his Albacete debacle, severely detuned him, and he was acutely aware that the fast and scary Osterreichring was not the place to have another big get-off. Fogarty took advantage in the most crushing possible way with pole position and two runaway wins. He crossed the line standing on the footpegs doing the same hand-jive with which Brazil's World Cup soccer players had been celebrating goals.

As Brazil were playing Italy in the World Cup Final that evening his Ducati mechanics weren't amused – even less so when Carl supported Brazil. However, the team, watching the match on TV, were very sporting. They took the water out of its bottles before throwing it over him. The team's spirits had also been lifted by the news that Falappa had been brought out of his coma and was out of danger. When his mechanics unfurled a banner on the start line reading 'The lion has awoken' there wasn't a dry eye in the house.

Russell meanwhile had only managed 14th and 12th so, for the first time since Donington, Carl was back at the top of the Championship. But he was now faced with the suddenly unwelcome prospect of another wild-card ride in the British GP.

Fogarty's presence on a Cagiva was important to the Donington promoters anxious to reverse the trend of falling gates. Carl wondered how he'd got himself into the situation where he could ruin his chances of the Superbike title in a one-off ride on a motorcycle he hadn't tested.

To make matters worse, Cagiva wanted Carl to ride the unproven and unraced fuel-injected 500. Everyone's worst fears were almost realised when he slid off in the first untimed practice session and damaged his right hand. No worries, everyone was told, he's only taken some skin off. Sure enough, Carl struggled through qualifying on a recalcitrant motorcycle to 11th on the grid, after which it was announced that he had in fact got a couple of cracked bones in his hand and would not be racing. He retreated into the Clinica Mobile for prolonged treatment while Slick warned lurking journalists and TV crews to stand well back when Carl emerged, which he did, in subdued mood, sporting an outsize icepack on the damaged hand.

It was all a charade. The hand was indeed only skinned but the team had to find a dignified way of withdrawing their man without incurring the wrath of the organisers and promoters. Carl played his part, giving a beautifully low-key interview to a suitably solicitous Sky TV crew before disingenuously hopping on his scooter and riding off without any apparent hand problems at all. He didn't hang around for race day either, earning the disapproval of Donington promoter Robert Fearnall.

The Superbikes then headed off on their Far Eastern excursion to Indonesia and Japan. But despite leaving Austria in the lead, Foggy now found himself second behind Aaron Slight after the FIM gave him back the points that had been confiscated after the Donington fuel tests.

It was the start of a totally frustrating Indonesian weekend for Carl that encompassed handling problems in practice, a certain win dematerialising when a valve broke in the closing stages of Race 1, and finally a win in Race 2. Slight's brace of seconds kept him in the lead, and Russell's two thirds put him exactly equal on points with Carl.

In Japan Russell fought back with two wins against Fogarty's fourth and second, but then it was back to Holland. The one thing you can guarantee about Assen is that it will rain at some point during the meeting. Thankfully, from Carl's point of view, the weather disrupted qualifying rather than the racing and he stormed to another Dutch double. Carl left Holland second in the Championship – but he arrived at the San Marino round at Mugello as leader after the FIM finally brought the 'illegal' fuel saga to a close by taking 17 points back off Aaron Slight. In the end natural justice prevailed and the Kiwi was only penalised for using illegal fuel in the one race after which the fuel was tested. Carl did not take such a charitable view. Indeed, he had now elevated the New Zealander into his personal hate figure in place of Russell. The relationship between Fogarty and Russell had now mellowed from open dislike into what looked suspiciously like mutual respect, despite the fact that the title chase was a three-horse race, and a close race at that.

It seemed that Russell would cancel out Fogarty's Dutch wins after he beat Carl fair and square in the first race at Mugello and looked to be on his way to victory in the second race – however, his Kawasaki broke for the first time that season.

A grateful Foggy left Italy with a second, a win, and a smile on his face at the prospect of another home race at Donington as a replacement for the cancelled European round at Jerez. But he was aware that the cancellation of the final scheduled round in Argentina meant that he could not afford the luxury of another crash or a mechanical breakdown.

Going into Donington Carl led the Championship with 255 points. Slight was still second with 237 after the FIM and Honda had finished their courtroom wranglings, and Russell was back in third with 223. There were 80 points still up for grabs from four races left (two at Donington and two in Australia).

It is often overlooked that the 916 was a brand new bike for 1994 and with the usual lack of pre-season practice the team took half the year to get it handling

Following pages: *Carl and the Ducati 916 – made for each other.* (Kel Edge)

properly. The problems were exacerbated in wet weather when Carl found it difficult to get the power down, so the last thing he needed was a wet race. Unfortunately for Carl and the Donington crowd, race day was soaking. He gambled on the weather drying for the first race and went for a relatively hard-compound rear tyre. The gamble didn't pay off. It stayed wet, Carl had precious little grip and ended up 14th, losing 18 points to Russell who held off new Aussie star Troy Corser who had been drafted in to beef up the Ducati challenge. It was a Russell-Corser one-two again in the second race, but this time Carl managed fifth place to limit the damage. But he wasn't happy.

Two factory Ducati riders finished in front of him – Corser and Mauro Lucchiari in second and third – which provoked a tabloid storm of synthetic outrage about the lack of organisation in the Ducati team. Corser had spent the whole event harassing Russell, trying to get past or force a mistake.

There was no exuberance, just utter relief, the demon of failure gone

There was no way he was going to drop back and give up a chance of his first World Superbike win: helping Carl was no doubt very much a secondary consideration. The question of Lucchiari is more complex, but he was well over 30 seconds in front of Fogarty in the second race, which would have made it difficult for him to move over and let Carl through. Interestingly, Carl didn't seem particularly interested in the subject until a journalist brought it up. When he realised that he now had just five points in hand over Russell he took a strong interest.

After a nerve-wracking four-week gap the Superbikes pitched up at the superb Phillip Island circuit for the Australian round. Carl was amazingly calm, relaxed even. He played a bit of golf, chatted to all and sundry, and generally chilled out. Where was the usual Fogarty, the one who always seemed to think that the world was against him, the driven man? He was now approaching the most crucial race of his career. Shouldn't he be even more tightly wound than ever? There was never a doubt in his mind: Michaela was equally certain, her first words to him on race-day morning being, 'You're going to be World Champion today.'

The Championship was going to be a straightforward showdown between Fogarty and Russell, with Slight having a tenuous mathematical chance of the title. No one else could win it, but the picture was complicated by the arrival of yet another new name. Teenager Anthony Gobert, the new Aussie Superbike Champion, had been poached from Honda by the Muzzy team and promptly set pole the first time he sat on a Kawasaki.

Most people would think that in Fogarty's position the best thing to do would be to take no risks, shadow Russell and make a move towards the end of the race if it were possible. This is not the Fogarty way. He pushed and shoved in the first corner like it was a six-lap sprint race, got to the front and put on a classic Foggy charge to break the field in the opening laps and control the race from the front. It wasn't conclusive, though. Gobert ran in second for most of the race before letting Russell through just before the chequered flag to make the gap eight points with just one race to go.

With 20 points for a win, Carl could afford to let Russell win, finish third and still be the champion. The issue was resolved by outside factors. With Gobert leading, Russell and Fogarty were dicing warily when, coming into a right-hander, Russell waved Carl through and effectively conceded the Championship. He pulled into the pits where it quickly

Celebratory photocall at Phillip Island, Australia, 1994. (Kel Edge)

became apparent that his tyres were completely ruined. Carl cruised to second place and the 1994 World Superbike Championship.

In the pits he was greeted by an enormous posse of journalists and photographers led by a microphone-toting Barry Sheene and his Channel 9 camera crew. They were all fighting for the first comment from the new World Champion. Carl took his helmet off, looked around anxiously and saw Michaela standing almost apologetically by the rear wheel of the Ducati. He pushed the assembled media aside to get to Michaela and embrace her. This was a touching moment and a rare public gesture from a man who can get embarrassed if you ask him to put an arm round his wife for a photo.

It showed how deeply the title affected him. So did the body language on the slow-down lap and the rostrum. There wasn't the standing-on-the-pegs, fist-waving exuberance of a Kevin Schwantz: it was the utter relief of a great weight being lifted off the shoulders, of the demon of failure being exorcised. Wayne Rainey reacted just the same way when he won his first World Championship. Carl later said he'd been crying – he used the Lancashire dialect term 'skryking' – around the last lap.

The title, and the season-long struggle that led to it, confirmed Carl not just as the British motorcycle fans' number one hero, but also as a racer of international status. In Italy fans followed him into the showers. In Spain – a country without a top Superbike racer – he is the only man from the class to have any public profile, the Ducati man with the dancing eyes. In America his feud with Scott Russell was rapidly turning him into an anti-hero.

The fact that he rode a Ducati helped.

Adam Ant World Champ? Surely some mistake.
(Fogarty family)

The Italian bikes have the same ability to tug at the heart strings as their four-wheeled compatriots from Ferrari, a characteristic that crosses international borders. Even in Japan a large section of the crowd were sporting Ducati regalia. It's a classic David and Goliath confrontation, the small Italian factory and their soulful, bellowing V-twins battling against the mighty Japanese corporations, their mega-Yen budgets and serried ranks of computer-aided designers.

The Fogarty character lent itself to that against-the-odds struggle. His more bloody-minded pronouncements seemed to fit the situation and endear him to the public rather than alienate them. The title also brought a subtle but distinct change in Carl's public persona. He became a much more relaxed guy to deal with. That old impression of being one man against the world faded – only slightly, but it faded nonetheless. He seemed happier.

Anders Andersson, the Ohlins suspension technician who moved to work for the Ducati team over winter, put it more bluntly. He saw a rider who was more confident in his abilities to set up a bike, happy to work with and learn from other people. The team was now getting really useful feedback from their rider. Anders also recognised the importance to Carl of Michaela and the kids. He summed the situation up with typical Scandinavian brevity: 'He's grown up – it happens to all of us.'

Jim Whitham also saw a change. 'He's not angry any more. He used to be the angriest bloke I've ever met.' He agrees that Michaela is the most important influence on Carl.

Slick saw a new dimension to Fogarty. 'He is the easiest rider I've ever worked with, he's like a blank sheet of paper, no preconceptions.' That means that Carl doesn't prejudge a change to his machine in practice sessions. He just asks what's been done since the last time he went out. If Slick replies, 'New front tyre, stiffer carcass, softer compound,' Carl never comes back with a negative remark of the 'But that'll make it worse/unrideable/lethal' variety, he just nods and gets on with it.

Slick was starting to see Carl thinking more deeply about his machinery, silently analysing what changes in set-up were doing. It was also noticeable that Carl had developed a more sensitive touch. Back in the F1 days his engine tuner, Tony Scott, used to build in massive piston-to-valve clearances because Carl was so brutal with his engines. Now Carl had very few engine failures, even when other works Ducatis were falling by the wayside. The kid who had been a typical rev-happy 250 headbanger had turned into the complete racer.

Virginio Ferrari was a more remote manager than Raymond Roche had been, largely because his English wasn't as good. According to Slick all he and Carl would get at some team meetings was 'Hello' and 'Goodbye'. But as with Roche, Carl says he learned a few things from Virginio.

Slick realised that he had to take over the psychological role that Roche had played so cleverly, and he did so both in testing and on race days. When Carl would come in and complain that the bike had no grip/was oversteering/wouldn't rev, it was Slick who broke the problem down to its component parts and got Carl to focus on the worst area. By now Slick was, like Jim Whitham, more like a brother to Carl than a friend.

With Foggy you are either an outsider or a brother. There is no in-between, no circle of acquaintances whom you'd call friends. 'James,' he says with feeling, 'understands me.' It would be too easy to characterise Carl as a bloody-minded automaton who only cares about winning. It isn't true. He cares about two things – winning races, and his family – and he is a far more complex character than many paddock inhabitants think. But on track he is driven by the sort of

Success has brought a few nice toys. (Kel Edge)

Michaela and Carl with Claudia and Danielle in their newly purchased Grade II listed house.
(Kel Edge)

will to win that only World Champions have.

At Sky, Martin Turner saw Fogarty as a champion who was also a star despite himself. 'He's not the now traditional media-friendly sportsman. He's self-contained, suspicious even, but the point about Foggy is that in the future he will be remembered for what he did on the track, for his astounding achievements, not because he was a media tart.'

Nevertheless, the non-specialist media started to take notice of Carl, high-profile British World Champions being thin on the ground. He was presented to the crowd at Blackburn Rovers' next Premiership soccer match, which happened to be against Tottenham Hotspur, so the ground was full. Carl seemed surprised by the enthusiasm of the reception he got: 'They went mad.' His reticence may have had something to do with the fact that he's been a Manchester United supporter since he was a kid, not something you readily admit to in Blackburn. When he found out that a couple of United's star players were fans of his Superbike exploits he was genuinely pleased and flattered as only a true fan can be when the object of veneration notices your existence.

There was also the matter of money. For the first time in his career Carl was making seriously good money and could command a basic signing-on fee of around £250,000 plus good contracts with leathers and helmet suppliers. His helmet manufacturer, Shark, started selling a Fogarty replica but without the red rose of Lancashire on the front in case it stopped residents of the ancient rival county of Yorkshire buying it.

This all helped in finishing the restoration of the new family home, a Grade II listed farmhouse on the moors outside Blackburn which was also home to an expanding menagerie of dogs,

What to do next . . . Carl contemplates his future.
(Mac McDiarmid)

ducks, Vietnamese pot-bellied pigs, geese and Michaela's horse. The star turn was still Arai who spends most of his time swinging on the rear leg of an amiable Great Dane called Bridgit. Carl cannot begin to understand how anyone could live in a city, 'especially London'.

There was also the arrival of daughter number two, Claudia, in August. Carl had been a quite modern, involved dad to Danielle, doing – he claims, and Michaela agrees – his fair share of nappy changing and other parental duties. He certainly dotes on his kids. Indeed, to find a photo of him looking totally relaxed and open you need to see a picture of him with his daughters. But you will not be surprised to learn that Claudia was thus named because of her dad's undisguised admiration for a certain supermodel.

But back to the business. Naturally there were more people than Ducati interested in Carl's services – and, of course, the number one plate – for 1995. Honda's Neil Tuxworth was still the man most likely to get Carl off Ducati, but his sales pitch was complicated by the situation with Doug Polen, who had not lived up to expectations in 1994 and was only half way through a two-year contract. One plan had Polen going back to race in the States, but nothing came of it, and amid much financial skulduggery he left the Castrol Honda team only weeks before the start of the season.

Carl says he would have stayed with Ducati in any case, but the prolonged intra-Honda wranglings meant that Tuxworth could not make him a proper offer.

Record breaker

It should have been as close as the previous year. Foggy himself reckoned that defending his 1994 title would be even more difficult than winning it. He pointed to fellow Ducati riders Mauro Lucchiari and Troy Corser as the men most likely to give him a hard time.

True to form he didn't mention Aaron Slight, and he slagged off the new Yamaha team of Yasutomo Nagai and young American Colin Edwards as 'one Japanese – they never go well away from home – and one rider no one's ever heard of.' Kawasaki's Anthony Gobert was good, he reckoned, but would start crashing when he got out of Australia.

The title might have mellowed him but no way was Carl going to give the rest of the field an easy time on or off the track during 1995. His new-found respect for Russell surfaced in a typical piece of double-edged Fogarty wit: 'I think I'll wind Scott up by saying he'll be no threat this year.'

There was no sign of humour after the opening skirmish of the season at Daytona. Scott won for the second year running in circumstances that only

Looking assured with his new status as World Superbike Champion, early 1995. (Kel Edge)

reinforced Carl's dislike of the place and his feelings about Russell. The British weekly tabloid *Motor Cycle News* stoked up the pre-season hype by quoting Carl as saying that he hated all Americans. The cutting was pinned to the wall in the

Starting at Daytona – for the last time.
(Kel Edge)

Daytona press office. What Carl had actually said was that he hated Daytona and the way the Americans run the place, but the crowd left Carl in no doubt as to how they felt about people who impugned their country, the flag and mom's apple pie.

In the race, Scott Russell tipped off on lap two, but incredibly didn't break a footrest or a handlebar, was push-started by marshals and got back in the race. Later on, with Carl leading, the pace car went out and Russell was alleged to have passed several riders under the yellow flag caution in force, an illegal move. The American rides Daytona as well as anyone and he charged to the front and won. Carl was incandescent with rage. As far as he was concerned he had been cheated, and he was still blazing when he got back to the UK after testing at Laguna Seca. Significantly, Michaela was equally adamant that her man had been cheated. Most neutral observers agree that Russell did pass under the caution but also point out that the Ducati pitwork was so sloppy that they lost nearly a minute to the Kawasaki in the pit lane, and the fact remains that Russell rode brilliantly. Carl, of course, doesn't quite see it that way and is very, very unlikely to return to the Speedbowl – if only because it's the sole place he's ever found himself riding round thinking about what would happen if he crashed.

Back home, Fogarty was getting an increasingly high profile in the world outside motorcycling. It was enough for Martin Turner to persuade Sky Sports to make a promotional commercial for the new season.

The image of Carl and the Ducati bursting from a cage in clouds of dry ice was perfect – and of course there was a close-up of those eyes. The bike used was actually Jim Whitham's, and after

repeated starting and stopping through-out the day's filming the machine was running at about 100°C. 'Jim did say it wasn't quite right the following week-end,' Carl remembers guilelessly.

There was no lack of motivation when the 1995 Superbike season started. For the first half of the season it looked as if no one was going to be any sort of threat to Carl. In the first six rounds he won seven out of 12 races, including doubles at the opening round at Hockenheim and the third round at Donington Park. The Donington double took Carl past Doug Polen's record of eight double wins in World Superbike, and his fastest laps in Hockenheim put him top of that list ahead of Raymond Roche. Only Polen's record of 17 pole positions survived: every other World Superbike Championship record now belonged to Carl Fogarty.

The British daily press were taking a keen interest in Carl. The tabloid *Sun* started running regular race reports, the august *Daily Telegraph* ran an interview after Donington, and the *Independent on Sunday* ran a full-page interview on race day. The *News of the World* picked up on the fact that Carl's Vietnamese pot-bellied pig had had piglets, which he'd named after various Superbike racers, including Scott Russell and James Whitham.

The first shock of the season came at Albacete where Aaron Slight cleverly conserved his tyres in the first race to beat Carl into second. Thereupon Foggy reasserted his superiority in the second race to take his 28th win in World Superbikes and go to the top of the all-time winners list in front of Doug Polen.

The post-race press conference saw Aaron take umbrage at some of Carl's comments: 'I was just trying to get over that my bike wasn't the fastest,' he now says, 'but Aaron thought I was having a

Having a slight disagreement with Aaron at the Albacete winners' press conference, Spain.
(Kel Edge)

go at him. I think he's all right about it now though.' Even if Carl didn't put it too diplomatically, his point about the relative performance of the bikes had some merit. At every track where a radar gun speed-trap was in operation, the Honda was shown to be the quickest thing out there. Ultimate top speed is academic on most race tracks, but it was an indication that the RC45 was a real threat and that if Aaron Slight had had a team-mate working alongside him for the whole season that threat might have been more consistent.

Back on track in Austria Carl won the first race and was joined on the rostrum by Gianfranco Castiglioni to celebrate Ducati's 100th victory in World Superbike.

Carl had some pithy opinions about the new regulations

Half way through the season things were looking good. It wasn't just that Carl had hit the ground running despite the usual lack of pre-season testing – there was also the total disarray of the opposition. Corser was unlucky, suffering a lack of power in Germany, a sheared sprocket while challenging Carl in the UK, and two crashes in Italy. The new Yamahas had so far only managed a single rostrum place for Edwards. Slight, now the sole Honda rider after the departure of Polen, was struggling, and despite the win in Spain he could only manage 16th and 13th at Misano with what was obviously still a difficult motorcycle to ride on bumpy tracks.

But the Kawasaki teams were in the worst shape. True to Fogarty's predictions, Russell didn't get on the rostrum in the first three races, then decamped to the Suzuki Grand Prix team to take the place of the retiring Kevin Schwantz.

Half way through the season Carl was a stupefying 114 points ahead of Slight, with Corser a further 27 points back. Of the 300 possible points (wins were now worth 25) Fogarty had scored 275.

But Carl's domination wasn't obtained by default, as his qualifying performances demonstrated. Two poles, two seconds and two thirds in the first six races, plus six fastest laps, showed his form. Corser's qualifying performances were nearly as impressive, but he had yet to set a fastest lap.

If things were going well on the track, the off-track politics were making up for it. Carl's domination, plus the way other Ducati riders were showing at the front, albeit sporadically, was giving ammunition to those who said that the regulations gave the V-twins an unfair advantage. Christian Sarron, the Yamaha team manager, was the most consistent complainer.

Entertainingly, Carl Fogarty had said in the close season that being World Champion relieved him of the obligation to suck up to sponsors. On the grounds that no one could ever remember him toeing any PR line or doing anything other than speak his mind, this remark provided some merriment for the paddock.

Carl now certainly had a few pithy opinions on the subject of the regulations. Having said, as usual, that the situation was doing his head in – he has a low tolerance for anything he sees as paddock politics – Carl defended Ducati vociferously, arguing that they were merely benefiting from the work they'd put in over the years and that if V-twins had such a big advantage, why didn't Honda or Kawasaki build one?

He also saw the complaints as undervaluing his own contribution as a rider. He pointed out that Ducati's success might be down to the riders, adding that the two best racers in the series – himself and Troy Corser – were on Ducatis and that he didn't remember anyone moaning about the rules when Scott Russell and Kawasaki were running away with the Championship at the start of the previous season. Nevertheless, in an unprecedented move the FIM changed the rules mid-season and raised the minimum weight limit for V-twins. It made no difference practically. Even the factory Ducatis weren't down on the minimum weight limit, but as the series is run by the Italian Flammini Group and many of the teams are Italian-based, making a political gesture was seen as important.

The defection of Scott Russell, for so long Fogarty's nemesis, affected Carl more than he will admit. His uncharitable parting shot, made with Daytona in mind, was that it didn't matter how well Russell went in GPs, he'd know that he'd be beaten if Fogarty was in the race. But Russell was greeted by the Grand Prix media as a gift from above. He quickly showed that he was going to be competitive and was hailed as a future contender.

Detractors of Superbike as a lesser formula had previously characterised the riders as second-raters. In many ways the American's superb showing in 500cc GPs underlined just how good a top Superbike rider has to be, thus validating both his own and Fogarty's World Championships.

Carl had previously shown very little interest in GPs, but through the second half of the season he didn't brush aside questions about a potential switch to 500 GPs, saying that he'd like to move – but of course only to a bike that was capable of winning. The praise being lavished on Russell obviously got to Carl, although he would of course deny it vehemently. He vastly enjoyed Pierfrancesco Chili's wild-card appearance at the Mugello GP where he put the Cagiva on the front row of the grid having not ridden a 500 for four years. That showed them what a good Superbike rider could do!

In the second half of the Superbike season the competition got their act together and gave Fogarty a much harder time. His only really bad meeting of the year came in, wouldn't you know it, the USA.

Carl was pleasantly surprised by the reaction of most American fans to him but there were a few exceptions, and some banners in the crowd showed Foggy in the cross-wires of a gunsight. That Daytona taunt just wouldn't go away. Typically, Carl rode around the very obvious problems in the races to score a fifth and a seventh, but the day belonged to the Aussies, with Corser and Gobert scoring a win and a second apiece. It was Gobert's first trip to the rostrum since he had burst on to the world scene in Phillip Island the previous season.

Normally, a home round at this juncture in the season would be just what a racer wanted. The European round at Brands Hatch didn't quite fit the bill, though. Carl had never won at the Kent circuit at any level. Indeed, he'd usually had appalling luck there, breaking down on the grid after getting pole in a British national race, and falling on the first lap in the World Superbikes two years before. Add in the expectations of the British public and you'd expect Carl to act like a man with the weight of the world on his shoulders. Maybe he would have done 12 months earlier. Two years before he certainly would have done. Instead there was the same relaxed Fogarty we'd seen at Phillip Island when the pressure was on in the biggest possible way. He gave the impression that he already had it won and took pole for the first time since Donington Park.

On race day the sun shone and nearly 50,000 fans packed into the circuit, turning the spectator banking into a sea of

Following pages: *Dominating style on the 916.* (Kel Edge)

red Foggy T-shirts. They weren't disappointed. Carl won both races. It was vintage Fogarty. He dealt with the field in the first few turns – Gobert was particularly troublesome – waited until he was sure the tyres were up to working temperature, then piled on the pressure, watching his pitboard and controlling both races from the front in a splendid display of track craft and concentration.

Brands Hatch hadn't seen a day like it since the Sheene-Roberts confrontations in the Transatlantic Trophy meetings of the late 1970s. The natural amphitheatre that frames the short-circuit section generates an atmosphere that compares with places like Assen and Hockenheim; and the crowd was much bigger than for the GP at Donington. It really did feel as though the good days of British racing were back. Carl was almost lost for words to describe how he felt, stuttering out 'All these people . . . wonderful' before

The Sugo highside: Carl was back on his bike three hours later for the second race which he won! (Sky Sports/Flammini Organisation)

declaring that it was one of the best days of his career. He realised that he could retain his title at the next round in Japan, but said that he would almost prefer to win it at the following round in Holland because there were always so many British fans at Assen. Once again, they were prophetic words.

Carl Fogarty took pole at Sugo, just as he'd done in 1993, and drew level with Doug Polen's record of 17 World Superbike pole positions. Unfortunately, there was to be another echo of 1993 in the first race. Yamaha use Sugo a lot for testing, so Yasutomo Nagai knew the circuit as well as anyone. He'd been edging his way into Carl's bad books by making a point of latching on to him in qualifying to get a tow to a fast time. It's not an uncommon tactic but Carl did not appreciate it, neither had he grown to like Colin Edwards, the other factory Yamaha rider. Foggy adopted a cockroach he found in the circuit hotel, housed it in a jam jar with a pierced lid and christened the unfortunate insect 'Colin'.

Nagai desperately wanted a win at his home circuit and led the early stages before Carl got past him after a short struggle. True to form Carl tried to make a break and was pulling away when he dived into the right-hander that had claimed him in 1993 and again suffered an enormous crash.

It was the classic highside in which the rear tyre breaks traction when the power is applied with the bike cranked right over; it slides, then grips again, flicking the bike upright. It's the worst way to crash a motorcycle and this was one of the worst highsides of the season. The bike flipped with such violence that its petrol tank detached itself in mid-air and Carl was flung out of the saddle and vertically into the air. He was flung so high that he had enough time to pedal a few times in mid-air like a long-jumper before hitting the deck. Hard.

Given the brutality of the crash, it was a relief to see Carl get to his feet and limp back to the paddock. His right hand, wrist, hip and ankle were seriously banged about and swollen. There was

doubt that he'd be able to come out for the second race. Surely he couldn't lose the Championship now – even if the injuries were serious?

But come out for the second race he did, and on the first lap he renewed his gloves-off fight with Nagai. Going into the very tight chicane for the first time he got past the Yamaha, then gave the Japanese rider a single-finger salute on the way out. Nagai, not noticeably intimidated, dived straight back under him, nearly removing Carl's right handlebar in the process. Now thoroughly annoyed, Fogarty dragged past on the following steep straight and was never headed again, leaving a frustrated Nagai to settle for second.

Fogarty later said that Nagai probably did him a favour by annoying him and taking his mind off his injuries. Neil Hodgson, the young English 500 GP rider watching in the Sky Sports TV studio back in the UK, had it right: 'That,' he said, 'is what World Champions do.' Gary Pinchin put it just as well in *RPM* magazine, headlining a Foggy interview:

'Eyes of a tiger, heart of a lion, instincts of a gunslinger.'

In Italy race reports now regularly called Carl *Cuor de Leon* – Lionheart – and *Moto Sprint* magazine cartooned him as leaping into the saddle of his bike with the aid of a trapeze. The scale of Fogarty's heroism soon became apparent. The crash had cracked two bones in his ankle, broken a small bone in his right hand and bruised his hip very badly. He was only able to race with the aid of a hefty dose of painkillers as a result of which he felt extremely queasy for a good while afterwards. The flight home was far from comfortable, but it could easily have been so much worse.

The hand was still giving Carl trouble when the Superbikes went to Holland.

Carl seemed surprised to be greeted as a hero on the ferry home

The good news was that Assen is Fogarty's favourite circuit. He hadn't been beaten there since finishing second in the second race of the 1992 round, and only Corser and Slight could now prevent him from taking the Championship. It was a matter of when, not if. Corser would have to win both races to postpone the inevitable, but showed that he was willing to fight to the finish by taking pole.

As soon as the lights went green for the first race it was obvious that the legion of British Foggy fans who'd made the journey were going to get what they wanted. Carl got to the first corner in the lead and only Simon Crafar, the Honda-riding New Zealander, was able to stay with him. For a while Carl worried about Corser, who was dicing for third, and wondered if he would do better to follow Crafar, who was harassing him. But, worried that he'd lose concentration if he slackened his pace, Carl pressed on to break Crafar's challenge and win by over three seconds.

He had retained his title. Union Jacks waved everywhere. Straight after crossing the line, as Crafar was giving him the thumbs-up, Foggy wasn't celebrating his own triumph, he was jabbing an index finger at Crafar and giving him the thumbs-up, saying how well Simon had ridden. It was a generous gesture, but he had plenty of time for celebrating.

As usual he stopped to take a flag from a fan, but the guy didn't hear Foggy's request to tie the flag round his neck and hopped on the back of the Ducati for a wild, celebratory ride back to the pits. Slick was impressed that the Ducati's rear subframe took the unforeseen load without breaking. Asked on TV how he would celebrate, Carl acidly recalled that Formula 1 driver Damon Hill had said he might stay up until 2am and a have a couple of beers after winning the British GP, adding that he might do the same. Assen town then turned into one big British party as the travelling army celebrated. Carl actually seemed surprised to be greeted like a conquering hero when he got on the ferry back to the UK on Monday.

Now the rumour machine started working overtime. There were still two rounds of the World Superbike Championship left, but it was common knowledge that every works Superbike team had already made Carl an offer for 1996. Carl had decided, though, that he wanted a move to 500 Grand Prix racing. Unfortunately for Carl, there were very few seats left. Suzuki had their two riders signed up, there was no chance of a Honda, and Cagiva had withdrawn from GPs. Which left Yamaha, specifically the Marlboro-sponsored Kenny Roberts team.

It seemed an unlikely marriage given that Roberts and Fogarty had hardly been polite about each other in the recent past, but GP promoters Dorna were offering a bounty of free TV advertising in their broadcasts for the team that got Fogarty into GPs. Carl made a very public visit to the final GP of the year in Barcelona, where he was flattered by the amount of media attention he received: 'More than I get in a year in Superbike, and more than Schwantz or Doohan got.'

But there were still two more Superbike rounds and until Carl decided which way he was going to jump no one was going to confirm what they were doing in 1996.

Indonesia came and went with a win and a breakdown, then came Phillip Island. The circuit announcer and the Sky Sports studio anchorman Keith Huewen did their best to drag information out of Carl about his plans, but all they could get was that this was his last race on a Ducati and that he'd probably be on a Superbike next year.

The world had to wait until the following Wednesday before it was officially announced that Fogarty would be on a Honda Superbike in 1996. In fact, Carl had made his decision during a short break on the Island of Bali before the Australian race when, he says, he had time to think.

There were many reasons for the decision to move to Honda. Money, of course, played its part, but the newly formed Suzuki team offered Carl more than Honda, and in many ways would have been the safer bet. If he were to finish third on the brand new Suzuki GSX-R, people would say what do you expect on a new bike, and if he won he'd be a hero. Ducati's offer reflected the company's increasingly rocky financial situation, and Carl admits that he was surprised at the low level of their bid. He was more annoyed, though, with the lack of communication from the team – not knowing which hotel they'd be in until the last moment, and details like not flying business class added to his dissatisfaction. The Castrol Honda team, he noted, seemed to be much better managed.

The major incentive for change,

Celebrating retaining the title at Assen 1995, with the aid of an unscheduled passenger. (Kel Edge)

though, was the prevailing opinion that the Ducatis had a major advantage. This was despite the fact that the Honda was always speed-trapped as quickest, and only one other Ducati rider made a major impression on the Championship. Carl was definitely irked by the paddock whisper that he was good but that the Ducati made him look better than he was. Scott Russell even went on record as saying that he wouldn't respect Fogarty as a rider until he won the title on a Japanese bike. Two other riders have won back-to-back World Superbike Championships, the Americans Fred Merkel and Doug Polen – but no one had won three, or won on different makes of bike, so there were still targets left to aim for.

Just a few years previously, even after his annus mirabilis in 1992, Carl had run up against the glass ceiling imposed by British under-achievement on the world stage. But his success had one important side-effect that pleased him greatly. Promising young British riders were now considered seriously by team managers. His friend Neil Hodgson took over Carl's seat at Ducati for 1996, Darren Barton – another Lancastrian – got a chance at 125 GPs, and youngsters Jamie Robinson and Chris Walker seemed on the verge of the big breakthrough. After years in the doldrums British racing could again pull the crowds, although it still needed the presence of Carl Fogarty to really pack them in.

One very important aspect of the Honda team is that it is run out of Britain, with Neil Tuxworth as manager. It was a standing joke in the Honda pit in 1993 and 1994 that if you couldn't find Tuxworth you looked in the Fogarty motorhome. Neil wasn't just Foggy's old manager, but a family friend as well.

I prefer to remember him for his extraordinary will to win

It would be wrong to assume that Fogarty had major problems with Virginio Ferrari; he didn't. The tearful final parting at Singapore Airport after Virginio had made an impromptu speech of thanks is evidence of that. Ferrari said he was sorry his English prevented them communicating more, but any problems that arose were really cultural (apart from Slick and Anders Andersson the whole team was Italian). For example, the English contingent, used to eating at 7pm, never really came to terms with Latin habits such as eating at 10pm. But the most difficult aspect was trying to organise testing in the close season. Apparently sometimes it took days, if not weeks, simply getting hold of Ferrari to find out what was going on.

Ferrari says: 'My team made every effort to give him every chance of victory. We even employed an English mechanic he trusted and a suspension specialist he had almost exclusive use of. There are many examples of Carl's strangeness. He is a great champion but a fragile man. He certainly gave much of himself and I prefer to remember him for his extraordinary will to win. I've been a racer myself and I know how difficult it is to motivate oneself.'

But as Ferrari himself then pointed out, there is no doubt that at Ducati Carl found a second family in which he knew everyone from the owners downwards – even the Castiglionis used to drop by the motorhome for a cup of tea.

With the 1996 Castrol Honda team Carl could keep that family feeling. There were also the advantages of living only two hours' drive from team HQ in Louth, Lincolnshire, and having a testing schedule laid out before the season started. Slick went to Honda with Carl, and there were no problems in having the family around him at the races.

Michaela only had one question before Carl signed on Honda's dotted line: she wanted to know if she'd still be allowed to watch from the pit wall. All the support systems that Carl needs so much if he's to give of his best could stay in place if he stayed in Superbike. If the Grand Prix deal had gone through Michaela was expecting to stay at home for the whole year. How would Carl's morale have stood up to the isolation? And would Kenny Roberts have taken Slick on too? We never got to find out because Roberts wasn't in a position to offer any sort of deal. Instead the paddock started wondering how Fogarty and Aaron Slight would get on.

Neil Tuxworth had taken Aaron over to the Ducati team's hotel the day after the Australian round and, in Carl's room, got the two to shake hands and pointed out that they'd both benefit from working together. The two had once been good friends, but Carl's insistence that Slight wasn't a good enough rider to challenge for the Championship, plus the Albacete incident, had not surprisingly alienated the Kiwi. Privately, both men said that they were glad the other was in the team so that they could finally settle the argument by beating the other on the same bike. The paddock predicted an interesting time for Tuxworth in the 1996 season.

Carl would have liked to ride for Roberts – he thinks Kenny appreciates straight talking – but he isn't going to lose any sleep over missing out on GPs. 'Five years ago I'd have been devastated, but Superbike is so big now that the Championships are of equal stature and the money's the same too.' In Carl's case, that would mean a signing-on fee of over £500,000.

The second Championship made Carl even more of a hero to the British bikers, but his success also took him out of the ghetto of motorcycle sport. He was featured on the BBC's 1995 *Sports Review of the Year* and was pleasantly surprised to find sportsmen like the boxer Chris Eubank coming up to him to offer congratulations.

The general public liked him, too. The car department at Honda UK undertake annual market research into the sports personality with whom the public identify. They favoured Damon Hill in 1994: in British eyes the Williams F1 driver had been robbed of the World Championship by foul deeds. In 1995 Hill was replaced as people's champion by Carl Fogarty. At that point the car people at Honda were not aware that Foggy had signed to ride a Honda in 1996.

chapter eight

To Honda and back

Was leaving Ducati a mistake? The record books make it look like one; fourth in the 1996 Championship with just four wins, his lowest placing and his lowest victory count since becoming a works rider. Carl is emphatic that it was not an error of judgement, although he does concede that breaking up a winning team – by which he means himself, Slick, suspension engineer Anders Andersson and Ducati engine man Ivo Bertoni – wasn't a good idea.

In public he said all the right things about being able to win on the Honda, but in private he accepted that the title was out of the question. The achievable target was to win races, but even that seemed a long way away after the first test session. Carl's first thought was 'What have I done?'; his style of using extreme angles of lean while carrying lots of corner speed just didn't work. Putting

Right: *Sometimes the Fogarty-Honda combination worked really well.* (Kel Edge)

Below: *The year (1996) with Honda included a ride in the Suzuka 8 Hours.* (Kel Edge)

power to the ground was the problem, or rather the lack of grip at the rear end, and it would dog him all year.

Just to add a bit of extra pressure, the first race of the year was at Misano, the track at which the Honda team had been humiliated the previous year. Carl promptly made things even worse by highsiding at around 80mph on cold tyres in qualifying, after which two points-scoring rides were seen as a bonus. However, a miserable Donington, which Carl described as the lowest point of his career, followed by Slick Bass's sacking by Castrol Honda team boss Neil Tuxworth two days later brought things to crisis point. The departure of Slick was an early indication that Carl wasn't finding life with Honda as comfortable as he had expected.

Both parties wonder what Carl could have done if he'd stayed

Foggy's old mate was a casualty of the different ways a giant Japanese corporation and a small Italian company do business. This was the second time Tuxworth had fired Bass; the first was in 1989 when he was working for Joey Dunlop. It wouldn't be long before Fogarty himself decided he wanted out, too.

But first he had to prove that he didn't need the Ducati to win. Hockenheim was next on the calendar, and to compound the misery it was Carl's team-mate Aaron Slight who gave the Honda its first win of the year in Race 1. Back in the motorhome Danielle made it clear to her dad that she didn't like him not winning. Carl consulted with his new mechanic Nick Goodison, and they decided that they had nothing to lose by gambling on some radical changes to the bike's set-up. They jacked the rear ride-height up to throw more weight over the front and Foggy went out to do battle with Slight and Superbike new boy John Kocinski, who had taken his seat at Ducati. It was a typical Hockenheim epic.

On the fastest track in the calendar it went down to the last lap and was decided when Carl outbraked his team-mate on the right-hander coming into the Motodrom and held on through the stadium section for his first Honda-powered win in Superbike.

There was a win at Monza, then one of the greatest races the Championship has ever seen; inevitably it was at Assen. The whole race was a battle between Carl and Kocinski, and again it was decided on the last lap, this time at the last corner, the Circuit Van Drenthe's infamous chicane. Carl led into it with Kocinski attacking on the brakes up the inside on the right of the track. But the American was carrying too much speed and went past the apex as Carl turned the RC45, stamped it down into first, got his weight over the front wheel and drag-raced to the line and an historic victory. Not only did it keep his run of wins at the Dutch track alive, but as he'd won the first race earlier in the day it was the first ever double win for the Honda RC45.

It couldn't have come at a better time, as Carl had announced during qualifying that he would be back with Ducati in 1997. He had thought the grass would be greener on Honda's side of the hill, but didn't like it when he got there. As well as the problems with the bike, he wasn't comfortable with the extra commitments and tighter organisation of the Honda squad. Lengthy debriefing meetings after qualifying to analyse information from the data logger are not Carl's style; having one or other of the brothers who own Ducati drop into his motorhome for a cup of tea is.

He wanted to get back to that family atmosphere, and there were no ill feelings. Neil Tuxworth is still a friend with whom Carl discusses both his professional life and what it'll be like when he stops racing. There were, however, some regrets. Both parties still wonder what Carl could have done if he'd stayed for another season; after all, the bike won the title in 1997 in the hands of John Kocinski. At the time there were also mutterings that staying with Honda would get him a 500 ride, but GPs were never mentioned in any discussions.

Did Carl prove that he could win on a four as well as a Ducati? One person who thought so was Colin Edwards. The young Texan had taken up Scott Russell's theme that Foggy didn't deserve any respect until he won on another bike, and was looking set to become Carl's next hate object. But he marched into the Fogarty motorhome and announced that he'd been wrong and Carl did indeed deserve respect. Foggy was impressed, and reckoned that making that statement in front of his whole family took some guts, before adding hurriedly, 'Doesn't mean I like him, mind.'

It was with some relief that Carl returned to Virginio Ferrari's Ducati team, a feeling that left him as soon as he rode the latest version of the Ducati 916. When he tried Troy Corser's 1996 Championship-winning bike, he went round Laguna Seca faster than he'd ever done before, but he found the 1997 bike

much more difficult, and he couldn't get on with Kocinski's 1996 bike at all. A massive increase in fuel-injector body size plus increased minimum weight simply made the bike more difficult to ride at exactly the same time that Honda did what they do best – making their bike much easier to ride. Which only went to underline Carl's conviction that as usual he'd been issued with the worst bike.

It didn't stop him grabbing six wins during the year, but he still says they had no answer to the Honda; he couldn't ride the bike smoothly and was 'stealing wins' by 'barging through', as his team-mate Neil Hodgson could testify after Carl mugged him on the last lap at Hockenheim. At least British fans got to see him win at home, once at Donington and once at Brands after a ferocious duel in the wet with John Kocinski. The American's strange off-track behaviour didn't endear him to the paddock, although Carl and James Whitham did derive considerable amusement from observing some of the more obsessive

With the new Ducati Performance team – Slick on the left, Tardozzi on the right. (Kel Edge)

habits associated with his cleanliness fetish. He may not be the most lovable personality, but Kocinski certainly has the admiration of those who rode against him. He is one of the few rivals for whom Carl has total respect and to whom he ascribes the will to win of Russell and Mick Doohan, the man every racer admires. That respect was expressed through gritted teeth after Kocinski won Honda the 1997 title and put an end to Carl's run of wins at Assen, a sequence of victories that went back to 1993.

Ducati, now under the ownership of an American conglomerate, the Texas Pacific Group, knew that they had to get their bikes back on course. In November 1997 they took the Championship-winning bikes from 1994 and 1995 plus the unruly 1997 model and the putative 1998 bike to Albacete for four days of intensive testing to try and work out where they'd gone wrong and what to do about it.

The Ducati factory wasn't too keen on paying Carl the £700,000 he wanted for '98, reckoning at least three other riders capable of winning who would come a lot cheaper. At this point Hoss Elm, boss of UK Ducati importers Moto Cinelli, who realised how vital Carl was to Ducati, hatched a cunning plan. He told the factory that he wanted a limited edition of Fogarty replica road bikes for the UK only. Putting an extra £1,000 on the price would generate the £200,000 difference between what Carl wanted and the half-million the factory wanted to pay. Grudgingly, the factory agreed. They would be glad they did, for more than one reason.

Over the winter Carl also explored the possibility of another form of racing, this time on four wheels. He tested the Vauxhall Omega used by John Clelland

in the British Touring Car Championship. It was a serious test, not a holiday excursion. Vauxhall hired Oulton Park for the day and Clelland was on hand to chauffeur Foggy round, then – bravely – go round as Carl's passenger. Foggy was quick enough to spin it and to scare Clelland into baling out after a couple of laps – 'He's as bad as Brundle!' Team management was impressed not just by Fogarty's speed but also by the way he looked, learned and avoided the usual novice errors, like stalling the motor. Carl and Vauxhall were keen to progress their relationship with a drive in the Vectra Challenge – a one-make series that featured a celebrity car for guest racers. Ducati didn't think this was a good idea, and Carl had other problems to worry about.

His right knee needed rebuilding. He'd ruptured the anterior cruciate ligament motocrossing a year earlier and while it was no problem on a road race bike, it repeatedly popped out of joint if subjected to any twisting forces, so squash and most other forms of fitness training were out of the question. Carl had no choice – the damage had to be repaired. The job was done three weeks before Christmas at the Droitwich Knee Clinic in Droitwich Spa Hospital by Mr Peter Turner using keyhole techniques. The South African-born surgeon took a 32cm length of semitendonosis (part of the hamstring), folded it in four and used to it replace the ligament inside the knee joint. This technique was pioneered by the Clinic and has a very high success rate. There was also plenty of collateral damage from the 1986 fractures and other detritus to remove. Adhesions (fibrous growths) were pulling down on Carl's kneecap and stopping him straightening his leg completely, and there were signs that arthritis was on its

Feeling at home again on the Ducati 916. (Kel Edge)

way. Carl has the whole thing on video and he is unstinting in his praise of the surgeon, who did a 'fantastic job'. Mr Turner's view is that it was a well-proven procedure the success of which depends on the patient's willingness to work hard at his rehabilitation during the vital first three months after the operation, and this is why Carl looks back on it as a serious episode.

He first rode a bike again in February 1998 and with some relief found that he didn't have too many problems. When he got off the bike he was in agony, but found that it was the thigh muscle going into spasm and simple stretching seemed to cure it. Carl's training had never been organised; he was used to doing what he wanted when he felt like it and now he had to concentrate on a specific problem for the first time. He was genuinely unsure of his ability to last a race. He did have problems for the first four races, the severity depending on the nature of the circuit, and even now you'll sometimes see Carl stretch his right leg during a race on a tight circuit just to shake off any nagging ache, although he is adamant that he has had no problems with the knee itself since half way through 1998.

If I keep riding like that I'll be looking for another job

There were, however, still problems with Ducati, both on and off the bike.

For 1998 the official works team was again run by Virginio Ferrari with Troy Corser and Pierfrancesco Chili as riders, with Foggy on his own in a new team, Ducati Performance, run by Davide Tardozzi. 'I wanted to be on my own – another mistake,' says Carl. 'I thought I'd be able to focus but I got distracted.' The main distraction was what Corser was doing with his own bike. Ferrari and Tardozzi had never been the best of friends and there was no exchange of information between the two teams, so Carl often let himself waste time and effort trying to work out what the Aussie's set-up was, especially at the new tracks to the Championship, Nurburgring and Kyalami. Not that you'd have known that Foggy had any problems in the first race of the season on Corser's home turf of Phillip Island, where he won from Troy. It would have been easy to assume that the 916 was back on top form, but the weather conditions masked the true picture; gale-force winds off the Bass Strait blew some riders off-line and one or two literally off their bikes. Carl said later that it was the toughest race he could remember, a test of nerve and concentration rather than of machinery.

Foggy left Australia joint leader of the Championship with Noriyuki Haga, but over the next two rounds he slipped to third as his problems became more apparent. A win in Race 2 in Spain put him back to second despite a miserable ninth in the wet in the first race, but the worst was yet to come. As usual rain visited the Nurburgring, but it came on race day and it came in torrents. Carl could only manage two miserable thirteenth places. He didn't blame the bike, he blamed himself: 'If I keep riding like that I'll be looking for a job.' He dropped to sixth in the Championship, the lowest point he'd reached since becoming a works rider. His state of mind matched the result; he was wondering what the hell he was doing slogging round the world for no reason. Carl has never been one just to make up the numbers, and the idea of retirement occurred to him. 'I had had enough,' he says with some feeling.

It was around this time that people outside the team started noticing Davide Tardozzi. His contribution to Troy Corser's 1996 Championship had gone unremarked outside the paddock, largely because it was a trouble-free season, although Corser himself made no secret of his admiration for Tardozzi's management skills. Like Roche, but unlike Ferrari, he concerned himself with detail of bike set-up and understood implicitly how to handle Carl. Tardozzi plays this down: 'I was surprised he did not want to win every race. I kick his arse.' Actually, it was more complicated than that because Carl is more complicated than that. The secret is knowing when to kick and when to leave well alone; outside of his family the only people who really seem to understand how Carl works are Jim Whitham and Davide Tardozzi. Other mere mortals risk permanent excommunication from the Fogarty consciousness if they misread him just once, as Frankie Chili would find despite the fact that he had become the only other rider Carl seemed pleased to see on the rostrum.

Tardozzi's close-knit young team all come from Bologna, they socialise together away from racing, and work hard together at the track. Very hard. Carl didn't appreciate their demands to start with, but quickly realised that if he wanted to win again then he too would have to knuckle down. George Fogarty has a typically generous view of Tardozzi: 'He's a gift from God for Carl.'

Half way through the season the tide started to turn with the arrival of a new bike based on a new model of Ducati, the 916SPS Fogarty Replica. Realising where the problems with the race bike lay, the factory opportunistically homologated the necessary modifications on the new model. Without the pre-season aggro about the size of Carl's pay cheque the new bike and those vital modifications would not have happened. Of the 200 road bikes that had to be made to homologate the model for competition, one went to Carl himself, one to Ducati's new museum and the rest were offered to British customers. If you were one of the lucky 198, congratulations: your

money helped keep Carl a Ducati rider. By the time mid-season came around, Tardozzi's team had sorted out the suspension and the sudden throttle action, and the new bike featured a frame modification that made room for a larger airbox as part of a total revision of the flow dynamics to and within a new cylinder head. It worked. The new bike's first outing was Kyalami where Frankie Chili creamed the rest in Superpole, then scored his first double win. This is the point that Foggy identifies as the start of things going right. Both he and the team – new for the season, remember – had made mistakes early on, but now they moved from strength to strength. Fifth place and a breakdown next time out at Laguna Seca don't look at all impressive, but it was in California that Carl maintains he learned a lot about the bike. The lesson? Stick to the base-line set-up and spend qualifying finding the right tyres. All of a sudden Carl recognised that the Ducati was 'so much closer to the Hondas'. He also realised that the Championship wasn't over and done with in spite of the fact that he was fourth in the running, the small matter of 33 points behind Corser with only four rounds left. None of the opposition was dominating the Championship and wins were being shared out between Haga, Slight, Chili, Edwards and Foggy, with Corser's consistency keeping him at the front. It was the signal for an epic Fogarty charge.

Eighty-two thousand people turned up to the next round at Brands Hatch, a record attendance for a World Superbike race, and saw Corser extend his lead by a few points. They also heard Foggy promise to return in 1999, the first time he confirmed that he wouldn't be retiring. Austria belonged to Slight; he won both races and closed to within one and

Following pages: *Carl leads Jamie Whitham at Brands '98.* (Kel Edge)

a half points of Corser, while Carl's third and second reduced his deficit to 19. Then came Assen.

Carl was not happy after the first race; Frankie Chili shadowed him before making his move on the last lap. At the post-race press conference Carl did a good impression of Mick Doohan complaining about his opposition's 'tow-truck' tactics. Race 2 shaped up to be a repeat performance, but the final act was very different. On the last lap Carl held off Chili where he'd passed earlier in the day and they arrived at the chicane side-by-side only for Chili to ask too much of his front tyre and slide off under braking, but the high drama was yet to come. While Carl was celebrating, an incensed Chili appeared and tried to hit him, at which point Foggy covered the scene in tyre smoke with a burn-out. Tardozzi appeared at the run and stopped Carl taking things further, hanging on to the chin-bar of his helmet with one hand and jabbing the other index finger into Carl's face shouting, 'Shaddup, fakkoff, shaddup, fakkoff!' On the rostrum, Fogarty made a point of raising Tardozzi's arm and inviting the thousands of British fans who turn Assen into a third home round for him to acknowledge his contribution. But it wasn't over. Chili was convinced that Carl had cut him up on the flat-out section on the back of the circuit and invaded the post-race press conference in a towelling dressing-gown to say so, threaten retribution and take another swing at the Englishman. Want an unbiased view of what went on? Try this from the ever-quotable Colin Edwards: 'I think Chili had a nervous breakdown!'

In fact, the Italian had seen his chance not just of the 1998 title disappear but also his works ride. His contract guaranteed a factory Ducati for 1999 only if he finished in the top three of the Championship, and that was now all but impossible. Chili lost more than his job at Assen, he lost a lot of fans too. Carl merely wrote him out of his consciousness: 'I don't care if I never talk to him again.'

All the shenanigans obscured the fact that Foggy was now third in the Championship, only six points behind Corser with just the Japanese round left,

Frankie Chili's front tyre is about to cry enough and start the Battle of Assen. (Kel Edge)

and to make it really interesting Slight was second, a mere half point behind the Australian.

The Championship had come down to a three-way showdown, a scenario made for Carl Fogarty. He discounted Corser from the equation – not through lack of respect for the ex-champion but because of his lack of results on the run-in. And when the Superbike circus got to Japan, an excruciating four weeks after Assen, Honda's chances looked rocky once Slight dropped from third in regular qualifying to tenth after Superpole – a third row start. Amazingly Shinichi Itoh, who was running away with the Japanese Championship on a works Honda, was one place behind. It looked as if Honda and Michelin had got their calculations badly wrong, but Carl simply saw it as Slight buckling under pressure. Corser was to start from pole, but an amazingly relaxed Fogarty had his best ever qualifying at a Sugo event and would start from

The three men who went to Sugo '98 with a chance of the title: Carl, Aaron Slight and Troy Corser. (Kel Edge)

the other side of the front row. Then the pressure got to Troy Corser. In Sunday morning warm-up he went down one gear too many at the end of the front straight and crashed; it was an innocuous-looking fall, but he landed with his elbow tucked under his body and broke three ribs. He would have ridden with the damage strapped up, but then his blood pressure suddenly went off the scale and spleen damage was diagnosed. He was immediately taken to hospital where a local specialist managed to save his spleen from being removed.

Back at the track Carl was having his own little crisis. Michaela found him in an emotional state with tears in his eyes; realisation had hit him, he really could be Champion again. Michaela knew what to do – she fetched James Whitham ('he really understands me') to talk Carl round. It worked. Foggy was having the 'easiest race of the season' after Haga crashed out of the lead when the rear tyre spun on the rim, setting up a major vibration and forcing him to back off and settle for third. With Slight only seventh, it was enough to put him on top of the

The third title is his – Carl lets it sink in at the post-Sugo press conference. (Both Kel Edge)

table by one and a half points, the first time he'd led the Championship since the first race of the season. In Race 2 he cruised round to fourth, six places in front of Slight, and his third World Superbike title. His first reaction was to stop the bike and slump over the tank – that release of tension again rather than celebration – as those ever-present Foggy fans with a flag of St George rushed to him. By the time he got back to the pits he had his emotions under control and was able to enjoy the celebratory T-shirts Davide Tardozzi, in a typical act of faith, had brought with him.

Three of the best riders ever to race a Superbike went to Sugo in 1998 with an almost equal shot at the title. The last of the gunslingers to blink was Carl Fogarty.

chapter nine

National hero

The third Championship did more than rewrite the record books; it made Carl a household name. Sure he'd become the first rider to regain (as opposed to retain) the World Superbike title and the first man to win it three times, but it also made him famous outside the small world of motorcycle racing. To his surprise, the 1998 win attracted more national media attention than the first two put together. BBC Television's trailer for their annual sports review of the year opened with footage of Carl on the Ducati, and he appeared on the ever-popular *A Question of Sport* quiz, both as a panellist and a mystery guest. British armchair sports fans who used to know the names of two British motorcycle racers, Geoff Duke and Barry Sheene, added a third to their list – Foggy.

This process had been moving slowly for a few years as demonstrated by Moto Cinelli's superb advertising campaign for Ducati streetbikes. A cut above the usual technical rundown for insiders, these ads were shot by a fashion photographer and featured Carl, Michaela and the girls, and of course some bikes. The end product was striking enough to be used in lifestyle magazines and the big-selling car mags, but the fascinating thing was that there was no text explaining who the people in the pictures were. It was assumed that if you were sassy enough to be reading the publication in question then you obviously knew who the Foggy family were; for instance, a smouldering shot of Michaela looking moodily at the front end of a Ducati carried the copy 'Carl Fogarty, Lucky Man'. The unwritten subtext being that if you didn't understand you were obviously a sad, out-of-touch nerd.

This was all part of the Ducati company's ten-year transformation from a small moribund company in protective receivership to a brand recognised world-wide for producing iconic machines. Put simply, they became the two-wheeled Ferrari with a similar tug on the heart-strings of enthusiasts, particularly in Italy where victory for the red bikes (or cars) matters more than the nationality of its pilot. The spearhead of this assault on our consciousness was the sublime Ducati 916, and the man who did the winning that put it there was Carl Fogarty.

Carl himself was rapidly coming to terms with his success and was able to relax more with the media attention, although it is worth noting that he has never failed to give a quote to a journalist even on his worst days at the races. His confidence manifested itself in answers to questions that would have done credit to his dad in their wordiness, and he seemed to assume a responsibility for speaking on behalf of not only the other riders but also the whole Championship. He was just as competitive as he'd been as a tongue-tied youngster, but the inner anger that drove him had dissipated or been channelled more constructively.

His contentment stemmed from the fact that he felt he was winning easily now that he was as comfortable with the bike as he'd been in 1995 and happier with the team than he'd ever been, so the most relaxed Carl Fogarty anybody could remember fronted for the 1999 season to defend his number one plate. He was pleased to find that he had a new sponsor, and a British one at that, although Slick thought it was a chocolate company when Davide Tardozzi told them about 'Nut Twist'. It was the NatWest bank…

This new sponsor, along with Shell International, came in specifically to be associated with Carl Fogarty. Amazingly, the factory had again been less than enthusiastic to re-sign him and he had gone to Sugo without a contract. When he came back, his price had gone up! Elements within Ducati wanted to employ Luca Cadalora, seemingly because they were concerned the bikes were getting less credit than the rider. The two new sponsors ensured Foggy was re-signed.

If the opposition thought that the old drive might have been diluted by the third title, they were mistaken. Carl had only won three races in 1998 and hadn't had a pole position since Sugo in 1995, yet he opened his campaign with a crushing double, and took pole at the third round to make himself the most successful Superbiker in that area, the only record that up until then had eluded him. He then took two more poles in the next three rounds, won at

With Davide Tardozzi on the rostrum at Monza after a stunning double win. (Kel Edge)

Another season, another team-mate, this time it's Troy Corser enjoying the team launch with Carl. (Kel Edge)

Donington, did the double at Misano, where he'd never won before, and won at Nurburgring under the shadow of personal tragedy. He was winning the second race too, but asked too much of

It wasn't all plain sailing . . . (Kel Edge)

the front tyre and crashed. Any other rider of his status would have walked away in disgust, but Carl wrenched his bike upright, restarted and just made it to the flag in 15th for one Championship point. No lack of motivation there. Even his wet-weather confidence seemed to return in Austria.

Then there was the astonishing crowd at Brands, most of whom followed Carl to Assen a month later to see him do the

Tyre problems? What tyre problems? (Kel Edge)

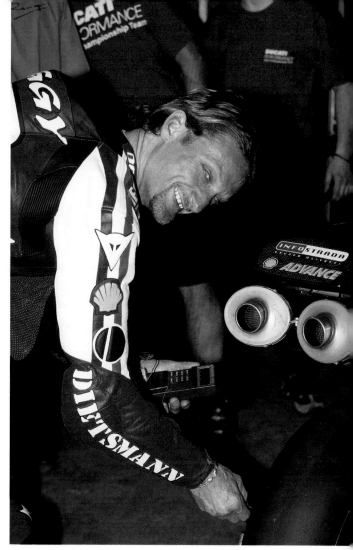

Tyre problems? What tyre problems? (Kel Edge)

double he promised them after the disappointment of the home round. After that it was simply a matter of staying on two wheels for the first race at Hockenheim and the fourth title was his.

There was always a prurient interest in his relationship with Chili to deal with. In Kyalami Chili had offered his hand on the slow-down lap, but with a throttle in one hand and a flag in the other Foggy couldn't shake on his victory so they touched gloves. Questions on the subject continued to be raised for the next two races, to Carl's irritation; he just didn't understand why anyone would care. The Italian media went nuts after he did the double again at Monza in front of 73,000 *tifosi*, beating Colin Edwards by a hair's breadth in Race 2 with an impossible

The mutual respect with Colin Edwards was becoming more obvious. (Kel Edge)

outside line at the fearsome Parabolica on the last lap. *Gazetto dello Sport*'s weekly count of photographs in the sporting press found that Carl was the fifth most illustrated personality of the week behind Michael Schumacher and Max Biaggi from motorsport plus two Brazilian footballers playing for Italian clubs. Weekly bike sport magazine *Moto Sprint* called him 'a force of nature' and 'the perfect racer', French magazine *Moto Revue* decided he was 'the Doohan of Superbikes'. When *Moto Sprint* did its annual survey of the GP paddock for opinions about the best rider in the world, no less a pair than Valentino Rossi and Loris Capirossi nominated Carl as

Following pages: Putting the number-one plate back at the front, where it belongs. (Kel Edge)

number one. In the UK, *Total Sport* magazine ran a feature asking who the most successful British sportsman of the 1990s was. Two men nominated Fogarty. One was football hero Michael Owen – the other was Carl himself!

Slick also saw a new-found confidence in Carl's set-up abilities. In the old days decisions were made by Carl, Slick and a Michelin man; nowadays it's a much bigger committee who decide what to do with the aid of reams of data. This sort of thing was never Carl's strong point, but at Misano he demanded to be allowed to use his choice of tyre against the advice of Michelin, and won. At Brands he went against his instincts but didn't win, and still wonders whether history would have been different if he'd stuck to his guns. Not that Tardozzi and the team always give in to Carl. He used to moan about being sent out to do race-distance testing on race tyres, but at more than one 1999 race the chosen rubber failed during qualifying and Carl went on to win on his second choice of tyre or wheel rim size. Tardozzi's insistence on thoroughness applies to every member of the squad, including the riders. He is, Michaela, Slick and the rest of Carl's inner circle agree, the best team manager Foggy has ever had.

It is, however, easy to lose sight of the fact that Superbike is still significantly less popular in most motorcycle-sport-aware countries than GPs despite the record crowds at Monza and Assen in 1999. Does that mean that Carl should have gone to the GPs to prove his worth? Does he need to? To the man himself it's a meaningless question that he only addresses when a journalist asks. He certainly doesn't brood on it, and takes the view that the right ride never came along at the right time. He certainly was never going to take any 500 ride just to make up the numbers. Speculation about a ride with or for Mick Doohan arose after the two found themselves on the same flight from Heathrow to California before the 1999 Laguna Seca race, and Foggy helped the injured Aussie with his bags and hire car. With the end of his career looming and Michaela saying that she is ready for Carl to retire, it would take someone of the status of Doohan, the man who's done even more in GPs than Carl has in Superbike, to lure him away from Ducati and the feeling of family he has for the Italian company.

When he does hang up his Daineses he will without doubt go down as the greatest British motorcycle racer of the modern era, but where does he stand in relation to other British sporting greats? If you look for achievement at the very highest level in the last decade, only the 110-metre hurdler Colin Jackson, sprinter Linford Christie and oarsman Steve Redgrave have comparable records to Carl. Perhaps Redgrave is the best comparison for he too has beaten the best over an extended period with little or no help from the establishment or publicity from the mass media.

Davide Tardozzi is convinced that Fogarty deserves to be ranked in the top five riders of the last 20 years, but he can't tell you what makes Carl a winner. He shrugs, then says, 'There are many fast riders but few champions. When you are in the presence of one, you know.'

So is it upbringing, dedication, training, determination or sheer bloody-mindedness that made Carl Fogarty what he is today? Ask him the question and you'll get the same answer you'd have got ten years ago, a shrug and a 'dunno really', and then a laser stare and a simple statement that encompasses the fundamental truth about Carl Fogarty: 'I can't stand losing.'

World Superbike Championship wins

1992

#1
Round 2, Great Britain, Donington Park
Race 2

After falling while leading Race 1, this was as gritty a performance as you could wish to see. Even in the early days of the Championship, wins by true privateers were rare, and to pull away from the factory Ducatis of Roche, Polen and Falappa

was simply magnificent. Once the break was made, Carl kept up both the concentration and the pace, only slowing on the last lap as realisation of what he'd achieved hit him.

2nd Raymond Roche, Fra, Ducati
+2.99sec
3rd Scott Russell, USA, Kawasaki
+3.07sec
Pole: Fogarty
1min 35.74sec/94mph
Fastest lap: Fogarty
1min 36.91sec/92.86mph

1993

#2
Round 3, Spain, Albacete
Race 1

Once Carl had disposed of early leader Bontempi it was another exhibition ride in front of a record crowd that had turned out to see local hero Juan Garriga in the middle of a short post-GP four-stroke excursion before retiring. It would be a long time before the 30,000 crowd was bettered

place man was well behind the battling pair. In Race 1 they were first and second by the third corner and continued their wheel-to-wheel battle until just before half distance when Russell hit tyre problems and couldn't stay with Fogarty's pace. He was always close enough to take advantage of a mistake – but Carl didn't make one. Race 2 was a mirror image with the deciding factor being Carl hitting engine problems. Although they scored the same number of points, Carl went from third to second in the title.

2nd Scott Russell, USA, Kawasaki
+2.09sec
3rd Aaron Slight, NZ, Kawasaki
+14.86sec
Pole: Fogarty
2min 6.18sec/95.69mph
Fastest lap: Fogarty
2min 6.44sec/95.43mph

– and when it was Carl Fogarty would win in front of it in a similarly decisive manner.

2nd Aaron Slight, NZ, +3.79sec
3rd Piergiorgio Bontempi, Ita,
Kawasaki +23.06sec
Pole: Slight
1min 32.94sec/85.13mph
Fastest lap: Slight
1min 34.33sec/83.92mph

#3
Round 3, Spain, Albacete
Race 2

Carl completed his first World Superbike double with an even more emphatic win than in the first leg. Again he took the lead early – he didn't get the holeshot – and again the rest didn't see which way he went. After falling off on the first corner of the first round (at Brands

Hatch) to not just win one race but both meant that a Championship challenge was a reality – even though he left Spain fifth in the Championship and 17 points behind the leader Scott Russell.

2nd Scott Russell, USA, Kawasaki
+10.48sec
3rd Aaron Slight, NZ, Kawasaki
+26.68sec
Pole: Slight
Fastest lap: Fogarty
1min 34.09sec/84.13mph

#4
Round 6, Czech Republic, Brno
Race 1

The whole meeting was a duel between Fogarty and Russell: they took a win and a second place apiece after qualifying first and second, and in each race the third

#5
Round 7, Sweden, Anderstorp
Race 1

Another storming win from pole position. It took him until Lap 2 to get the lead but by Lap 5 he was well ahead of a memorable battle for second involving Falappa, Pirovano, Whitham, Slight, and local hero Christer Lindholm. While the mob traded paint, Foggy controlled the race from the front, his only worry being – probably imaginary – noises coming from the motor in the closing stages.

2nd Giancarlo Falappa, Ita, Ducati
+7.30sec
3rd Fabrizio Pirovano, Ita, Yamaha
+7.85sec
Pole: Fogarty 1min 33.76sec
Fastest lap: 1min 33.81sec

#6

Round 7, Sweden, Anderstorp
Race 2

This time Foggy didn't wait until Lap 2; he was in front at the end of Lap 1. And this time he didn't even have to worry about any engine rattles. The major effect of Carl's second double of the year was to close the gap on Scott Russell at the top of the table to 11 points.

2nd Scott Russell, USA, Kawasaki
+2.47sec
3rd Giancarlo Falappa, Ita, Ducati
+9.66sec
Pole: Fogarty
Fastest lap: Fogarty
1min 33.48sec

#7

Round 8, Malaysia, Johor
Race 1

The first Malaysian race was just like Sweden only a lot hotter and more humid. Carl was on pole again and it took him until Lap 2 to get past Falappa, who fought with Russell for second until he crashed out. But all the fighting was well behind Foggy.

2nd Scott Russell, USA, Kawasaki
+3.46sec
3rd Fabrizio Pirovano, Ita, Yamaha
+12.15sec
Pole: Fogarty
1min 29.83sec/96.12mph
Fastest lap: Fogarty
1min 30.46sec/95.44mph

#8

Round 8, Malaysia, Johor
Race 2

This time a grimly determined Russell clawed his way back up to Carl's back wheel after he'd disposed of the battered Falappa. He gained most ground on the brakes only to lose most of it again as the Ducati powered away out of the corners. With four laps to go Fogarty put in his big effort and broke Russell's challenge. The double win put Carl within five points of the American at the top of the points table.

2nd Scott Russell, USA, Kawasaki
3rd Fabrizio Pirovano, Ita,
Yamaha
Pole: Fogarty
Fastest lap: Russell
1min 30.45sec/95.46mph

#9

Round 9, Japan, Sugo
Race 1

Fogarty took his fourth consecutive pole followed by his fifth consecutive win, but this one wasn't the type of runaway he'd managed in the past few rounds. After a bad start he was first involved in a fight for fourth place, then in a three-man battle for second place before he got on terms with leader Keiichi Kitagawa. He took the lead on Lap 3 but the local man dogged his wheel tracks until Foggy made the decisive break in the closing stages. Russell's new motor could only take him to eighth, so Carl went to the top of the Championship table. Unfortunately, he lost the lead when he crashed out of Race 2.

2nd Keiichi Kitagawa, Jpn,
Kawasaki +2.16sec
3rd Shoichi Tsukamoto, Jpn,
Kawasaki +24.78sec
Pole: Fogarty
1min 32.37sec/90.50mph
Fastest lap: Kitagawa
1min 33.17sec/89.73mph

#10

Round 10, Holland, Assen
Race 1

Foggy couldn't have picked a better place to get over his Japanese crash; the Circuit Van Drenthe could have been built for the way Carl rides a motorcycle. From his fifth consecutive pole position Carl took the lead

from Russell at the first corner and was never headed again. For the first half of the race he was harried by the Kawasaki rider, again especially on the brakes, but before half distance Fogarty lit the blue touch-paper and pulled away as Russell suffered some vibration from the front end of his bike.

2nd Scott Russell, USA, Kawasaki
+2.80sec
3rd Aaron Slight, NZ, Kawasaki
+27.46sec
Pole: Fogarty
2min 6.20sec/107.22mph
Fastest lap: Russell
2min 5.95sec/107.43.mph

#11

Round 10, Holland, Assen
Race 2

The race was over by the end of Lap 2. Fogarty was simply awesome: he even managed the holeshot this time and was never headed. Uncharacteristically, he was waving to the fans – many of them British – on the last lap. Again he closed the gap at the top of the table, and from Russell's grim countenance on the rostrum you could tell where he thought the Championship was headed.

2nd Scott Russell, USA, Kawasaki
+6.41sec
3rd Stephane Mertens, Bel, Ducati
+15.31sec
Pole: Fogarty
Fastest lap: Fogarty
2min 5.75sec/107.60mph

Round 13, Portugal, Estoril
Race 2

Russell now held the whip hand, having beaten Fogarty at both Donington and Monza and started Estoril with a 32-point lead. After neither man finished the first race, Fogarty won the second easily once he'd passed fast-starter Bontempi on the first lap. Russell finished second, so the lead was only reduced to 29 points with one round left. Unfortunately for Carl, that round never took place.

2nd Scott Russell, USA, Kawasaki
+8.91sec
3rd Fabrizio Pirovano, Ita, Yamaha
+11.85sec
Pole: Aaron Slight, NZ, Kawasaki
1min 54.01sec/88.64mph
Fastest lap: Fogarty
1min 52.18sec/90.99mph

1994

#13
Round 1, Great Britain, Donington Park
Race 1

The first race of the season and a debut win for the new Ducati 916, but it didn't come without a fight, first with the Kawasakis of Russell and Rymer, then with fast-starting

Falappa until Carl took the lead on Lap 5. There was no escape, though – both Corser and Pirovano led briefly before Carl repassed and made his decisive break. Behind him, Slight on the new Honda RC45 recovered from a bad start to a storming second place, which he repeated in Race 2 behind Russell. Fogarty's third place meant that he left Donington with the slimmest of Championship leads: one point. Much better than his usual start to a season.

2nd Aaron Slight, NZ, Honda
+1.33sec
3rd Fabrizio Pirovano, Ita, Ducati
+2.01sec
Pole: Scott Russell, USA, Kawasaki,
1min 34.96sec/94.76mpg
Fastest lap: Troy Corser, Aus,
Ducati, 1min 35.52sec/94.21mph

#14
Round 4, Spain, Albacete
Race 1

Fogarty arrived in Spain only fourth in the Championship following injuries at Round 2 and Russell winning three races in a row, then finishing second to Falappa. But Albacete is track that Carl likes almost as much as Assen, and from pole position he got the holeshot and was never headed. The most significant event of the race was

Scott Russell crashing out on oil while holding a comfortable second place. Fogarty later said he was lucky to have used a different line from the American.

2nd Aaron Slight, NZ, Honda
+8.80sec
3rd James Whitham, GB, Ducati
+15.42sec
Pole: Fogarty
1min 33.34sec/85.05mph
Fastest lap: Fogarty
1min 33.08sec/84.81mph

#15
Round 4, Spain, Albacete
Race 2

Doug Polen surprised the field with a demon start from the third row and led until Fogarty got by on Lap 2. Foggy then repeated his disappearing act of Race 1. Russell had to use his second bike but his luck didn't improve, and he crashed again. This time he was only in eighth place when he lost the front end in a slow corner. However, he didn't lose the Championship lead. Despite Foggy taking 40 points to Russell's zero, the Briton only jumped to second overall, still 24 points adrift.

2nd Aaron Slight, NZ, Honda
+6.97sec
3rd James Whitham, GB, Ducati
+17.79sec

Pole: Fogarty
Fastest lap: Fogarty
1min 33.67sec/84.51mph

#16
Round 5, Austria, Osterreichring
Race 1

Carl's only real problem of the whole weekend was taking pole position from local hero Andy Meklau. Pirovano did head him in the first race of the day but Carl was in front at the end of the first circuit. By the end of the third lap he had a significant lead and the rest were involved in a spectacular battle for the lower placings. Just as in qualifying, Meklau used his local knowledge to good effect to win that battle.

2nd Andy Meklau, Aut, Ducati
+2.33sec
3rd Doug Polen, USA, Honda
+3.19sec
Pole: Fogarty
1min 50.18sec/118.82mph
Fastest lap: Meklau
1min 50.40sec/118.58mph

#17
Round 5, Austria, Osterreichring
Race 2

After a restart due to a first-bend pile-up, Fogarty was never headed. After three laps he had a three-sec-ond lead and by half-distance (nine laps) it was four seconds, after which he controlled the race from the front while Meklau and Polen again disputed second, again with the same result. Russell only managed 14th and 12th, his confidence badly damaged not just by Albacete's crashes but by a testing crash the week after. He also lost the Championship lead to Fogarty.

2nd Andy Meklau, Aut, Ducati
+2.33sec
3rd Doug Polen, USA, Honda
+2.46sec
Pole: Fogarty
Fastest lap: Fogarty
1min 50.77sec/118.20mph

#18
Round 6, Indonesia, Sentul
Race 2

Despite leaving Austria as the Championship leader, Carl arrived in Indonesia second to Aaron Slight who had been given back all the points he lost after testing for illegal fuel at Donington. To add to his grief, Carl broke down in Race 1 while holding a comfortable lead, handing a debut World Championship win to his best mate James Whitham. However, Race 2 went how Carl was hoping the first one would: he led every lap for a comfortable victory. But with two second places, Aaron Slight out-scored him to extend his Championship lead.

2nd Aaron Slight, NZ, Honda
+2.80sec
3rd Scott Russell, USA, Kawasaki
+10.98sec
Pole: Fogarty
1min 28.02sec/100.77mph
Fastest lap: Fogarty
1min 28.06sec/100.71mph

#19
Round 8, Holland, Assen
Race 1

As expected, Carl took his fourth pole of the season at this, his favourite circuit. Equally predictably he got the holeshot and was never headed; he was even able to ease down a little towards the end of the race. Unexpectedly, Paolo Casoli did Foggy a favour by pushing points leader Slight back to third place.

2nd Paolo Casoli, Ita, Yamaha
+3.81sec
3rd Aaron Slight, NZ, Honda
+5.15sec
Pole: Fogarty
2min 7.38sec/106.24mph
Fastest lap: Fogarty
2min 6.75sec/106.75mph

#20

Round 8, Holland, Assen
Race 2

Slight managed to hang in Fogarty's slipstream from the flag but never managed to pass him. Once his Dunlops went off Slight had to concede victory and again Fogarty was able to cool it on his way to the flag. With Slight in an equally safe second, the real battle was for third. Carl's third double of the season put him to within eight points of Slight as Russell, who only managed sixth and eighth, had another bad day.

2nd Aaron Slight, NZ, Honda
  +6.55sec
3rd Mauro Lucchiari, Ita, Ducati
  +8.20sec
Pole: Fogarty
Fastest lap: Fogarty
  2min 6.40sec/107.05mph

#21

Round 9, San Marino, Mugello
Race 2

Despite being second after Assen, Foggy arrived at Mugello leading the table as the lawyers finally settled the fuel issue from Donington and Slight once again lost points, but only 17 for the race after which he was tested. Carl's luck was further in when he won the second race of the day after Russell broke down while leading. The American had won the first race by over four seconds and looked set for a double that would have put him right back not just into Championship contention but on top of the points table; instead he was third, 32 points behind Foggy.

2nd Aaron Slight, NZ, Honda
  +6.12sec
3rd Mauro Lucchiari, Ita, Ducati
  +11.29sec
Pole: Fogarty
  1min 56.07sec/101.09mph
Fastest lap: Russell
  1min 56.30sec/100.88mph

#22

**Round 11, Australia,
Phillip Island**
Race 1

Russell's double at a second hastily arranged Donington round after Mugello left Carl with a scant five-point lead. With 20 points for a win and 17 for second, two second

places would be no use to Carl – so he went for the win. Russell led for half a lap before Foggy charged past and headed for the hills. Russell meanwhile was left to fight with his new team-mate, a teenager called Anthony Gobert whom Kawasaki had poached from Honda's Australian team and put on the absent Terry Rymer's bike. Russell only got second place when the Aussie moved over just before the flag. Second place behind Gobert in Race 2 after Russell's rear tyre disintegrated was enough for Carl's first World Superbike title.

2nd Scott Russell, USA, Kawasaki
  +13.75sec
3rd Anthony Gobert, Aus,
  Kawasaki +14.77sec
Pole: Gobert 1min 35.51sec
Fastest lap: Fogarty 1min 35.57sec

1995

#23

Round 1, Germany, Hockenheim
Race 1

Fresh from Daytona and convinced that he'd been cheated of a win, Foggy did everything except get pole at the track where he broke his wrist in 1994. The only rider who made the break with him was Pirovano, while third place was disputed by a bunch of ten riders. Six laps into the race Pirovano was beaten and Fogarty took nearly a second out of him for the remaining eight laps to win comfortably. Chili nearly skittled the pack fighting for third at the Sachs Curve last time round.

2nd Fabrizio Pirovano, Ita, Ducati
  +9.59sec
3rd Jochen Schmid, Ger, Kawasaki
  +11.52sec
Pole: Troy Corser, Aus, Ducati
  2min 2.28sec/124.24mph
Fastest lap: Fogarty
  2min 2.59sec/123.94mph

#24

Round 1, Germany, Hockenheim
Race 2

It was a repeat of Race 1 with Fogarty making a break straight away and doing a disappearing act. This time the bunch were fighting for second four seconds behind him, with Slight at first looking as if he could go with Carl before being

caught by the eight other racers who were covered by less than two seconds at the flag. Schmid's brace of rostrums represent the only top-three finishes by a German rider in the whole history of the Championship.

2nd Jochen Schmid, Ger,
  Kawasaki +4.23sec
3rd Aaron Slight, NZ, Honda
  +4.46sec
Pole: Corser
Fastest lap: Fogarty
  2min 2.61sec/123.92mph

#25

**Round 3, Great Britain,
Donington Park**
Race 1

A crowd of over 22,000 got what they wanted: Foggy led from the start but Scott Russell went with him, making his point by taking the lead at the Old Hairpin before being outbraked at Goddards. Carl built up a lead of over four seconds before easing off towards the end of the race. Corser, who finished second, lost his chances of the win when he made a terrible start.

2nd Troy Corser, Aus, Ducati
  +1.00sec
3rd James Whitham, GB, Ducati
  +12.58sec
Pole: Fogarty
  1min 34.85sec/94.88sec
Fastest lap: Fogarty
  1min 35.43sec/94.30mph

#26

**Round 3, Great Britain,
Donington Park**
Race 2

This was the last that Superbike saw of Scott Russell for a while; he pulled in early on when an improperly fitted carburettor clip worked loose. Meanwhile Fogarty and Corser annihilated the field, pulling out a lead that was big enough for them to only worry about each other. They swapped the lead a couple of times and spent as much time looking at each other as the track, as they prepared for a last-lap showdown. That treat was denied fans at the track and in front of their TVs when Corser's Ducati sheared its sprocket bolts three laps from the flag, leaving Foggy to do his first double in front of his home fans.

2nd Pierfrancesco Chili, Ita,
   Ducati +10.80sec
3rd Aaron Slight, NZ, Honda
   +11.60sec
Pole: Fogarty
Fastest lap: Fogarty
   1min 35.41sec/94.33mph

#27
Round 4, San Marino, Monza
Race 1

A weekend of firsts. The first ever
dry World Superbike race at
Monza, the first pole for the Honda
RC45 and – in Race 2 – a first win
for Chili. And in Race 1 Fogarty
couldn't do his usual escape act and
had to work for his win. Corser,
carrying injuries from a heavy
practice crash, led early on before
running out of brakes and tailgating Gobert. That left only Slight to
challenge Fogarty, but his rear
Michelin had already given its best
and he had to settle for second.
Edwards got his first World
Championship rostrum with third
place.

2nd Aaron Slight, NZ, Honda
   +1.95sec
3rd Colin Edwards, USA, Yamaha
   +7.97sec
Pole: Slight
   1min 48.22sec/119.89mph
Fastest lap: Fogarty
   1min 48.33sec/119.77sec

#28
Round 5, Spain, Albacete
Race 2

This one was revenge for the first
race, in which Aaron Slight did a
clever job of conserving his tyres to
beat Foggy off. This time Carl
didn't give the rest a chance, but
made an early break and forced the
four-cylinder bikes to use up their
tyres chasing. There was more
action in the post-race press-
conference than on the track as
Fogarty and Slight each maintained
the other had a machinery advantage, making their disdainful view of
each other's opinions quite obvious.

2nd Pierfrancesco Chili, Ita,
   Ducati +4.76sec
3rd Aaron Slight, NZ, Honda
   +6.37
Pole: Troy Corser, Aus, Ducati
   1min 33.45sec/84.71mph
Fastest lap: Pierfrancesco Chili,
   Ita, Ducati
   1min 33.78sec/84.42mph

#29
Round 6, Austria, Salzburgring
Race 1

This was the first and only time the
Superbikes visited the daunting
Salzburgring, and it was Foggy who
had the best weekend with second
in Race 2 as well as this win. Troy

Corser's first ever win prevented
another Fogarty double after he
dealt with backmarkers better, but
no one laid a punch on Carl in Race
1 after he got the holeshot and –
vitally – reached the tricky first-cor-
ner chicane in the lead. Carl left
Austria with a lead of over 100
points at the top of the table after
Aaron Slight lost more ground with
a brace of fourth places.

2nd Anthony Gobert, Aus,
   Kawasaki +5.55sec
3rd Troy Corser, Aus, Ducati
   +5.88sec
Pole: Yasutomo Nagai, Jpn,
   Yamaha
   1min 20.27sec/118.24mph
Fastest lap: Fogarty
   1min 20.15sec/118.42mph

#30
Round 8, Europe, Brands Hatch
Race 1

British bike fans had their best day
out for years – and they got exactly
what they wanted right from King
Carl taking pole position through to
his two dominating victories. Over
45,000 fans, most of whom appeared
to be wearing red Carl Fogarty T-
shirts and sweatshirts, revelled in
their hero's domination. They also
got the bonus of a strong showing
from John Reynolds, especially in
the first few laps before Fogarty

broke the tow and opened up an unassailable lead of eight seconds. All the action was in the fight for second place.

2nd Troy Corser, Aus, Ducati +2.93sec
3rd Anthony Gobert, Aus, Kawasaki +4.05sec
Pole: Fogarty
1min 27.83sec/106.58mph
Fastest lap: Fogarty
1min 28.27sec/106.04mph

#31
Round 8, Europe, Brands Hatch
Race 2

Very few of the massive crowd minded that they got an action replay of the first race three hours later. British bike fans had had very little to cheer about since the days of Barry Sheene and they revelled in another runaway victory. Again it was John Reynolds who provided the bonus with third place, although he didn't get to stand on the rostrum. Yasutomo Nagai thought he was third but was deemed to have passed under a yellow flag on the last lap and the second added to his race time put him fourth.

2nd Colin Edwards, USA, Yamaha +1.15sec
3rd John Reynolds, GB, Kawasaki +3.84sec
Pole: Fogarty
Fastest lap: Fogarty
1min 28.34sec/105.96mph

#32
Round 9, Japan, Sugo
Race 2

After crashing spectacularly and heavily in Race 1, Carl was lucky to be able to get to the grid for Race 2. His mind was taken off his bruises during a furious first-lap dice with Yamaha-man Nagai before Carl pushed through coming out of the last corner, the chicane, made his opinion of the Japanese rider clear with a few hand gestures, and pulled away for an unchallenged win. At Brands Carl had said he would rather take the title at Assen than in Japan because there would be thousands of Brits in Holland. It looked like he'd get his wish now.

2nd Yasutomo Nagai, Jpn, Yamaha +5.47sec
3rd Katusaki Fujiwara, Jpn, Kawasaki +12.99sec

Pole: Fogarty
1min 30.89sec/91.99mph
Fastest Lap: Fogarty
1min 31.61sec/91.26mph

#33
Round 10, Holland, Assen
Race 1

Carl got his wish and retained his World Superbike Championship with a hard-fought win. First he had to deal with his fast-starting team-mate Mauro Lucchiari, then he was harried for half the race by Simon Crafar on the Rumi Honda RC45. Crafar never led but he certainly gave Fogarty something to think about. In the end it was a comfortable win and the enduring image is of Carl on his victory lap with that spectator perched on the seat hump waving the flag for the now double World Champion.

2nd Simon Crafar, NZ, Honda +3.79sec
3rd Troy Corser, Aus, Ducati +5.15sec
Pole: Corser
2 min 14.99sec/100.24mph
Fastest lap: Pierfrancesco Chili, Ita, Ducati
2min 5.94sec/107.44mph

#34
Round 10, Holland, Assen
Race 2

The second race was like a lap of honour for Carl; a lead of over a second at the end of the first lap and a lead of over eight seconds before Foggy eased up slightly and enjoyed the crowd's adulation for his sixth consecutive win at Assen. John Reynolds got his second rostrum finish, and this time was able to savour it standing on the rostrum. Tragically one of the race's many crashes resulted in the death of Yasutomo Nagai, the Championship's first fatal accident.

2nd Aaron Slight, NZ, Honda +7.41sec
3rd John Reynolds, GB, Kawasaki +7.84sec
Pole: Corser
Fastest lap: Fogarty
2min 6.21sec/107.21mph

#35
Round 11, Indonesia, Sentul
Race 1

Despite having the Championship

in his pocket there was no mercy for the opposition. In Race 1 Carl ran away for his 13th win of the season, a total only exceeded by Doug Polen in his first Championship year. He looked set for number 14 and his fifth double of the year in Race 2 when he suffered his only mechanical failure of the year thanks to a blocked fuel pump.

2nd Troy Corser, Aus, Ducati +5.38sec
3rd Aaron Slight, NZ, Honda +8.63sec
Pole: Slight
1min 28.03sec/100.76mph
Fastest lap: Corser
1min 28.67sec/100.14mph

1996

#36
Round 3, Germany, Hockenheim
Race 2

The first Superbike win on a Honda came after a terrible Donington meeting followed by the sacking of Carl's long-time mechanic and friend Anthony 'Slick' Bass. Carl's career had never been at a lower point. To add to his misery, he'd finished a lack-lustre fifth in the first race and – worse still – his team-mate Aaron Slight had won. In the three hours between races, Carl and his crew gambled on some radical alterations to the chassis set-up. They worked well enough for Carl to run with Slight and Kocinski. And when it came down to the last-lap showdown it was Carl who blinked last for his first Honda-powered Superbike win, the first RC45 one-two finish and the first time the bike had won both of the day's races.

2nd Aaron Slight, NZ, Honda +0.30sec
3rd John Kocinski, USA, Ducati +0.55sec
Pole: Pierfrancesco Chili, Ita, Ducati 2min 0.33sec/126.29mph
Fastest lap: Slight
2min 1.59sec/124.97mph

#37
Round 4, Italy, Monza
Race 1

The Hondas' power on the long straights of the Milan parkland circuit negated any of the traditional usability of the Ducatis – in fact there wasn't a Ducati on the rostrum

149

But Carl again defied the odds, first dealing with the challenge of Corser and Chili, then with Slight and Kocinski when they joined the leading group. Ten laps in – two-thirds distance – Carl made the break and, riding the Circuit Van Drenthe as only he can, won handily.

2nd Pierfrancesco Chili, Ita,
   Ducati +3.04sec
3rd Aaron Slight, NZ, Honda
   +5.93sec
Pole: John Kocinski, USA, Ducati,
   2min 4.41sec/108.76mph
Fastest lap: Fogarty
   2min 4.90sec/108.34mph

#39
Round 10, Holland, Assen
Race 2

Once Frankie Chili had dropped off the pace three-quarters of the way through the 16 laps, this was a three-man fight: Fogarty versus the Ducatis of Corser and Kocinski. The lead swapped several times each lap and it was obvious that the race would be decided at the last corner – the chicane. Fogarty led into it, Kocinski went through on the inside but was too hot, Foggy dropped the bike into first, got over the front wheel and won the drag race to the flag taking Corser through with him. If there had been a better World Superbike race no one could remember it. It was also the first double for the RC45.

2nd Troy Corser, Aus, Ducati
   +0.06sec
3rd John Kocinski, USA, Ducati
   +0.07sec
Pole: Kocinski
Fastest lap: Kocinski
   2min 4.63sec/108.57mph

in the first race. Both races provided the usual drag race to the line out of the fearsome last right-hander, the Parabolica. The 0.6sec winning margin of Fogarty's victory in Race 1 was a country mile compared to Race 2. In that Fogarty was just over a tenth of a second behind the winner and finished third. Race 1 marked another small milestone in the RC45's struggle towards competitiveness, the first time the bike had won two consecutive races.

2nd Aaron Slight, NZ, Honda
   +0.007sec
3rd Colin Edwards, USA, Yamaha
   +1.02sec
Pole: Pierfrancesco Chili, Ita,
   Ducati 1min 47.09sec/120.53mph
Fastest lap: Chili
   1min 47.22sec/120.38sec

#38
Round 10, Holland, Assen
Race 1

Kocinski's pole position showed that

Carl's Assen hegemony was in danger, and the fact that he could no longer run away from the opposition underlined it. Add in a broken rib from a crash in the previous round previously diagnosed as merely bruised, and a bookmaker would have given you long odds on a Foggy victory, let alone a double.

1997

#40

**Round 3, Great Britain,
Donington Park**
Race 2

Kocinski got the holeshot but was soon passed by Foggy and Chili. The Italian gave Carl a hard time for half the race but soon dropped back and had to fight off Race 1 winner Slight. Fogarty was well aware that he was reaching yet another career milestone, and as he took the flag he was sat upright in the saddle showing four fingers to his team and family on the pit wall.

2nd Pierfrancesco Chili, Ita,
  Ducati +3.89sec
3rd Aaron Slight, NZ, Honda
  +4.14sec
Pole: Neil Hodgson, GB, Ducati
  1min 33.75sec/95.99mph
Fastest lap: Fogarty
  1min 34.64sec/95.09mph

#41

Round 4, Germany, Hockenheim
Race 2

Another typically scary slipstreaming battle went down to the last lap, although this was the race that Neil Hodgson should have won after he opened up a significant lead. But he rode a shaky last lap and coming into the stadium for the last time he was mugged by Foggy, then overtaken by most of the rest of the leading bunch. Fogarty professes not to like this track, but you'd be hard-pressed to tell from this ride.

2nd Akira Yanagawa, Jpn,
  Kawasaki +0.70sec
3rd James Whitham, GB, Suzuki
  +1.40sec
Pole: Simon Crafar, NZ, Kawasaki
  2min 0.81sec/125.76mph
Fastest lap: Fogarty
  2min 2.59sec/123.93mph

#42

Round 7, Europe, Brands Hatch
Race 2

After falling and taking down Simon Crafar in Race 1, Foggy needed a result. He got his chance in a two-part race interrupted by rain. Surprise package Michael Rutter ran away with the soaking second part while Carl duelled with Kocinski far more ferociously than the conditions should have allowed. Kocinski finished ahead on the track but Carl's advantage from the first part was enough to give him the win on aggregate time.

2nd John Kocinski, USA, Honda
  +4.75sec
3rd Michael Rutter, GB, Honda
  +15.87sec
Pole: Pierfrancesco Chili, Ita,
  Ducati 1min 25.96sec/108.91mph
Fastest lap: Fogarty
  1min 26.36sec/108.39mph

#43
Round 8, Austria, A1-Ring
Race 1

Chili started from pole for the third consecutive time at the revised Austrian track. He was one of the early leaders along with Carl and Akira Yanagawa. That bunch was soon joined by Slight, Kocinski and Crafar in a typical Superbike scrap that looked as if it was going to be won by Yanagawa. But Carl got him on the last lap and made the pass stick. The Japanese had to wait until Race 2 for his debut World Superbike win after Carl rammed Kocinski and crashed while the two were dicing for the lead.

2nd Akira Yanagawa, Jpn,
    Kawasaki +0.30sec
3rd Aaron Slight, NZ, Honda
    +0.61sec
Pole: Pierfrancesco Chili, Ita,
    Ducati 1min 30.80sec/106.39mph
Fastest lap: Yanagawa
    1min 30.94sec/106.23mph

#44
Round 9, Holland, Assen
Race 2

The unthinkable happened in Race 1: Carl got beaten at his favourite circuit, but it took probably the greatest ride in the history of the

Championship to do it. Kocinski got a terrible start off pole and rode past every other works bike to win. In Race 2, Kocinski made an even worse start and never got on terms with the leaders. Whitham was the early leader but incurred a stop-and-go penalty for a jumped start. Foggy was past Jim before he was called in and towed Chili away. It looked as if Chili was putting Ducati's interests ahead of his own as he shepherded Foggy home to the win, which put him within five points of the American at the top of the Championship table.

2nd Pierfrancesco Chili, Ita,
    Ducati +0.93sec
3rd John Kocinski, USA, Honda
    +2.99sec
Pole: Kocinski
    2min 4.06sec/109.07mph
Fastest lap: Chili
    2min 4.65sec/108.55mph

#45
Round 12, Indonesia, Sentul
Race 2

This is one race that Carl should never have won. He was well behind Kocinski and the leader Crafar when, on the last lap, the American made a kamikaze dive up the inside at a left-hander and both riders went down. As Kocinski had

made almost as tough a pass on his team-mate Slight in Race 1, despite having clinched the Championship at the previous round, the paddock was less than amused. Foggy made his feelings quite clear by handing the winner's trophy to Crafar's Kawasaki team.

2nd Akira Yanagawa, Jpn,
    Kawasaki +7.77sec
3rd Noriyuki Haga, Jpn, Yamaha
    +7.80sec
Pole: Kocinski
    1min 26.84sec/102.14mph
Fastest lap: Kocinski
    1min 27.15/101.77mph

1998

#46
Round 1, Australia, Phillip Island
Race 1

Frankie Chili headed Carl for two laps, but that was the Englishman's only challenge. Corser soon established himself in second, leaving Haga and Slight battling for third, a dispute that was settled when back-marker Jean-Marc Deletang nerfed the Kiwi off on the last lap. It looked like one of his easier wins, but Carl later said that the wind – gale would be more accurate – blowing in off the ocean made it

one of the most difficult races of his life. Haga got the second race, his first victory outside Japan.

2nd Troy Corser, Aus, Ducati
  +1.04sec
3rd Noriyuki Haga, Jpn, Yamaha
  +3.13sec
Superpole: Corser
Fastest lap: Fogarty
  1min 35.77sec/103.94mph

#47
Round 4, Spain, Albacete
Race 2

After a dismal ninth place in a wet first race, Carl beat them all to the first corner in Race 2, thus avoiding the Yanagawa-initiated mêlée that took out Hodgson, Lavilla and Edwards. That was the decisive moment; as usual the field spread out round the tight circuit and the only real race was Corser and Slight's dispute over second place.

2nd Aaron Slight, NZ, Honda
  +6.03sec
3rd Troy Corser, Aus, Ducati
  +8.81sec

Superpole: Noriyuki Haga, Jpn,
  Yamaha
Fastest lap: Slight
  1min 32.84sec/85.26mph

#48
Round 11, Holland, Assen
Race 2

Everyone remembers the confrontation between Chili and Fogarty after Race 2, which Foggy won when Chili crashed at the final chicane. What happened before it was that Chili won Race 1 after shadowing Carl right to the final lap before making his move. Fogarty was determined that there would be no repeat in Race 2 and Chili crashed without touching Carl. His tantrum was due to what he claimed was dirty riding by Carl earlier in the lap. The result was Chili dropping out of Championship contention and Carl closing in on Corser and Slight to set up the showdown in Sugo.

2nd Aaron Slight, NZ, Honda
  +5.28sec

3rd Troy Corser, Aus, Ducati
  +5.42sec
Superpole: Pierfrancesco Chili, Ita,
  Ducati
Fastest lap: Fogarty
  2min 4.55sec/108.64mph

1999

#49
Round 1, South Africa, Kyalami
Race 1

Carl got the holeshot, taking Corser, Haga and the Hondas with him, but only Troy could stay with him as the race unfolded. Haga, having amazed everyone by qualifying the new Yamaha R7 on the front row, further amazed them by fighting with Slight for third. Carl was never headed in a processional race and Troy never looked like being able to get to him.

2nd Troy Corser, Aus, Ducati
  +5.26sec
3rd Aaron Slight, NZ, Honda
  +9.78sec
Superpole: Corser

Fastest lap: Colin Edwards, USA,
   Honda 1min 43.80sec/91.96mph

#50
Round 1, South Africa, Kyalami
Race 2

Kyalami is supposed to be a difficult track on which to overtake, a
fact agreed on by all the top riders.
Yet Carl was third into the first corner behind Slight and Corser, but
first across the line to start Lap 2.
From then on it was another pro-
cession, only enlivened for spectators by the quite astounding speed
and confidence of Carl and the
Ducati. The wining margin doesn't
do justice to the manner of Foggy's
win; it was utter domination and a
fitting way for the most successful
Superbiker ever to bring up his
half-century.

2nd Aaron Slight, NZ, Honda
   +6.07sec
3rd Troy Corser, Aus, Ducati
   +7.28sec
Superpole: Corser
Fastest lap: Fogarty
   1min 43.48sec/92.25mph

#51
**Round 3, Great Britain,
Donington Park**
Race 1

Chili led off pole – his first on the
Suzuki – and it took Carl two laps
to get past. From then on it was
business as usual, and the 60,000
crowd, many of whom were still
caught in the gridlock outside the
circuit, got what they wanted. Carl
was never headed again. Actually, it
was more difficult than it looked.
When Slight got into second he
relentlessly applied the pressure
and Carl could not increase the
gap, but the Briton didn't crack
and took his third win of the
season. The big surprise was that
Corser couldn't challenge for a
rostrum position.

2nd Aaron Slight, NZ, Honda
   +3.43sec
3rd Colin Edwards, USA, Honda
   +16.48sec
Superpole: Pierfrancesco Chili, Ita,
   Suzuki
Fastest lap: Fogarty
   1min 33.70sec/96.02mph

#52
Round 5, Italy, Monza
Race 1

Corser led for five laps before
Carl went to the front. The next
leader was Edwards who rapidly
made up for a bad start from pole
and took both Ducatis at the first
chicane. Three bikes wouldn't fit –
Corser ran over the kerbs and
did not challenge again. Chili
had hitched a lift to the front in
the Honda's slipstream but didn't
look like he had the vital last
element of top-end power on
this high-speed circuit. Edwards
was in the right place on the last
lap – right behind Carl – but he
couldn't make a pass at the
Parabolica and Foggy won on the
slower bike.

2nd Colin Edwards, USA, Honda
   +0.12sec
3rd Pierfrancesco Chili, Ita, Suzuki
   +0.55sec
Superpole: Edwards
Fastest lap: Troy Corser, Aus,
   Ducati 1min 46.53sec/121.16mph

53

Round 5, Italy, Monza
Race 2

Race 2 was just like Race 1 only more so with the same three riders battling for the rostrum positions. This time Chili did go to the front at the start of the last lap, but only to make a point rather than with any real hope of the win. At the Ascari chicane for the last time Foggy got sideways and dropped to third, and it looked as if any chance of a double was gone. But he went straight back past Chili and went into the fearsome Parabolica, the last corner, right in Edwards's wheel tracks, picking up the slipstream and driving right out on to the old track to cross the line right beside the American. After some confusion, the verdict went to Carl by five-thousandths of a second, equivalent to the width of a tyre.

2nd Colin Edwards, USA, Honda
 +0.005sec
3rd Pierfrancesco Chili, Ita, Suzuki
 +0.54sec
Superpole: Edwards
Fastest lap: Chili
 1min 46.55sec/121.14mph

#54

Round 6, Germany, Nurburgring
Race 1

Carl's 200th World Superbike race should have been a cause for celebration, but a tragic accident at his home nine days previously cast a heavy shadow. The young daughter of the Fogartys' best friends drowned in their swimming pool. After an understandably lacklustre qualifying, Foggy's Superpole lap was nothing short of awesome, putting him nearly half a second ahead of the Hondas. In the race he was happy to run in third at the start before Jerman's blown engine dumped oil on the approach to the first turn. Unbelievably, the marshals didn't put out oil flags and many top contenders, including the leader Edwards, came to grief. Carl's tighter line kept him out of trouble and he won from a resurgent Slight. He crossed the line, pointed to the heavens and slumped over his tank. There was no champagne on the rostrum.

2nd Aaron Slight, NZ, Honda
 +7.62sec

3rd Troy Corser, Aus, Ducati
 +30.18sec
Superpole: Fogarty
Fastest Lap: Fogarty
 1min 39.70sec/102.22mph

#55

Round 7 San Marino, Misano
Race 1

On a track he'd never won on and dislikes heartily, Carl notched up his 20th pole position before not just breaking his duck but doing the double. In the first race he didn't start well, having to work his way past Haga, Ulm and Yanagawa before closing on Troy Corser. The two Ducatis then ran away from the field leaving the two Hondas some 20 seconds in arrears on the circuit where Slight did the double last year. Fogarty duly passed Corser under braking at the end of the long back straight but was unable to break away. The Aussie repassed in the same place on the last lap but he'd got in the corner too hot, ran wide and Fogarty went back up the inside and held his small advantage to the flag.

2nd Troy Corser, Aus, Ducati
 +0.13sec
3rd Akira Yanagawa, Jpn,
 Kawasaki +10.94sec
Superpole: Fogarty
Fastest Lap: Aaron Slight, NZ,
 Honda 1min 35.04sec/95.56mph

#56

Round 7 San Marino, Misano
Race 2

This time Carl made the start, led into the first corner and was never headed. Behind him Haga provided the entertainment, especially with his attack on Corser, until the inevitable happened and he slid off after losing the front end. Yanagawa took third again to make the day's two rostrums symmetrical but though Slight got a few seconds closer to the winner than in Race 1 the great surprise of the day was how uncompetitive the Hondas were.

2nd Troy Corser, Aus, Ducati
 +6.50sec
3rd Akira Yanagawa, Jpn,
 Kawasaki +10.66sec
Superpole: Fogarty
Fastest Lap: Corser
 1min 34.76sec/95.85mph

#57

Round 11 Holland, Assen
Race 10

He missed out on pole thanks to an astonishing Superpole lap from Troy Corser, but that's the only thing Carl missed out on all weekend. He all but clinched his fourth title with two masterly displays, the first of which was almost untroubled. There was to be no repeat of the '98 aggro with Frankie Chili, his Dunlop-shod Suzuki couldn't find the grip to stay with the top three. Carl inexorably pulled out a lead over the Aussie and strung out the rest of the field too with Edwards, who knew he must win to keep alive his slim hopes of the title, over 12 seconds back in fifth. There was even time to take the chicane slowly on the last lap to set up a massive wheelie for the travelling army of fans packing the grandstands.

2nd Troy Corser, Aus, Ducati
 +4.44sec
3rd Aaron Slight, NZ, Honda
 +5.82sec
Superpole: Corser
Fastest Lap: Fogarty
 2min 03.91sec/109.20mph

#58

Round 11 Holland, Assen
Race 2

Once Chili and a very rapid looking Corser had been disposed of it was the same again, although the heightened track temperature meant lap times were down. Carl again rode untroubled to his twelfth Assen victory with Corser again in second. Slight was third again but only after a fight which was resolved at the last chicane when the Kiwi and Yanagawa shoved past Edwards. Most of the 78,000 crowd were already celebrating Carl's win and the massive British contingent - conservatively estimated at 30,000 - staged a genial track invasion to get near their hero. And then they got back behind the barriers to see Steve Webster win the sidecars to round off the best day British fans had had in years, for British riders won all five races on the card.

2nd Troy Corser, Aus, Ducati
 +6.32sec
3rd Aaron Slight, NZ, Honda
 +14.59sec

Superpole: Corser
Fastest Lap: Fogarty
  2min 04.11sec/109.03mph

#59
Round 12 Germany, Hockenheim
Race 1

When Troy Corser's rear tyre disintegrated less than a third of the way into the race all Fogarty needed to do was cruise round to 12th place to be champion for an unprecedented fourth time. Instead he was embroiled in a slipstreaming battle with Slight, Chili and Yangawa which came down to a head-to-head with Slight on the last lap, and when the Honda man led over the line everyone thought he'd got his first win of the season. Carl certainly thought he'd come second but a red flag had gone out due to a massive crash on the run out to the Ostkurve and the results were therefore taken from the lap before the chequered flag was shown. Carl didn't want to take the victory but the rule book said he had to. Slight protested but to no avail, and boycotted the rostrum in protest. Carl Fogarty just got on with celebrating his new championship.

2nd Aaron Slight, NZ, Honda
  +0.25sec
3rd Akira Yanagawa, Jpn,
  Kawasaki +5.03sec
Superpole: Slight
Fastest Lap: Fogarty
  2min 00.42sec/125.79mph

Photographs in the Appendix were supplied by the Fogarty family, Kel Edge and Honda Racing Corporation.

Acknowledgements

It's only right that I should first thank Carl Fogarty for his tolerance over the years. He has never failed to answer a question, either from me or any other journalist in the paddock. What's more, he's answered them honestly.

His family have been equally helpful in preparing this second edition, specifically Carl's wife Michaela who raided the family album and filled in a lot of background information. Carl's parents Jean and George were equally helpful.

I must also thank the photographers who have done justice to Carl's achievements: Phil Masters for the early years, Don Morley for some epic TT shots, and Kel Edge for the Endurance and Superbike illustrations.

One of the nice things about being involved with motorcycle racing is that because there's so little money in it, the people in the paddock are, almost without exception, there because they love the sport. Many of them have helped me over the years, there isn't room to list them all, but you know who you are.

Finally, my thanks and gratitude to my wife Wendy for her tolerance of the strange way I make a living.

Julian Ryder
Cheshire, 1999

Index

Other Haynes titles of interest

WORLD SUPERBIKES
Julian Ryder ISBN 1 85960 404 8

DUCATI: 50 GOLDEN YEARS
Motociclismo ISBN 1 85960 618 0

WAYNE RAINEY
Michael Scott ISBN 1 85960 401 3

HONDA'S V-FORCE
Julian Ryder ISBN 1 85960 421 8

DUCATI SUPER SPORT
Ian Falloon ISBN 1 85960 412 9

MICK DOOHAN
Mat Oxley ISBN 1 85960 635 0

THE DUCATI STORY (2nd edition)
Ian Falloon ISBN 1 85960 442 0

For more information please contact: Customer Services Department,
Haynes Publishing, Sparkford, Nr Yeovil, Somerset BA22 7JJ
Tel. 01963 440635 Fax: 01963 440001
Int. tel: +44 1963 440635 Fax: +44 1963 440001
E-mail: sales@haynes-manuals.co.uk Web site: www.haynes.co.uk

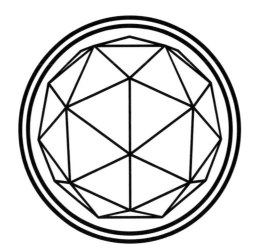

THE CRYSTAL MAZE

CHALLENGE

First published in Great Britain in 2017
by HEADLINE PUBLISHING GROUP

1

Cataloguing in Publication Data is available from the British Library

Hardback ISBN 978 1 4722 5041 4

Designed by Lynne Eve, Design Jam
Illustrations by Will Tubby

Printed and bound in Germany by Mohn Media

HEADLINE PUBLISHING GROUP
An Hachette UK Company
Carmelite House
50 Victoria Embankment
London EC4Y 0DZ

www.headline.co.uk
www.hachette.co.uk

THE CRYSTAL MAZE

CHALLENGE

Neale Simpson with Anna Kidd, Chris Lore,
Toby Smith and Meral Taze

HEADLINE

CONTENTS

LET THE GAMES BEGIN!

LET THE GAMES BEGIN!

THE CRYSTAL MAZE

INTRODUCTION

The Crystal Maze is back! It's been twenty-one years and one incredible adventure for many of us lucky enough to be involved in its return. We hope you've loved seeing the show back on Channel 4, or even for the first time, meeting the incredible new Maze Master and, of course, shouting at the screen as teams make a complete mess of what really is a very simple game.

For many years we've been plotting to try and bring this legendary show back. Unfortunately it turns out that building a 2787 sq m set featuring four epically themed zones and a giant Crystal Dome is a tad expensive.

Then, in summer 2015, a small miracle happened. A group of brilliantly talented and completely bonkers young chaps decided to build a live experience of the Crystal Maze. Having obviously never done anything like this before they decided to post the frankly barmy idea on Indiegogo, a crowd funding website. They asked the public for £500,000 and by the deadline in July, they'd raised an astonishing £938,798. In April 2016 Little Lion Entertainment opened a live experience in Angel, north London. It was a phenomenal success and within four weeks they'd sold out their initial run of tickets and received glowing reviews.

We met with the Little Lion gang in spring 2016 and together with Channel 4 we hatched a plan to produce a one-off special in aid of the fantastic charity Stand Up To Cancer. This plan was riddled with logistical challenges. The venue was open to the public six

▶ Stephen Merchant, the magnificent Maze Master for the Stand Up To Cancer special in October 2016.

days a week, and already sold out, so there was only one day in September that we were able to film. We couldn't rig the shoot until 11 p.m. the night before, and had to be completely clear by 9 a.m. the the day after the record. No pressure then. It was the most challenging and rewarding production we'd ever worked on, but a brilliant team and a fantastic turn from the terrifyingly talented Stephen Merchant as our Maze Master made it all possible.

Over 4.3 million viewers tuned in to the special, making it the third most-watched programme on Channel 4 in 2016.

When the show aired on Sunday 16th October we sat watching the stream of social media comments roll in with trepidation. People seemed to love the show and were calling for more. When the ratings came in the next morning over 4.3 million viewers had tuned in, making it the third most-watched programme on Channel 4 that year. What was most exciting to see was that over a third of the audience were too young to remember the original. Soon after the show aired we began the conversation with Channel 4 to bring the show back properly.

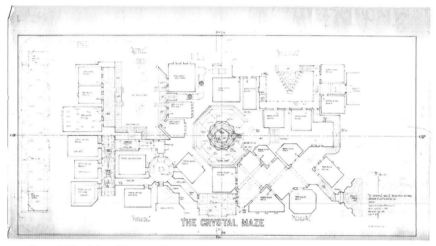

▶ James Dillon's hand-drawn plan for the original maze.

The first thing we did was call James Dillon, the mastermind who designed and built the original maze. He came into our office and rolled out a large and faded piece of paper onto the table. It was the original hand-drawn plan for the maze. Once we'd finished staring in wide-eyed wonder we asked him if he fancied building it again. James said he couldn't imagine anyone else doing it. Neither could we.

The second thing we did was discuss with Channel 4 who could possibly host the new series. Stephen Merchant had done a remarkable job of the special, but had only ever agreed to it as a one off. We had a long debate about finding someone with a strong character who would take ownership of the maze in a way that didn't feel like a pastiche of Richard O'Brien. Our first choice was Richard Ayoade. We're so lucky he agreed to buy some gold lamé boots and join us. There's no one else quite like him, and his energy, eccentricity and remarkable wit have all made for a Maze Master we've absolutely loved watching in action.

Our first choice was Richard Ayoade and we're so lucky he agreed to buy some gold lamé boots and join us.

The third thing, and the thing we've spent the most amount of time debating, is the games. We have assembled some of the most exciting and experienced game developers in TV who have set themselves the daunting task of reimagining the games for a new audience. From fiendish physical challenges, mind-bending puzzles to nail-biting tasks ... and, perhaps most importantly, the return of the wet log ... we've unleashed around forty games on a variety of unwitting and sometimes completely hapless teams all hoping to win a crystal or two.

Now it's time to share our incredible time-travelling adventures with you. We hope that with the weird, wonderful and frankly ridiculous games contained in this book you will have just as much fun creating your own maze at home ...

LET THE GAMES BEGIN!

Neale Simpson (Executive Producer), Anna Kidd (Series Games Executive), Chris Lore (Series Producer), Toby Smith (Development Executive) and Meral Taze (Games Producer)

▶ HOW TO MAKE THE MOST OF THIS BOOK

We designed this book so you can create your very own maze experience with friends and family in the comfort of your own home (or school, or office ...).

The grand idea is that you should spend an hour or two preparing various game rooms using this book as your guide. Once you've set everything up you can lead your band of adventurers (hopefully willingly) around your own maze to see if they're as hopeless as the teams in the series.

Some of the games in the TV series involve complicated set builds featuring smoke machines, laser beams, disappearing bridges, swinging planets, fire-breathing dragons and, of course, a giant wet log. We suspect you probably won't have these to hand. Therefore, we've developed all of the games so that hopefully you can play almost all of them using everyday objects you'll find lying around the house (or can easily pick up at your local DIY store).

Start by inviting a group of friends or family over. Ideally five or six will do. Try to avoid any annoyingly overbearing characters unless you are confident you can lock them in early on.

Look through the games in this book and choose how many and which games you'd like to play (we recommend 10–12 in total). Make a note of all the props/items you need and plot which rooms or environments are best suited to each. Some games are quick (so you can have a spontaneous game at home if you fancy) whilst others are more complicated to set up so follow the guide to preparing each game and do as much as you can in advance so when your friends arrive you're ready to begin.

The 'GAME SIGN' for each game is the text you should use to create the instructions that should be placed inside each room or environment,

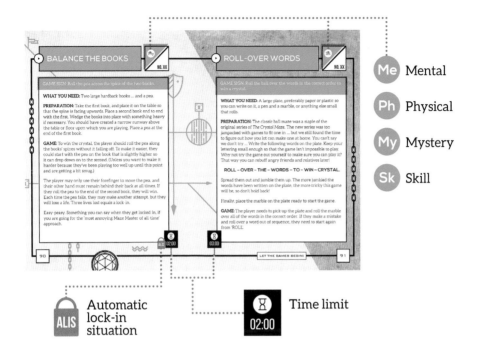

somewhere that is always easy for the players to find. If there is no game sign, then part of the game itself is for the player to work out what to do ... please do feel free to give them a hint or two if they're floundering.

Wait! What to use as those precious time crystals? We expect you probably haven't got a box of these lying in a cupboard so you should consider what you'd like to place in each game room. We think satsumas make perfect time crystal substitutes; they're bright, small and round and easy to spot. They also make a healthy treat for victorious players. Alternatively, how about rustling up a batch of crystal cupcakes?

Once you're ready to go, make sure you've got a running order of which game and room you're travelling to next. Have this book to hand at all times, perhaps bookmarking each game you're planning on playing, so you always have the answers ready. Trust us, teams can quickly become mutinous if not kept in check ...

HOW TO BE A MAZE MASTER

Arguably the most important role when playing your own version of the Crystal Maze at home is that of Maze Master, the mischievous and mysterious guide through this time-travelling adventure.

For maximum enjoyment we recommend that one of you commits to being Maze Master for your whole time playing these games rather than changing over for each challenge. That way one person can embrace the role, develop their own running gags and, if things go as planned, completely alienate themselves from all friends and family.

The role of Maze Master has been held by only four people: the truly extraordinary Richard O'Brien, wild-eyed punk hero Ed Tudor-Pole, comedy legend Stephen Merchant and the mighty nerd-meister Richard Ayoade.

It's hard to compete with these hugely talented folk, so let's take a moment to explore what makes a great Maze Master. You should be slightly stand-offish, to the point that some might even consider rude. You want to demonstrate a lack of empathy, and appear at times to be totally uninterested in a team's success or failure. You should always be on hand to point out where people are making mistakes and never ever accept any suggestions that you are at fault for anything that goes wrong.

In short, a teenager would be ideal for this role. If such a stroppy young individual isn't to hand, then look for the meanest family member or a friend that you all suspect secretly enjoys it when things go wrong for others. You've probably identified them before you finished reading that last sentence. Whoever takes on this

▶ Maze Master Richard Ayoade, complete with extended wooden hand to ensure that no physical contact takes place at any time.

cherished role doesn't have to shave their head, but garish clothing is strongly advised.

MAZE MASTER: You are the team's guide. Make sure you know all the games inside out before you introduce them; the team will look to you for clues and advice. Use your own judgement as to how much information you give to nudge players along if they're struggling. Lastly, don't hold back – your energy and enthusiasm will determine how much fun everyone else has. Good luck!

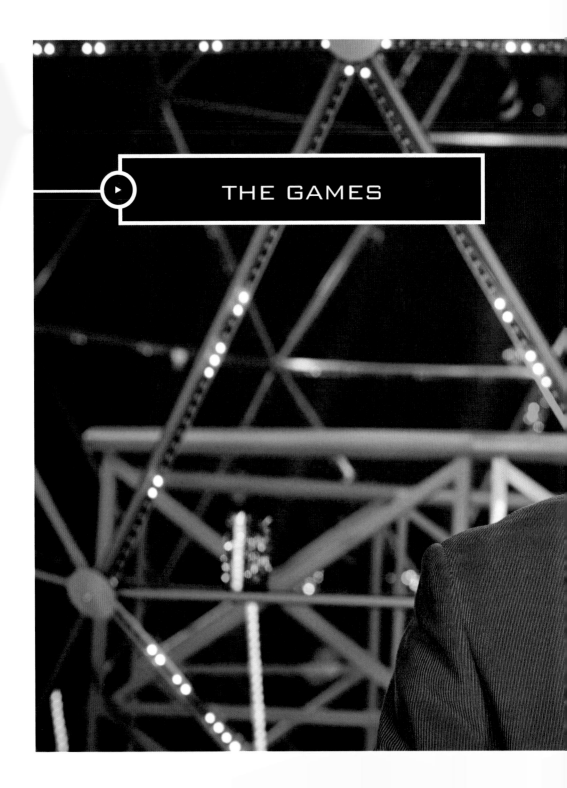

THE GAMES

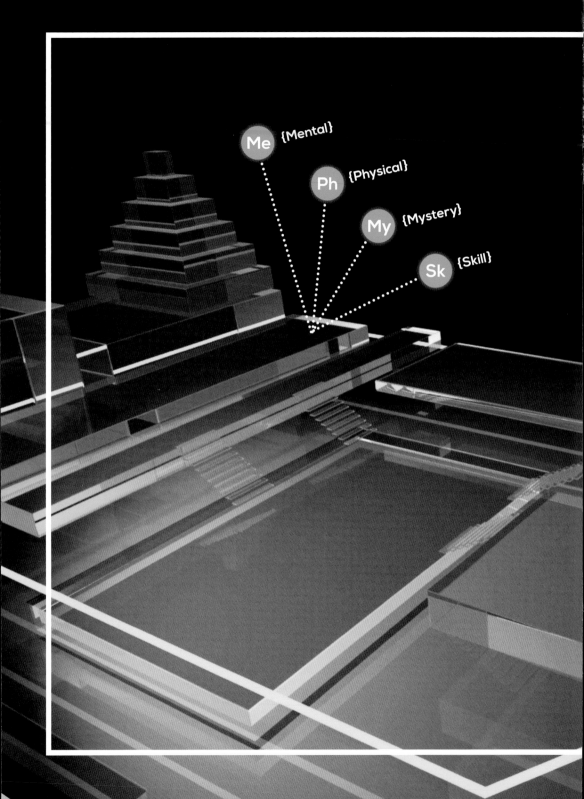

THE AZTEC ZONE

Welcome, team, to your first zone in the Crystal Maze, which contains the many mysteries of the ancient Aztecs.

You now stand in a giant temple located somewhere in Mesoamerica, a region in the Americas that spanned from Mexico to Belize and which thrived in the thirteenth and fourteenth centuries. The Aztec empire was a loose union between three cities known as the Triple Alliance: Tenochtitlan, Texcoco, and Tlacopan. And we definitely did not type 'Aztec' into Google to cobble this bit together.

Feel the sand in your shoes, notice the sweltering hot sun beating down on your backs, witness the marvels of the ornate carvings from nomadic tribes etched into stone over 700 years ago. Prepare yourselves for a zone of wonder, wisdom and a wet log.

Inside this cavernous kingdom of clever conundrums lie puzzles, games and challenges that will test you to your very limits. Some of you will fail. Some of you will face hours, perhaps even days, of mockery. Some of you, especially some of the older males of the group, will take it all a little too seriously and have a proper strop. Then everyone else will get upset that you've spoilt the fun of the whole thing. An argument may well ensue and the reader will wonder why they ever bought this book in the first place if this is how people are going to behave.

Gather your team together, crawl through the cave entrance (or under the dining-room table, if you don't have a cave to hand) and turn the page to discover your first game in the Aztec zone ... Let the games begin!

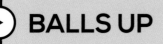
BALLS UP

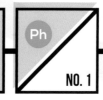

NO. 1

GAME SIGN: Collect the crystal without dropping any balls. Three balls dropped is an ALIS.

WHAT YOU NEED: A sturdy plastic plate, some string, tape, a variety of balls (e.g. round fruit, tennis balls, marbles or a mix of balls of different shapes and sizes), and a variety of soft items that can be used as obstacles.

PREPARATION: Create an obstacle course that requires a player to move slowly and steadily from the door to one end of the room and back again – things like pillows to step over, or string taped to walls to duck under.

Because you design the layout of the room and the obstacles within, you determine how difficult the game is.

GAME: A player, with a plate attached to the top of their head, must start by collecting a variety of balls, placing them on the plate on their head, and then slowly and steadily make their way around the obstacle course you've created so they can collect the 'crystal' and then return with it to the door within the allotted time.

Should the player drop a ball from the plate on their head then they lose a life. If they drop three balls, it's an ALIS.

MAZE MASTER: Don't forget to take photographs, as people tend to look quite funny with plates on their heads. If you're feeling especially mean, you can also dock points for bad language when balls drop to the floor.

ALIS 02:00

LET THE GAMES BEGIN!

27

WHAT'S IN THE BOX?

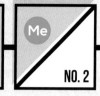

GAME SIGN: Identify all the objects by touch alone.

WHAT YOU NEED: One medium-sized cardboard box with the back open and an arm-sized hole cut in the front.

PREPARATION: Cut out a hole large enough for a hand to go inside the box without a player being able to see inside. Place a variety of objects inside the box. The number and type of items you choose will determine the difficulty of the game. We suggest eight items. For example: sponge, coins, SIM card, CD, Grandma's false teeth (ask Grandma first), playdough, pine cone, leftover porridge from breakfast.

GAME: The player must be directed to place their hand inside the box and attempt to guess all of the items contained within. The team can, of course, assist – shouting out suggestions based on the descriptions given by the player.

MAZE MASTER: The number of items you place in the box will determine the level of difficulty. We recommend no less than six, but feel free to add more and add more time if you feel like it. Make sure you have a checklist to hand so you can tick off all the items correctly identified.

{Time dependent on number of items} 02:00

BOTTLE-CAP BONANZA

GAME SIGN: Turn over all the bottle caps in the time allotted to win a crystal.

WHAT YOU NEED: A stick, some string, a large paperclip, a bucket or bin filled with water (or use your bathtub) and at least ten milk bottle lids or plastic bottle caps.

PREPARATION: Make a fishing rod and line with the stick and string. Fashion a hook by bending the paperclip. Place all the lids in the water with the rims facing down.

GAME: The player must simply pick up the fishing rod and use the hook on the end of the line to try to turn over all the bottle tops in the time allotted.

NOTE: If you want to play this as a mental game all you need is a permanent marker and some imagination. For a maths game, write numbers on the bottom of the caps as well as various symbols, such as -, + and x. Then come up with the sums that must be realised by flipping the lids. Or add a letter to each of the lids for a flippy-over anagram game!

{2–3 MINUTES
depending on number of bottle caps}
02:00

TOTEM POLE

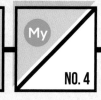

GAME SIGN: Build a tower in the correct coloured order. Ask the dragon how many boxes are correctly placed after each attempt.

WHAT YOU NEED: Four large boxes of different colours that can safely be stacked on top of one another.

PREPARATION: Position the four boxes next to each other. As Maze Master, decide a correct order from top to bottom and keep note of it so the team can't see.

GAME: This game is based on our Totem Pole puzzle in the new series. Once a player enters the room they must stack the four boxes in the correct order from top to bottom.

After each attempt the player should ask 'the dragon' how many boxes are in the correct placement. In the show we have a dragon statue that breathes fire for each of the four parts in the right order. You can choose your own method instead of a fire-breathing dragon; it could be to bang a drum, toot a horn or just ask an overbearing mother-in-law. Only when all four boxes are in the correct order can the crystal be released.

MAZE MASTER: This is not a skill game; it's really a test of memory. Ultimately the team should try to remember which order the boxes are in each time they learn how many are in the right or wrong position. Do feel free to nudge them about this as Maze Master.

⧗
03:00

GREAT GARDEN GUNSHOW

GAME SIGN: Knock seven objects over to release the crystal. Avoid objects with a red mark.

WHAT YOU NEED: Ten objects you are happy to be knocked over with jets of water, red marker pen, paper and a garden hose (ideally with a water-gun attachment).

PREPARATION: Place ten objects in the garden in a line. Put the objects as high or as low as you choose – the further away and harder they are to aim at determines the difficulty of the game. Clearly place a red mark on three of the objects (stick on red-marked paper if you don't want to write directly on the objects).

GAME: It's a straightforward game of skill. A player must use the hose to shoot at the objects with jets of water to try to knock them over. To stop the player indiscriminately firing with one stream, and therefore make the challenge all the more tricky, place the three red-marked objects close to some of the others so the player has to aim carefully.

Each of the red-marked objects knocked over loses the player a life. Three lives lost means a lock-in.

Turning the hose on mouthy and unsupportive teammates is not part of the game, but is deemed acceptable behaviour.

02:00 ALIS

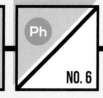
UNLOCK THE GODS

GAME SIGN: Match the symbols to release the crystal, starting with blue.

WHAT YOU NEED: Four pieces of paper, a blue marker pen, scissors, a red marker pen and a garden or large outdoor space.

PREPARATION: Use the blue pen to divide a piece of paper into eight equal sections and draw eight different symbols in each. Cut the eight sections out. Repeat the process on different paper with the red pen. On a third piece of paper copy four of the blue symbols into four equal blue sections and do the same with the red symbols on the same page. You should now have a page with four blue and four red symbols on it and sixteen small pieces of paper compromised of eight different blue and eight different red symbols.

Position the blue and red grid near the door, and hide the smaller pieces of paper around the garden. Where you put these will make the game easier or harder.

GAME: The aim of the game is for the player to memorise the four blue symbols on the grid before running around the space to find the right four pieces of paper to place on it. If any are wrong they have to head back out to find the right ones. Only when the four symbols have been verified as correct can they repeat the process with the red symbols to unlock the crystal.

You may well need to remind the player that it's a colour-coded game. Or if you enjoy seeing people run aimlessly around while their teammates shout angrily at them you can just keep quiet.

03:00

LET THE GAMES BEGIN!

33

APPLE-BOBBING ANAGRAMS

Sk

NO. 7

GAME SIGN: To solve the anagram, pick out the apples using only your mouth.

WHAT YOU NEED: A large bucket/bowl, five apples, plain white stickers, a waterproof marker and a towel.

PREPARATION: It wouldn't be the Aztec zone without someone getting soaked, would it? For health and safety reasons we can't encourage you to buy a giant wet log, but we have come up with an alternative ... Fill the bucket/bowl with cold water (add ice if you're feeling especially mean). On each of the five apples attach a sticker and use your marker to write a letter on each of the apples to make a five-letter word of your choosing. Have a towel handy so the player can dry themselves afterwards.

GAME: The player must apple-bob to remove the apples from the water as quickly as possible. Only when the player has successfully removed all five apples are they allowed to inspect them for the letters so they can attempt to work out the anagram. Correctly shouting out the five-letter word means victory! If you're feeling plucky, you could go for six- or seven-letter words and make the player work even harder.

During the game do feel free to encourage the team to shout things like 'Do it faster!' and 'Go quicker!' while the player is bobbing away. It won't make them perform any better but it does seem to be what everyone does in *The Crystal Maze*.

02:00

GAME SIGN: Hit three potatoes into the dustpan.

WHAT YOU NEED: A dustpan and brush, sticky tack, twelve small potatoes and a marker.

PREPARATION: Play this game on the biggest flat floor you have available. All you need to set up is a dustpan and brush, and a pile of your finest Maris Piper potatoes.

Place the dustpan at one end of the room and fix it to the floor with some sticky tack or wedge it into position with some heavy books. Place the brush and potatoes at the other end of the room and place a marker on the floor so the player knows where they are allowed to swing from.

GAME: When their time starts, the player must take their first potato and attempt to hit it into the dustpan, using only the brush and a single strike. It's like a game of mini-mini-golf.

The player must wait until the previous potato has stopped rolling to make their next attempt. If one potato hits another potato, and knocks it into the dustpan that way, it counts as a valid score. Three potatoes in the dustpan equals one shiny crystal.

After the game, give the tatties a wash, peel them and make some chips for your tea. Talk about the great times you had playing this game, or just ponder why real golf takes far too long to play.

02:00

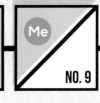
GAME SIGN: Every cube face must bear every symbol. Identify the correct cube shape to complete the cube.

WHAT YOU NEED: This book!

In *The Crystal Maze* there's a game called Four Symbols in which the players had to put eight large cubes into a two-by-two-by-two formation whereby all four sides bore all four Aztec symbols. If you think that sounds hard, just wait till you try to play the game without the cubes, using nothing but brainpower.

GAME: Once you start the timer, hand this book to the player. They must choose which of the cube diagrams pictured would make up the missing cube. Remember, the missing cube needs to complete the diagram so that all four sides of the formation bear all four symbols.

MAZE MASTER: Make sure you know the correct answer. And don't forget to shout things like, 'Remember, all faces must have four different symbols' or 'Don't swear, it's not in keeping with the show'.

02:00

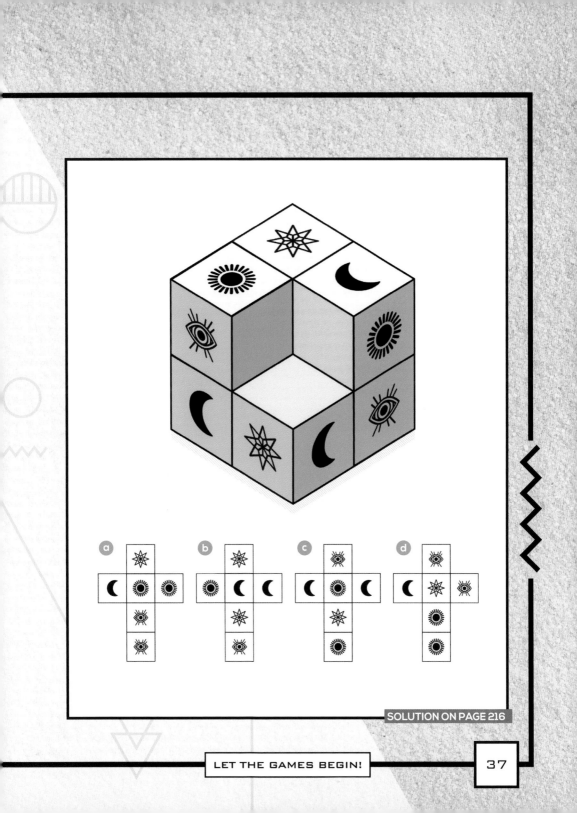

SOLUTION ON PAGE 216

LET THE GAMES BEGIN!

GAME SIGN: Collect the crystal without bursting the balloons.

WHAT YOU NEED: Two or three packets of balloons, six dining room chairs, some thick string, an old, reasonably large bra, a packet of drawing pins and two honeydew melons (or equivalent – e.g. kids' toy balls could work).

PREPARATION: Inflate the balloons and put two chairs back to back about a metre apart (and a metre from the door) and tie a length of string between the backs of the chairs at the top of each. Then fill the gap between the two chairs creating a hoop of balloons, tying them across the top, down the backs of both chairs and along the floor using the string.

Repeat this with another two sets of chairs at approximately one metre intervals. Place the crystal at the far end of the room.

Then, it's costume time. Take the bra and push the drawing pins through the cups so that the spikes are facing away from the wearer. Naturally, it will depend upon the size and style of the available bra, but the more pins you can get in, the better.

Finally, place a melon (or equivalent) inside each side of the bra, and make the adventurer carefully put the bra on, adjusting the straps to ensure the melons are tightly strapped to their chest and cannot slip out.

ALIS 02:00

If you have set things up correctly, then there should be a gap in the middle of each 'hoop' that's big enough for an adventurer in a spiky melon-filled bra to be able to make their way through without bursting the balloons ... but only just!

GAME: The adventurer has two minutes to make their way through the three gaps between the chairs, under the strings, and above the balloons, collect the crystal, and get out again.

If they don't make it out again in time, they're locked in. Plus, they have three lives and lose one every time they burst a balloon – so the third 'bang' equals an automatic lock-in.

GAME SIGN: Follow the rules to release the crystal:

1. **Every piece of string must cross through one green square and one crystal.**

2. **No square can have more than one piece of string on it.**

3. **Every square must be covered by string.**

WHAT YOU NEED: A large piece of paper, two pens (one green), scissors and string.

PREPARATION: Take a large piece of paper and draw a 5x5 grid. Draw crystals on four of them and colour four of them in green as in the formation opposite. Cut your string into four pieces of different length: two pieces should be long enough to span seven squares, one piece to cover six squares and one piece to cover five squares. Lay the paper out on a table and place the string next to it.

GAME: When the time starts, the player must lay down all four pieces of string on the squares, adhering to the rules stated on the game sign.

We recommend getting started as quickly as possible. Just get those pieces of string on the board and start moving them around. OR the player can try that other approach of staring at the game for a minute and hoping the answer will magically come to them, like a few of our contestants tend to do on the TV series.

⏳
02:30

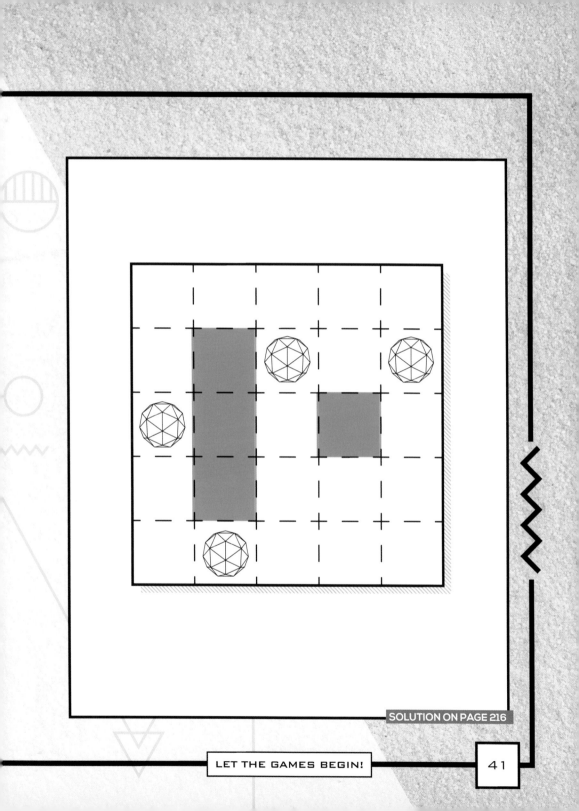

SOLUTION ON PAGE 216

LET THE GAMES BEGIN!

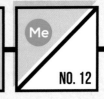
GAME SIGN: Arrange the boxes so the river runs unbroken through all four squares on the five visible faces.

WHAT YOU NEED: Eight identically sized plain square cardboard boxes and a thick green felt-tip pen. Note: If you don't have eight identical boxes you can easily make your own following a printable guide online.

PREPARATION: Stack the boxes in two layers of four boxes and use the pen to draw a continuous thick line (a 'river') through all four squares on all five visible faces of the stack (i.e. the top and four sides – not the base). Then take the stack apart and draw decoy lines on all the other faces of all eight boxes. Finally, leave the boxes scattered in the centre of the room for the player to find.

GAME: The player has to move the boxes around until they have recreated the continuous line or run out of time.

ILLUSTRATION: Fig.1 opposite shows is what the eight blocks would look like stacked as a cube (four boxes on top of four), when the 'river' is complete.

Fig.2 illustrates how each of the faces of the individual boxes might look with 'decoy' lines. NB: the squares highlighted in yellow are the ones on which you as the Maze Master will have drawn 'decoy' lines.

03:00

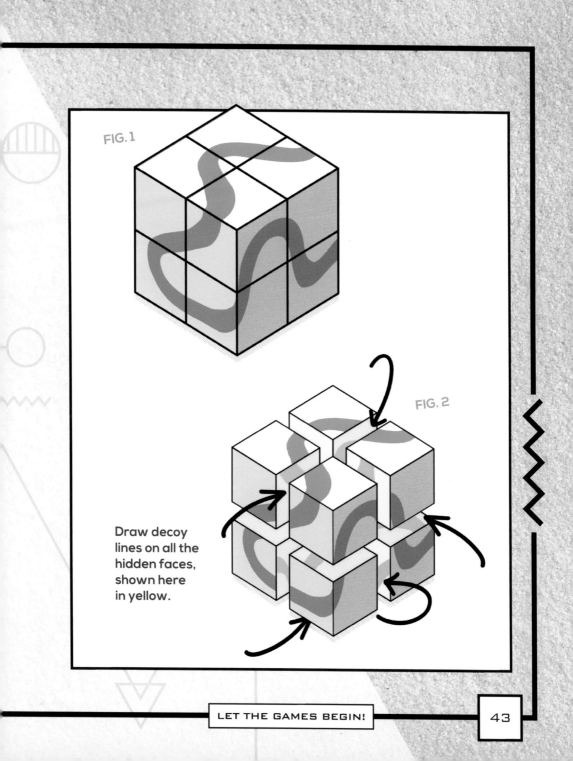

FIG. 1

FIG. 2

Draw decoy lines on all the hidden faces, shown here in yellow.

WALK THE LINE

Ph

NO. 13

GAME SIGN: Walk blindfolded without crossing the lines.

WHAT YOU NEED: Two lengths of string and some tape.

PREPARATION: This game is essentially the Crystal Maze version of a sobriety test. Except it replaces the alcohol with a blindfold, and the police with your friends and family.

The Maze Master should find a long, clear section of floor with no obstacles in the way. Then tape down two lengths of string, positioned parallel to one another and about 30cm apart.

GAME: The player is blindfolded and led to the end of the runway. To win the crystal, all they have to do is walk back down the runway without crossing either piece of string. If they step on or over a string, they lose a life. And you can guess what happens if they do this three times – that's right, it's an ALIS.

When the two minutes begin they can lift their blindfold and study the line. They can spend as much time scrutinising the line as they like, and when they are ready they can lower the blindfold. However, once it is lowered, they cannot raise it again, and must commit to walking the line.

Teammates can help with this one – so hysterical cries of 'Left a bit!' and 'Not THAT far left!' should be deployed. If the player gets to the end without crossing the line, they win the crystal.

ALIS 02:00

LET THE GAMES BEGIN!

45

GAME SIGN: Discover which package the crystal is in by joining the solutions.

WHAT YOU NEED: Some scrap paper, brown paper, string, two thick felt-tip pens (different colours) and two big bits of paper (ideally A1 or A2).

PREPARATION: Crumple the scrap paper into four balls the same size as the crystal, then use the brown paper and string to wrap each one. Use a felt-tip pen to draw a different Aztec-style symbol on each parcel, e.g. a crescent moon, a feather, an arrow and a snake. Then wrap the crystal the same way and draw a five-pointed star on it.

On one of the big bits of paper, write up the following list of sums:

1) $(88 \div 11) \times 3 =$
2) $(3 \times 3 \times 3) - (2 \times 2 \times 2) =$
3) $(56 \div 8) \times (49 \div 7) + 1 =$
4) $(6 \times 8 \times \frac{1}{2}) \div (15 \div 5) =$
5) $1 + 2 + 3 + 4 + 5 =$
6) $(100 \div 4) - (43 \div 43) =$

Then use the same colour pen to mark five dots that are arranged to be the five points of a large five-pointed star, like this ...

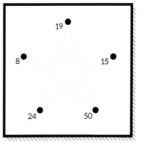

03:00

Once you have these marked in, add at least ten more decoy dots wherever you like, and put a number next to each of them. It doesn't matter what these numbers are so long as they are not any of the five numbers by the initial five dots.

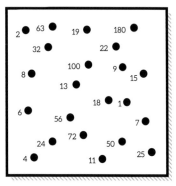

Use the sticky tack to stick both of the pieces of paper up on the wall. Place the five small parcels on a table. And, finally, have the other colour felt-tip pen ready for the player to use.

GAME: The player has to solve the sums in order to find the five dots to join (the last answer takes them back to the first dot to complete the symbol). When they draw lines to join these dots, they'll see a star – and so will know to open the star-marked parcel to get the crystal. They are allowed to open only one parcel – but if they've failed to solve the sums and join the dots correctly to work out the right symbol, it is up to you as Maze Master to decide whether you want to let them have a 'lucky dip' or not. Naturally, if the sums given above feel too easy or too hard for your adventurers, then feel free to replace them with ones you think are more fitting.

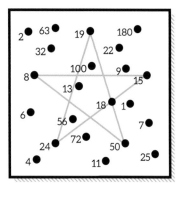

HEADS UP

Sk

NO. 15

GAME SIGN: Get and keep six balls in the bowl only by throwing them in.

WHAT YOU NEED: Elastic, a bowl, sticky tape and ten soft balls.

PREPARATION: Attach elastic to the underside of a bowl with sticky tape to create a strap that enables a player to comfortably and securely wear the bowl on their head. Place the soft balls around the room on the floor (or on objects that require further movement if you want to be especially unpopular).

GAME: A player must place the bowl on their head before they enter the room. This is mainly so they can be mocked by the rest of the team.

Once the player enters the room they must pick up balls from around the space and throw them up into the air to attempt to catch them in the bowl on top of their heads. Collect and keep six balls in the bowl to be able to unlock the crystal.

There are no penalties for balls falling back out of the bowl, but you can deduct lives for cheating. Only throwing and catching is allowed!

02:00

SLIDING PLANKS

GAME SIGN: Move the matches between the coins to reach the crystal and then return to the start.

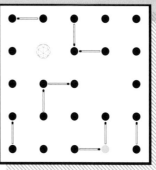

WHAT YOU NEED: A box of matches and 23 same-sized coins.

PREPARATION: Set out your matches and coins in the exact formation pictured on the right on a table. Take care not to place a coin where one is absent in the diagram. Clearly mark one coin as the starting position (gold in our picture) and one for where the crystal lies (blue in our picture).

GAME: If you don't have your very own foggy bog at home, then fear not! There's a simple way to play your own version of the game we call Sliding Planks from the series. The matchsticks are planks, and the coins are stepping stones. The gold coin represents the player's starting position. The blue coin represents the crystal. They can only travel between stepping stones by sliding the planks from one to the other, either horizontally or vertically, but diagonally. The player must work out the route to the crystal and back again within the time limit … or it's an ALIS!

MAZE MASTER: For an authentic foggy bog experience do feel free to create your own pungent smells throughout the game.

02:00 ALIS

SOLUTION ON PAGE 216

SPONGE SUIT

NO. 17

GAME SIGN: Raise the ball to the marker using only water from the sponges.

WHAT YOU NEED: This is ideally a game for the garden or outdoors. A paddling pool or small tub or bucket for a start position, a small bucket or large plastic glass for the finish position, a ping-pong ball or something similar, as many household and/or kitchen sponges as you can get you hands on and some string or tape.

PREPARATION: Pick a start line, put the largest receptacle there and fill it with water. Pick a finish line and put an empty receptacle there. Add the ping-pong type ball to the empty receptacle. Attach the sponges to the player (anywhere and everywhere!) with the string and/or tape.

GAME: The player must successfully raise the ping-pong ball to the top of the finish receptacle (or agree on a 'win' level before play commences) by transferring water from the start to the finish receptacles utilising the sponges on their person. When at the finish receptacle, the player must attempt to wring the water from their sponge suit and continue back and forth until they either succeed or the time runs out.

MAZE MASTER: Do have a towel ready to help them dry off. I'm guessing your Aztec zone isn't as hot as ours ...

{2-3 MINUTES depending on course size}

02:00

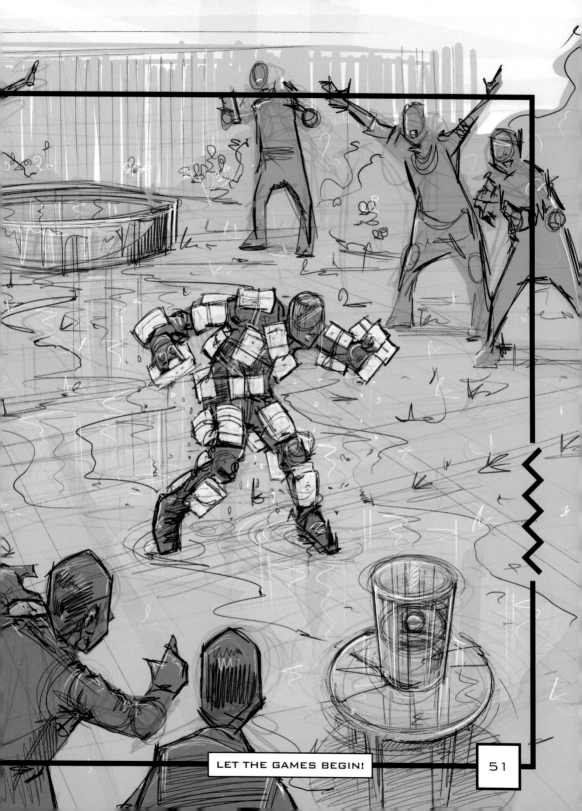

LET THE GAMES BEGIN!

AZTEC RIDDLES – AKA 'QUESTIONSCOATL'

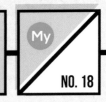

My

NO. 18

GAME SIGN: Solve two of the three riddles.

TIME: There is no time limit here. Apart from the limit that comes with boredom. Do please remind people of this when playing the game.

PREPARATION: It's a question of what lengths you want to go to. Maybe you'd like to make a feather-covered suit (e.g. by putting glue on a onesie, cutting open a feather pillow and rolling around in the downy contents?) and take on the feathered-serpent-form of Quetzalcoatl, the Aztec god of knowledge? If this sounds too highbrow, bear in mind he was also the god of wind – and so you'd have licence to go for some flatulence-based humour to undercut the historical accuracy. Then again, you might just want to use a permanent marker to draw a face on a corn on a cob and use it as a kind of maize-based riddle-setting stick puppet. Or you might just want to do nothing other than say, 'Here are some Aztec riddles,' and run the risk of your friends thinking you're a teeny bit lazy and not really as into *The Crystal Maze* as much as you claim to be.

GAME: Tell your adventurer that they must correctly answer two of three riddles to win a crystal. Some example riddles follow, but why not make your own up, spicing them up with Aztec terms you've learned from Wikipedia (just like the writers of this book did)?

EXAMPLE RIDDLES:

1. Chimalpopoca, the Aztec king, is getting desperate to find a husband for his daughter Centehua, but she is proving very picky. After initially trying to find the very best suitors for his little darling, he's now decided it's all about quantity. He's going to double the number of brave(ish), handsome(ish), young(ish) soldiers he puts before Centehua every week until she finally says 'Yes' (or even 'You'll do ...') to any of them. If he introduces her to three plucky hopefuls today, six next week, twelve the week after, etc., how many men will she have met – and, inevitably, rejected – in seven weeks' time?

2. Amoxtli, the Aztec high priest, has a massive collection of multicoloured skulls. All the green ones are carved out of jade. All the white ones are real skulls. But the red ones are a mixed bunch – half are real and half are terracotta. If he has 400 green skulls, 100 red skulls, with equal numbers of real and fake skulls, how many skulls does he have in total?

3. Chimalpopoca absolutely loves to eat. He has chocolate nine times a week, eggs four times a week, and beans five times a week. How often does he have sweetcorn?

SOLUTIONS ON PAGE 217

GAME SIGN: Every face must bear all four symbols.

WHAT YOU NEED: Paper, pen, scissors and glue or tape.

PREPARATION: Maze Master, it's time to get your arts and crafts on to prep for this game, and, if your players are predisposed to impatient outbursts, it's one you might want to do the night before to avoid a mid-maze riot. Opposite are a series of cube diagrams that you need to use to create eight cubes. Copy them accurately (or scan and print them), and then fold along the lines, before placing glue on the shaded edges and sticking them together. You might find it easier to tape the cubes shut.

Now we're not going to lie, preparation for this game is on the time-consuming side, but may we suggest you pop an episode of *The Crystal Maze* on whilst you cut and stick to keep you both amused and motivated.

GAME: This game is essentially a lo-fi version of a game we call Four Symbols in the show. The task is simple – the player needs to take the eight blocks and assemble them to make a two-by-two-by-two larger cube. To win the crystal, they must assemble all the small blocks so that each visible side of the larger block has one of the four symbols – a snake, a bird, a frog or a fish. There can be no two symbols the same on any visible side. Trust us, they're going to need every single one of those 180 seconds.

⌛ 03:00

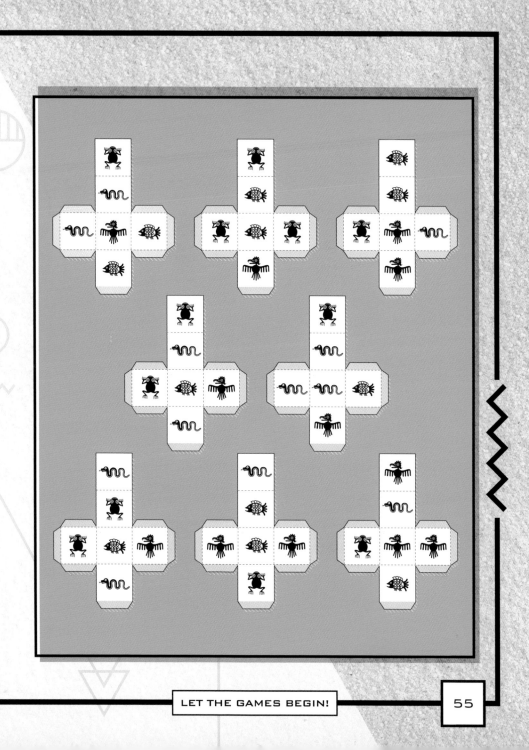

FOUR IN A ROW

GAME SIGN: Throw the balls in the cups to create a line of four in a row.

WHAT YOU NEED: Thirty-six plastic cups, some tape and twenty ping-pong balls.

PREPARATION: To set up this game, lay the plastic cups out in a grid formation that is roughly square – so, six rows of six. Tape the cups down so they don't move around.

The player plays the game from behind a line at a pre-determined distance away from the cups. Decide where this is going to be, depending on the player's age, height and how much you want them to win or lose.

GAME: To win the crystal, the player must simply throw the balls into the cups so that they get four in a line. The line can be vertical, horizontal or diagonal, but all four must be adjacent.

Each ball can only be thrown once, which means that the player has just twenty attempts. Four in a row wins a crystal.

02:30

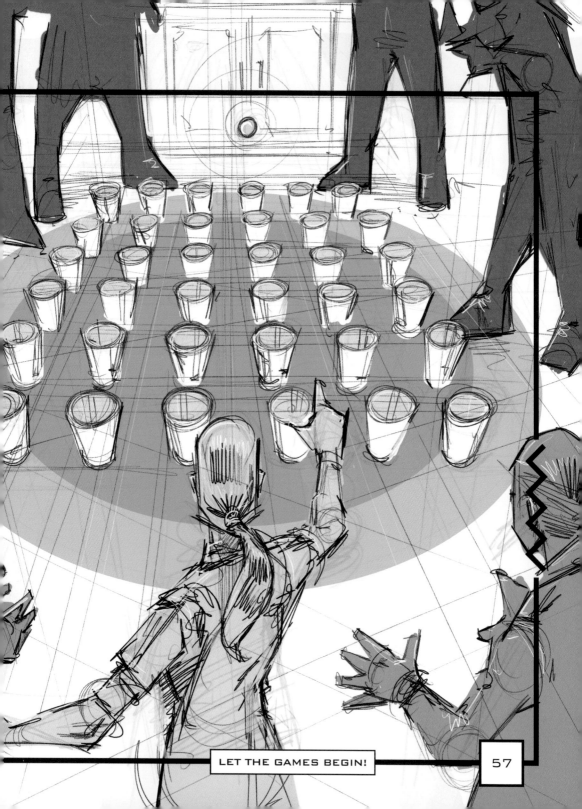

LET THE GAMES BEGIN!

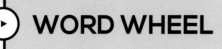

WORD WHEEL

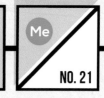

NO. 21

GAME SIGN: Turn the wheels to spell twelve words simultaneously.

WHAT YOU NEED: Paper, pen and scissors.

PREPARATION: Recreate the diagram opposite, either by sketching it out on to paper (scale it up in size), or by photocopying and enlarging it. There's no clear evidence of the Aztec people utilising photocopiers, but we like to think this is how they mass-produced temple plans.

Make sure the letters all line up correctly, and then you'll need to cut it up along the dotted lines to create four interlocking wheels. If you have a large piece of stone, chisel and literally oodles of time, then feel free to go fully Aztec in your re-creation and carve the wheels into rock, but we are not liable for you lot losing your jobs or minds.

GAME: The player is given the four interlocked wheels. The Maze Master should be familiar with the correct words in order to steer them in the right direction (or wrong direction as they choose), but should ensure the order is jumbled up; the player's got to work for their crystal.

Following the instructions, the player's task is to rotate the four wheels until the letters line up, spelling an eight-letter word along each of the twelve segments simultaneously. If they find the opposite solution in two minutes, they will win a shiny new crystal.

02:00

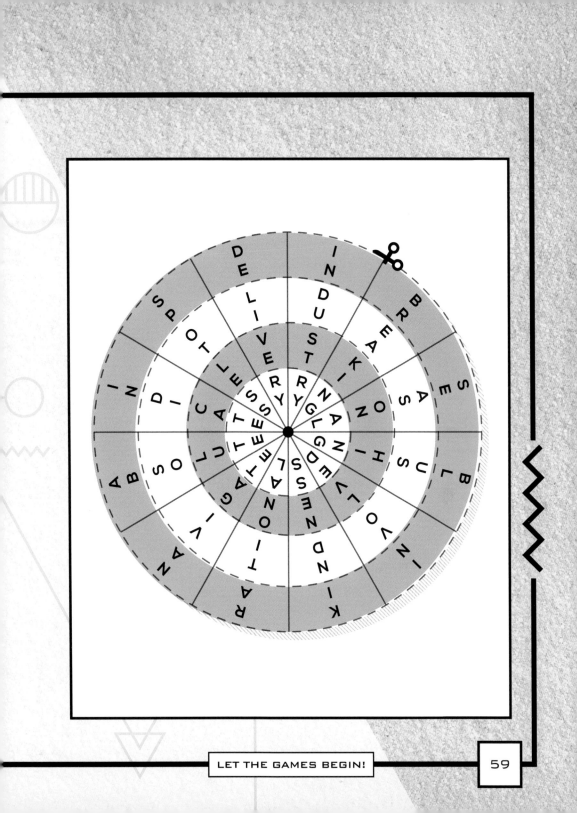

I WANT MUMMY

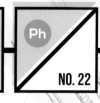

Ph

NO. 22

GAME SIGN: Create a mummy with no gaps in the paper.

WHAT YOU NEED: One full loo roll and a willing volunteer.

PREPARATION: Procure the loo paper and move to the designated Aztec zone in your house or flat. Find a room where someone can stand and there is room for the Maze Master to walk around them for inspection.

GAME: After the player has been chosen, identify another teammate who will be the willing volunteer.

The aim of the game is for the player to cover the volunteer from head to toe with loo roll. Crucially, they must do so in such a way that there are no visible gaps. This must be inspected by the Maze Master (who can be as pedantic or as lenient as they choose).

The roll of loo roll can break as it's being rolled around – all that matters is that there are no gaps. If every bit of tissue is unfurled and reasonably bound on the 'mummy' before the end of time, a crystal is won!

02:00

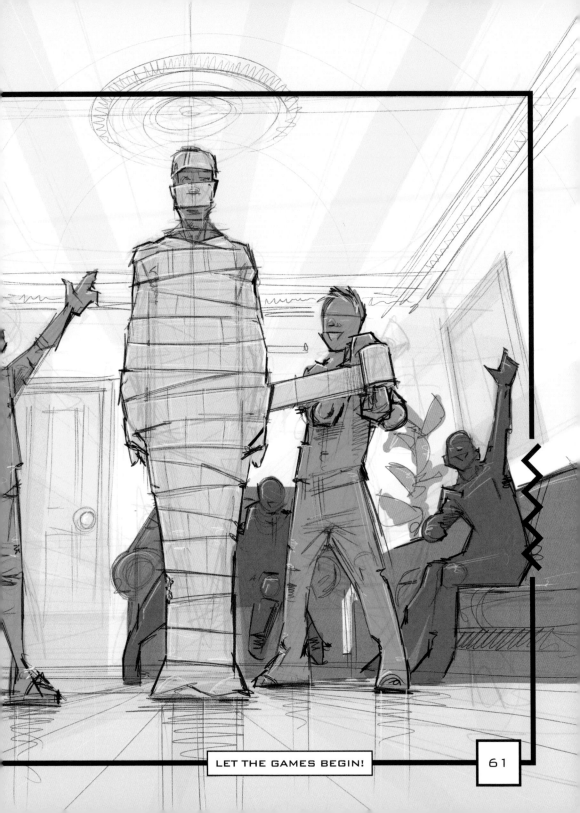

LET THE GAMES BEGIN!

61

GAME SIGN: Spell out words to cross the floor.
Do it fast or we'll lock the door.
Collect two keys and then you're set.
Free the crystal and out you get.

WHAT YOU NEED: Some chalk, a box, a length of chain and two padlocks with keys.

PREPARATION: This game is best played on a paved/tarmac area. Take the chalk and draw a 9 x 9 grid, filling in the letters and arrows as illustrated opposite. Then place the crystal in a box, wrap the chain around it, and padlock it twice. Place the crystal and the keys in the squares indicated.

GAME: The player starts at the arrow pointing into the grid of letters. They must step on letters to spell out a long word to get to the first key, then from that key to the second, and from the second key to the locked box. They use the keys to unlock the crystal and must then step on to letters to spell one final word to reach the 'out' arrow before their time is up.

Diagonal steps are not allowed and only unbroken English words will get them from point to point. As Maze Master, armed with the answers, you can give the player and their team some helpful hints if you feel so inclined.

ALIS 03:00

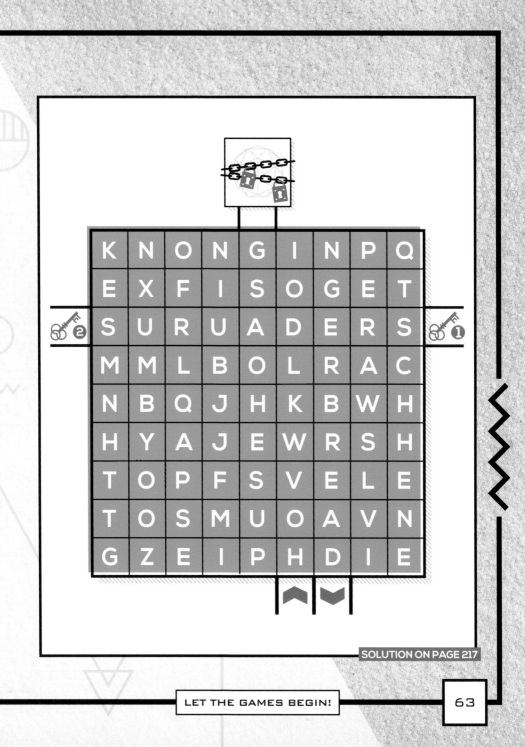

K	N	O	N	G	I	N	P	Q
E	X	F	I	S	O	G	E	T
S	U	R	U	A	D	E	R	S
M	M	L	B	O	L	R	A	C
N	B	Q	J	H	K	B	W	H
H	Y	A	J	E	W	R	S	H
T	O	P	F	S	V	E	L	E
T	O	S	M	U	O	A	V	N
G	Z	E	I	P	H	D	I	E

SOLUTION ON PAGE 217

LET THE GAMES BEGIN!

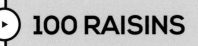 # 100 RAISINS

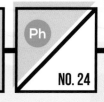

NO. 24

GAME SIGN: Transfer all 100 raisins individually to the other bowl using only your thumb and forefinger.

WHAT YOU NEED: Two bowls and 100 raisins.

PREPARATION: To set up, you need to fill your first bowl with 100 carefully counted out raisins (sultanas or any small shrivelled fruit will also work). Place that bowl at one end of the room.

Place the second empty bowl at the far end of the room. And if you want to place an obstacle – such as a pile of cushions or broom handle suspended between two chairs – bang in the middle of the two bowls, we won't stop you.

GAME: The player has two and a half minutes to transfer the raisins from the first bowl to the second. However, nothing is ever that simple in the Crystal Maze! The raisins can only be transported one at a time using the thumb and forefinger on one hand. If any other digits are used, it's a straight-up lock-in.

If any raisins are dropped, the contestant may pick them up, but again only using their thumb and forefinger. If they successfully transfer all 100 raisins, they will win their crystal.

02:30

LET THE GAMES BEGIN!

65

HOW TO BUILD YOUR OWN MAZE (TO SCALE) BY JAMES DILLON

First you will need to find 3019 sq m of spare floor space. If you live in London then it might fit in your basement extension. Otherwise three and a half football pitches would be about right. Bear in mind that you will also need around 8m of headroom.

THE MEDIEVAL ZONE

280 sq m of flooring is needed here. We used a recycled faux-flagstone floor with an MDF interlocking subfloor and a wool base layer to help deaden sound. You could try a padded stone-effect linoleum. The walls have a vac-form castle-stone finish. This comes in 2.4 x 1.2m sheets and you'll need about 450 of them. If that sounds like a lot, it's because the walls are 4.2m high and stretch 97.5m around the main set (excluding the game rooms).

To illuminate the Medieval zone about 200 large candles and twenty-five gas-flame torches are required to give the otherwise gloomy atmosphere a bit of a glow.

We use around thirty cans of cobweb in Medieval. Employing real spiders would take longer, but save money. If there aren't enough in your own house or garden, you could try crowdsourcing them.

The obstacle at one end of the zone is a swampy, murky water tank that holds 10,000L of cold water and twenty-four viciously pointed spikes. Make sure your tank is watertight and ask the bill payer's permission if you are on a metered water supply. Your local park

keeper might be helpful when it comes to sourcing wooden spikes, although ours are sculpted from foam. We treat the water with chemicals as plague-carrying rats were a problem in medieval times and the producers don't want contestants to contract Weil's disease.

To dress the set, you'll need four bales of straw, ten bags of earth, eight wooden barrels, a scramble net, 45m of chain, four 1000kg bags of dead ivy and a dry ice machine (try your local nightclub), plus some large sand timers.

INDUSTRIAL ZONE

Most factories in the UK have now shut, so plenty of the things needed for this zone will be readily available at your local scrap merchant.

Industrial has the highest walls of any of the zones: the main set is 6m high. It uses real corrugated iron sheets and you will need 250 of them, although you could try the garden shed plastic version and paint them silver. There is a 24m-long metal walkway surrounding the set with access stairs and ladders. Make sure the ones you use aren't too rusty – it's all too easy to fall through an unsafe handrail and land in the highly polluted central tank that occupies the middle of the zone. The tank contains 4100L of liquid waste, which bubbles and steams away, and it's not a good idea to inhale its toxic fumes. You can simulate the effect using compressed air pumped into your pool and use poster paints to give a nice green tint to whatever waste liquids you can find.

▶ The perilous plank across the foggy bog at the edge of the Medieval zone.

▶ The metal ladder, leading to the gangway out of the Industrial zone.

▶ The Aztec zone, featuring a 262 sq m scenic painted cloth with distant views of the Andes.

There are around 45m of ductwork vents and pipes around the zone. We use custom-built galvanised steel pipes, but cardboard tubes painted to suit will also work. Illuminating Industrial requires a large number of bulkhead lights (minimum seventy-five), coolie shades and floodlights. Most of this you can get from Homebase, B&Q or from any multistorey car park. Ensure that your electrical supply is robust enough to cope. It also helps to have some big industrial fans that have spotlights and smoke coming through, because the shafts of light always look good on camera and they also help disorientate the contestants. A big desk fan might be a start.

To watch the games in progress we have six high-grade monitors on the set, which are wired into the cameras that are recording the show (you can simulate this with a CCTV set-up from a high-street electronics provider). We also have specially adapted analogue photographic timers to count down the games but an egg timer would probably work. The set has 60m of electrical conduit struts, a recycled submarine hatch, eight heavy-duty electrical switchgear mechanisms and all sorts of dials, switches, pallets and trolleys as dressing. Most of this will be available on eBay or in your local canal.

AZTEC ZONE

The Aztecs and Mayans were incredible builders and the Aztec zone is a nod to their skills and achievements. They also liked a human sacrifice, something that we try to emulate with as many lock-ins as possible. (Health and Safety have cracked down on anything more permanent.)

The walls of the zone are constructed on large wooden frames. Sculpted panels and stonework made from moulded foam are applied and painted to look like a lost temple. We used about 325 sq m of these panels on the main set and also created a cave entrance and a waterfall. You could try using insulating foam boards from your attic, but you will need 600 of them and you will also need to carve them by hand. Difficult, maybe, but if the Aztecs could do it for real with blocks of stone, then carving a few foam panels shouldn't be impossible.

To cover the floor, you will need 18,000kg of sand. This is readily available from builders' merchants in one-tonne bags (ensure you have a forklift) or in smaller bags of 25kg from DIY stores, in which case you will need about 720 bags. We have a large scenic painted cloth that surrounds one end of the set. This is 265 sq m and it's painted to look like a jungle with distant views of the Andes. It's 8m high, so challenging to work on, and you'll need about 100L of paint.

The Aztec zone has around 200 real and artificial plants to create an overgrown-jungle feel. Lots of palms, creepers and bamboos are needed. Most will be available from your local garden centre, although 4m-high palms are not always a stock item.

> **To cover the floor, you will need 18,000kg of sand.**

The water game room in Aztec has a tank with 18,200L of water. Again, check with the bill payer before filling this up. You will also need a heater and filtration system to purify the water and make it comfortable for the twenty-first-century competitor (twentieth-century competitors were hardier). Any high-street swimming pool shop should have this equipment. Aztec water clocks are not easily available, even on eBay. A plastic container with some bamboo stuck through the bottom which empties into a jam jar would make a good substitute.

▶ The view from the revolving platform looking down the three spaceship corridors in the Futuristic zones.

FUTURISTIC ZONE

The new Futuristic zone requires a lot of silver paint. We'd advise at least 50L for the walls, floors and ceilings. The corridors in Futuristic have LED display panels inset behind the walls. There are thirty-nine panels arranged in groups of three. They are linked together and use a media server to display the electronic signals that control the space station. Try a local football stadium as they sometimes have them round the pitch and might lend you some spares. Thirteen flat-screen television sets would also do if you can't get the panels, and you will need another four LCD TVs for the control room. Two of these sit on a desk on a computer-controlled revolve. You could use an old roundabout mechanism from a closed-down playground (ask your local authority for the nearest).

Futuristic is lit with a type of fluorescent light called an encapsulite. We have about 150 of these hidden around the set in various sizes and an abandoned office block will have lots of them. There are also many light-up LED control panels. These perform the vital functions of providing flashing LED lights and looking space station-y. We have twenty of these from a specialist hire company. You could try second-hand or charity shops for old hi-fi amplifiers, which also have lots of useless flashing lights.

Outside the window of the control room is a large image of planets taken from space. This is a Translight on a frame. It's like a giant backlit photo and measures 17.6 sq m. If you decide to print yours at home, you will need 283 sheets of A4 taped together.

We have eight split doors on the set. These can be operated using electronic, pneumatic or hydraulic rams. However, as in the original series, we actually use rope and a highly skilled man concealed round the back of the set to pull them open and shut. The door sections alone are composed of 120 different elements. We used CNC (Computer Numerical Control) machines to cut most of the complex shapes needed for construction. These cost up to £50k; a decent electric jigsaw will give a similar result but take a lot longer.

THE CRYSTAL DOME

The Crystal Dome is 4.5m high and sits on a 1.2m rostrum that contains the fan system. It's basically a big greenhouse and we use it to grow plants for the Aztec zone when we're not filming. You can easily create your own dome by checking out www.domerama.com. If you go to the calculator page and key in your parameters, it will give you all the strut sizes and angles you need.

For the classic Crystal Maze look install a circular water tank around the dome and a waterproof hydraulic bridge, or go for the twenty-first-century-all-singing-and-dancing LED system with moving lights.

Please remember to anchor your dome down.

To blow the gold and silver tokens around you will need a fan system. We use nine fans of the type used in bouncy castles to create a vortex effect. If you want to go retro, one big aeroplane propeller blade under your dome might do it. Please remember to anchor your dome down, though.

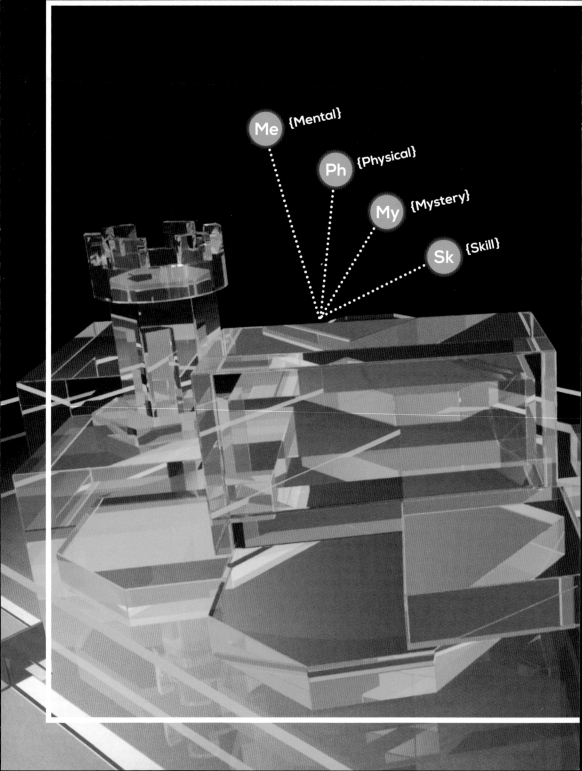

Me {Mental}

Ph {Physical}

My {Mystery}

Sk {Skill}

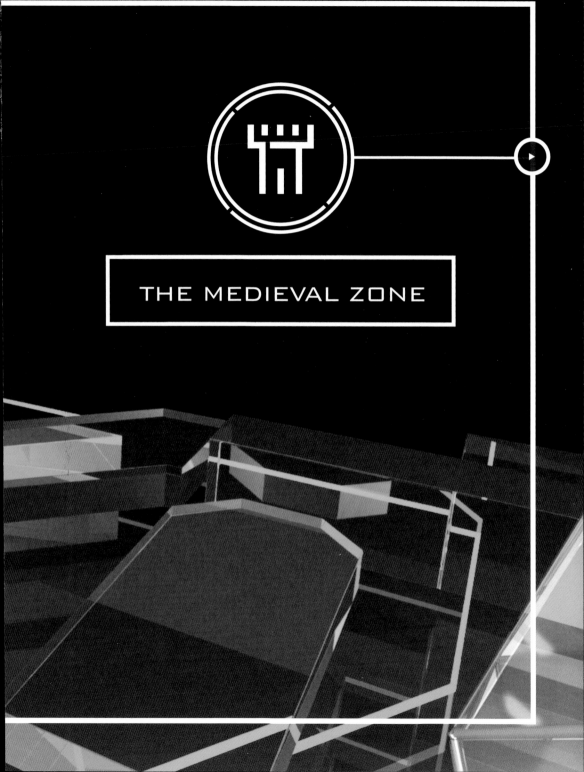

THE MEDIEVAL ZONE

Team, your second zone awaits you within the brooding castle walls of Medieval ...

The word 'medieval' comes from the Latin phrase *medium aevum*, which means 'middle age' – but have no fear. This zone is not themed around cardigans, estate cars, worrying about pensions and a burgeoning interest in wine/real ale/vinyl/yoga/DIY/etc. No, thankfully it's actually set in the dank dungeons and flame-lit hallways of a moody old castle. Phew.

If you were born into royalty, have become a tech billionaire or are currently a squatter in a little-visited National Trust property, then there is a good chance your current surroundings will be sufficiently castle-like to work for this zone 'as is'. If not, then you might want to make attempts to medieval-up your home before asking your adventurers round.

An easy first step is not to clean it for twelve to eighteen months – the dust, cobwebs and curious stains will all feel grimly authentic (plus, think what you'll do with all that hoovering time you'll have saved). Secondly, if you're playing in winter, turn off the heating and open enough doors and windows to allow a chilly breeze to blow through. And if you're playing after dark, turn off all the lights and instead set up sputtering candles on all available flat-ish surfaces. What fun.

It is now time for the team to embrace these primitive times, gird their loins accordingly, and prepare to face the puzzles that await them within these ancient castle walls ... Lead on, Maze Master!

ROMAN NUMERALS

GAME SIGN: Place all the squares in the grid. The numerals on the four squares surrounding each circle should total the numeral inside that circle.

WHAT YOU NEED: Two pieces of paper, a pen and scissors.

PREPARATION: Draw the layout below on to a piece of paper.

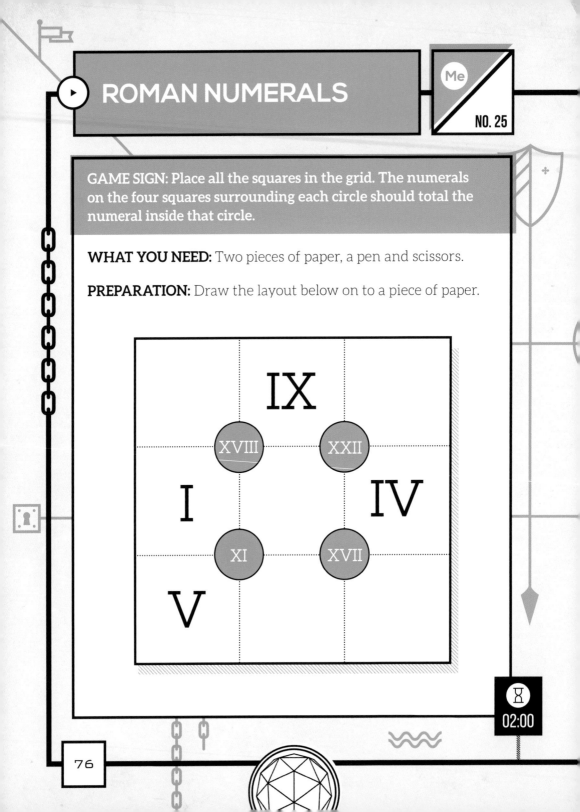

02:00

On a separate piece of paper write and then cut out these Roman numerals into squares that will fit into the grid.

II	VI	VII	III	VIII

GAME: This fiendish puzzle combines the twin terrors of maths ... and remembering Roman numerals. As we all know, everyone thinks they know their Roman numerals, but few people actually do. So please bear that in mind when Uncle Keith starts barking numbers with absolute conviction while the answer in this book doesn't quite tally.

When you start the two minute timer the player's task is to place the missing numerals into the grid in the correct places. The four spaces surrounding each golden circle must add up to the numeral inside it. So, players need to first work out the Roman numerals then how to place them in the right position.

MAZE MASTER: It obviously helps if you have made a note of the correct answers before the game begins so you can tell them when they've got it wrong.

And don't forget (purely for your own amusement) to encourage the player to show everyone else in the team the grid so they can all unhelpfully share their questionable Roman numeral knowledge.

SOLUTION ON PAGE 217

POCKET MONEY PILES

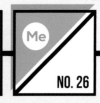

GAME SIGN: Arrange the money into piles as follows: (followed by your own chosen monetary amounts and rules – see below).

WHAT YOU NEED: A sizeable pile of loose change including 1p, 2p, 5p, 10p, 20p and 50p coins.

PREPARATION: Use the coins you have to work out five different amounts you would like a player to create. To make the task more challenging add rules about which coins must feature in specific piles.

Here are some examples:

12p – using only 2p coins and 1p coins
23p – with at least three 5p coins
61p – using no 5p or 20p coins

GAME: The player must arrange the coins into five piles following the specified instructions correctly. Only once the Maze Master has verified the five piles can the crystal be released.

ATTENTION, KIDS: This game is really a ruse to get money from other family members. Using the excuse 'But, Dad, I'm trying to make a fun activity for all the family'. It will never be questioned and after humiliating themselves the parents are likely to drink wine and forget you ever borrowed money in the first place. Winner.

02:00

BLOW BY BLOW

GAME SIGN: Blow the ball to the end of the maze.

WHAT YOU NEED: Some items to build a maze from (such as wooden blocks), a ping-pong ball and a straw.

PREPARATION: It's up to the Maze Master to build a tabletop maze for this game. You can make the maze out of anything solid, so get creative. If you've got a lot of kids' building blocks to hand, try those, or use a mixture of books, kitchen roll tubes or even pens. Tack the maze to the table to keep it from moving during the game.

It's up to you how hard to make the maze – the player's going to be guiding a ball around it, so if you're feeling a bit mean, put a tricky route in to flummox them or some dodgy openings in there so their ball might fall off the table.

When you're all set, place a ping-pong ball at one end of the maze.

GAME: When the timer starts, the player should use the straw to blow the ping-pong ball through the maze, attempting to get it to the end within the time limit, but without it going off the table (or they have to start again). Definitely a game for someone full of hot air …

03:00

DO OR DIE

NO. 28

GAME SIGN: Roll the dice over the finish line until you have done so with all six sides facing up.

WHAT YOU NEED: Paper to mark start and finish lines and one regular six-sided dice.

PREPARATION: Create a start and finish line in a room. Place the dice next to the start line.

GAME: The object of the game is for the player to roll the dice so that they roll every possible number at least once. The player begins behind the start line and must roll the dice across the finish line. Dice rolled short do not count.

After each roll, the Maze Master must verify the side on top and announce the number to the player. The player can then retrieve the dice and attempt another throw. They should continue until they have rolled each number on the dice (that's one, two, three, four, five, six, in case you need clarification). They must do this in the time allotted to gain a crystal.

02:00

LET THE GAMES BEGIN!

81

BALANCE THE BOOKS

My

NO. 29

GAME SIGN: Roll the pea across the spine of the two books.

WHAT YOU NEED: Two large hardback books ... and a pea.

PREPARATION: Take the first book, and place it on the table so that the spine is facing upwards. Place a second book end to end with the first. Wedge the books into place with something heavy if necessary. You should have created a narrow runway above the table or floor upon which you are playing. Place a pea at the end of the first book.

GAME: To win the crystal, the player should roll the pea along the books' spines without it falling off. To make it easier, they could start with the pea on the book that is slightly higher so it can drop down on to the second. (Unless you want to make it harder because they've been playing too well up until this point and are getting a bit smug.)

The player may use only their forefinger to move the pea, and their other hand must remain behind their back at all times. If they roll the pea to the end of the second book, they will win. Each time the pea falls, they may make another attempt, but they will lose a life. Three lives lost equals a lock-in.

Easy-peasy. Which is something you can say when they get locked in, if you are going for the 'most annoying Maze Master of all time' approach.

ALIS 02:00

ROLL-OVER WORDS

GAME SIGN: Roll the ball over the words in the correct order to win a crystal.

WHAT YOU NEED: A large plate, preferably paper or plastic so you can write on it, a pen and a marble, or anything else small that rolls.

PREPARATION: The classic ball maze was a staple of the original series of *The Crystal Maze*. The new series was too jampacked with games to fit one in ... but we still found the time to figure out how you lot can make one at home. You can't say we don't try ... Write the following words on the plate. Keep your lettering small enough so that the game isn't impossible to play. Why not try the game out yourself to make sure you can play it? That way you can rebuff angry friends and relatives later!

ROLL – OVER – THE – WORDS – TO – WIN – CRYSTAL.

Spread them out and jumble them up. The more jumbled the words have been written on the plate, the more tricky this game will be, so don't hold back!

Finally, place the marble on the plate ready to start the game.

GAME: The player needs to pick up the plate and roll the marble over all of the words in the correct order. If they make a mistake and roll over a word out of sequence, they need to start again from 'ROLL'.

03:00

COINING IT IN

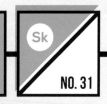

GAME SIGN: Throw coins into the cups to the values displayed.

WHAT YOU NEED: Three labels, three cups, a pen, a 1p piece, three 2p pieces, two 5p pieces, two 10p pieces and a 20p piece.

PREPARATION: The person playing this game shouldn't see the values on the three cups until their time starts. Label the cups as follows: one should have '5p' written on it, one should have '35p' written on it, and the last should have '17p' written on it. Place the cups a metre away from where the player will stand. The cups should be at least 10cm apart for this to be a true test of skill.

GAME: To successfully complete this game, the player must land three coins into each cup before their time is up. Those three coins should add up to the total written on the cup.

A player can retrieve coins that miss their target, but once a coin is in a cup it cannot be removed. If the coins go over the value of the cup, it's an ALIS.

This isn't your run-of-the-mill skill game as it comes with a mental twist. We'd love to supersize this but the publishers refused to back our suggestion to give away a free cannon with every book.

ALIS 02:00

TRICKY LICKY STICKY

Sk

NO. 32

GAME SIGN: Stick twenty sweets to your face.

WHAT YOU NEED: Loads and loads of unwrapped small sweets (a mixture of jelly and sugar-covered) and a mirror.

GAME: The medieval period was a time before hygiene as we know it today. Hands were never washed, effluent flowed uncovered through the streets, and bubonic plague was a popular lifestyle choice. Luckily for your adventurer, we have not chosen to create a game based around sharing bodily fluids with pestilent rats, but instead a game based on playing with your food.

The aim is simple – at the end of the two minutes, the player must have twenty sweets stuck to their face; if they achieve this, they'll win the crystal. Anything less, and they leave empty-handed.

MAZE MASTER: The only thing the player can use to attach the sweets to their face is their own saliva, so you have the joyful task of alerting them to the fact that they need to lick the sweets and stick them on. It doesn't matter if some fall off, they just have to keep going until they have twenty or more on their face that stay on for five seconds (it's your job to count) before the clock hits zero.

You might want to take a photo of the confection-visaged adventurer at the end of the game. Not for game verification, just so you can pop it on social media. (#crystalmaze)

⧗
02:00

GAME FACE

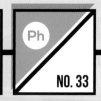

NO. 33

GAME SIGN: Turn over cards one at a time to find all the face cards and place them on the table face-up. All non-face cards must be left where they are, face-down.

WHAT YOU NEED: Standard deck of cards.

PREPARATION: Remove the jokers from the pack. Spread the cards face down on the floor and all over the furniture throughout the room. Clear a table in the centre of the room.

GAME: The player may turn over only one card at a time. The player must hunt to find all the face cards (Jacks, Queens, Kings) and place them on the table, face-up.

Each time they find a non-face card (Aces, and twos through to tens), they must replace it face-down and leave it where it is. But they'd better remember where it is, or they'll waste a lot of time.

If they successfully transport all twelve face cards to the table within the time limit, they'll win a crystal.

{2–3 MINUTES depending on course size}

02:00

LET THE GAMES BEGIN!

LETTER PICKER

GAME SIGN: Place an item beginning with each of the ten letters next to its corresponding letter.

PREPARATION: You'll need a room with a lot of items (a kitchen would be good), a large table/counter/surface and a set of letters. These need to be quite big and easy to read.

The simplest set of letters is a chunk of the alphabet, perhaps the first ten letters: A–J. No one will thank you for including X or Z. In the spirit of fairness you should make sure that there is something in the room that begins with each of the letters.

Place your letters down on the table so that the adventurer and the rest of the team can clearly see them. Make sure that there is room next to each letter for a small/medium-sized household item to be placed next to it.

GAME: The player has three minutes to identify and retrieve ten items, each of which begins with one of the letters you've selected. If the adventurer finds ten suitable items in the time, they earn themselves a crystal.

Because they have to place the items next to the letters it does mean that, for instance, they can't select things that are immovable (like 'cooker' for 'c') or intangible/abstract ('boredom' for 'b'). Once an item's been selected, it can't be played again for another letter. That's to say, if a mug of tea has been declared a 'cup' for 'c', it can't then also be declared a 'drink' for 'd'.

03:00

GAME SIGN: Find the six words to form a sentence.

WHAT YOU NEED: A pen and paper.

PREPARATION: While the chosen player is off making a round of tea (being a Maze Master is thirsty work), take a quill and some parchment paper and divide what you have into six equally cut pieces. If these are unavailable, regular pen and paper will suffice. Create a six-word sentence, e.g. you must praise your Maze Master, with one word written on each individual piece of paper.

Hide each of the pieces of paper around the room. Tucked into a picture frame, popped behind a cushion, poking out of your uncle's shirt pocket ... Well concealed or just hidden in plain sight, how difficult you want to make this is up to you.

GAME: Once you're ready, get your tea off the player and send them into the room. If the brew isn't exactly as you'd like then bring them back out and get them to remake it. Yes, let the power go to your head.

The player has three minutes to find the six pieces of paper, and must then rearrange them to form the sentence.

If they get the sentence formed correctly within the time limit, they win themselves a crystal.

03:00

ANAGRAM MAZE

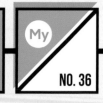

GAME SIGN: Make a pathway to the crystal by solving the anagrams to move forward.

WHAT YOU NEED: This book, or a printer to scan and copy the maze.

GAME: What kind of people would we be if we published a book that didn't have a maze in it? We sadly can't pop you in with our epic Medieval Knights maze from the show (those knights are high-maintenance by the way), but we've worked tirelessly to bring you the printer-friendly anagram-based alternative ... and this is how it works.

MAZE MASTER: Start the timer when you pass this book to the person playing. The player must work their way through the maze from the start to the crystal by solving anagrams. Only the paths that make a word can be travelled. When the player hits a letter jumble they can't solve, they need to turn back and try a different route.

There are a few dead ends along the way so quick thinking is a must.

03:00

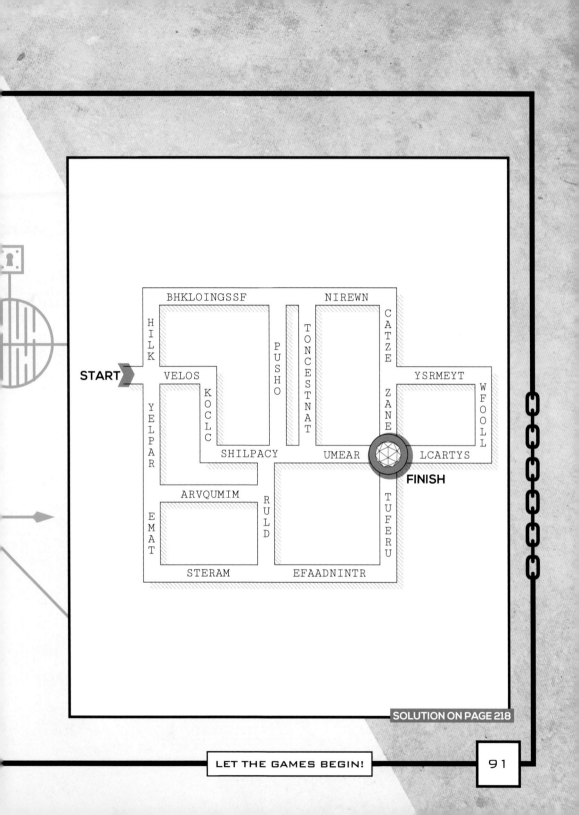

START

FINISH

BHKLOINGSSF

NIREWN

HILK

CATZE

PUSHO

TONCESTNAT

VELOS

YSRMEYT

KOCLC

ZANE

WFOOLL

YELPAR

SHILPACY

UMEAR

LCARTYS

ARVQUMIM

RULD

TUFERU

EMAT

STERAM

EFAADNINTR

SOLUTION ON PAGE 218

FLICK OFF THE MARK

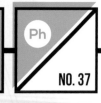

Ph

NO. 37

GAME SIGN: Flick the coin to the opposite edge of the table with just one finger in three moves. Then flick the coin up into the air and catch it to release the crystal.

WHAT YOU NEED: A table and a coin.

PREPARATION: All you need for this game is a table and one of your finest British coins, ideally a large one (physically speaking rather than monetary-wise), so a 2p, 50p or £2 coin would be perfect.

Place the coin on the edge of the tabletop so that it is half on and half off. Clear your drinks, TV remote and even this book off the table so nothing gets in the way.

GAME: All the player needs to do to win a crystal here is to flick the coin across the table to the opposite side using one finger. Using a maximum of three flicks, the coin must end up partially on and partially off the edge of the other side of the table.

Here comes the tricky part: the player must, in one final smooth move, flick the coin off the table, up into the air, and catch it. If it hasn't reached the edge in three flicks, the player can't attempt the final part and will need to give it another go. If the player drops the catch they also need to start again. We know, ruthless isn't it?

The player has as many attempts as they wish to complete this, but steady hands will be essential as the clock is ticking ...

02:00

LET THE GAMES BEGIN!

93

PUT YOUR FOOT IN IT

NO. 38

GAME SIGN: Bare your toes and cover your eyes:
It's time for a sensory surprise.
Identify three substances with your feet.
And a crystal will be your treat.

WHAT YOU NEED: Five shallow boxes or trays, five mystery substances (e.g. cornflakes, crumpled tinfoil, baked beans, paper clips and coins), a blindfold, tissues/wipes/flannels and towels for afterwards.

PREPARATION: Arrange the five boxes/trays in a row (so they're easy to step into) and in each one put a quantity of one of the mystery substances. Make sure that if you use anything wet/sticky/messy you put it in a waterproof box/tray and play this somewhere that can get messy rather than on top of, for instance, an enormously valuable Turkish rug.

GAME: Ask the player to remove their shoes and socks and put on the blindfold before they enter the room. Once inside the team should guide them to step into (up to) five boxes/trays, each of which contains a substance that they have to identify. They have one chance to give a final answer for each box and can only make two mistakes, as they must get three right to garner the crystal.

The rest of the team may help direct the player into the boxes but not give any clues as to the nature of the mystery substances. The order in which the player tackles the boxes is up to them and their team but, if one of the mystery substances is wet/sticky/messy, then it would be wise to leave it till last.

02:00

GAME SIGN: Build a seven-card tower. To use a card you must correctly answer the following sum for each you turn over: CARD NUMBER x 5 – 7

WHAT YOU NEED: Ten numbered playing cards.

PREPARATION: Jumble up the cards and lay them face down on a table.

GAME: This is another challenging game of skill and brainpower. To win the game, the player must successfully build a seven-card tower without it falling down (as we all know a steady turret was essential during the Middle Ages).

To make this game even more tricky, the player must solve an equation every time they turn over a card. So, for example to use the 7 of Hearts they would need to say '28' (7 x 5 = 35, and 35 – 7 = 28). Once they've given a correct answer they can keep that card, and add it to their tower.

As with any Crystal Maze game, they need to try to keep calm under pressure. If they have a maths wobble, then they're going to have a wobbly tower, if they get more than three answers wrong then the tower can't be built and their game is over. Thank goodness they've got their team and you as Maze Master on hand with words of encouragement ...

03:00

GAME SIGN: Solve two of the three riddles.

TIME: There is no time limit here other than the real-world ones imposed by people having buses and trains to catch, babysitters to let go, school in the morning, etc.

PREPARATION: It's another one where it's up to you how far you want to go. To be the knight, you could just adopt a courtly stance, pop a pan on your head for a helmet, and wear that grey jumper your gran knitted for you (which looks a bit like chain-mail if you squint a bit). Or you could spend ages making your own set of armour out of papier-mâché/painted cardboard/actual sheet metal. Or, if you don't feel that your thespian powers are up to this, why not write the riddles on rolls of paper, wear a black hoodie, pull the hood down over your face, and generally adopt aggressive body language to take on the – frankly, rather less demanding – role of the Jailer?

There are some example riddles below – but why not try writing your own? For reasons entirely unknown, Medieval = mathsy riddles on the whole in the Crystal Maze – but just make sure you've done your sums correctly (or be ready for someone to have a massive mid-Maze meltdown if you fail to accept the actual answer).

GAME: If you're the Knight, demand that your adventurer answers two of three riddles correctly before you'll award them a crystal. If you're the Jailer, let the adventurer pick up a crystal before you then lock them in with you (NB: to avoid embarrassment, do remember to have the key in there with you!) and refuse to let them out until they've correctly solved two of the three riddles-on-scrolls.

EXAMPLE RIDDLES:

1. The queen demanded that the palace cook bake her an incredible multi-layered game pie for her birthday banquet – and he served up one with a plum inside a cygnet inside a blackbird inside a duck inside a chicken inside a goose inside a marrow inside a swan inside a thick hot-water crust that was decorated with edible roses. How many different types of bird were in the pie?

2. The king wants to order a new fleet and has three bids in from different boatyard owners. Tristram the Trustworthy says he'll charge 2400 groats for every 8 ships he supplies, Reginald the Reliable says he'll charge 7800 groats for every 13 ships he supplies, and Penelope the Prudent says she'll charge 1300 for every 2 ships she supplies. To whom should the king award the contract?

3. The prince loves archery but he's not brilliant at it, which is a shame, as he hates losing. He's noticed that he tends to hit the bullseye with one arrow in every five. Before he enters another archery competition, he wants to know what the chances are of him hitting three bullseyes in a row. Can you tell him?

SOLUTIONS ON PAGE 218

TUTTI FLUTE-Y

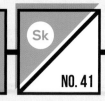

Sk

NO. 41

GAME SIGN: Reverse the order of the fruit in the glass using only the spoon and the glass.

WHAT YOU NEED: Champagne flute, three differently sized fruit and a teaspoon.

PREPARATION: For this game you're going to need a champagne flute. The flimsy plastic stick-the-stem-and-glass-together-yourself kind will do just fine. Don't risk the crystal for a crystal.

Next you're going to need three differently-sized fruit. If you don't have a medieval banqueting table to hand, try raiding the fruit bowl or fridge. All three fruit should be of varying size, and must fit in a champagne flute, so put that banana down. A perfect trio would be a blueberry, a grape and a slice of lime.

Pop the fruit in the champagne flute in size order, with the largest fruit at the bottom – so the lime sits at the bottom, the grape goes in the middle and the blueberry rests on top.

GAME: When the mocktail is ready, the chosen player should take the teaspoon. They have three minutes to simply reverse the order of the three fruit keeping them inside the champagne flute. They're not allowed to touch the fruit with their hands or any other part of their body. The fruit can only be moved using the spoon and the champagne flute.

After the game feel free to use the props to make a tiny fruit salad as a snack.

02:00

My

NO. 42

GAME SIGN: Spell out ten words whilst balancing on one leg.

WHAT YOU NEED: Pen, paper and this book.

PREPARATION: Make a place marker with the paper and leave it on the floor in the centre of the room. Have this book to hand.

GAME: When the player enters the room guide them to stand on one leg on the marker to play the game.

As Maze Master you are armed with a book with twenty tricky words to spell (see right). Choose any ten and one by one shout out a word when the player is standing on one leg. They must correctly spell that word before moving on to the next.

If the player puts their leg down for any reason, you must pause play while the clock continues to tick down. Do remind them of this fact every time they start to wobble.

Their teammates, of course, can't help them. They are free to groan, though.

01. weird
02. accommodate
03. handkerchief
04. indict
05. cemetery
06. conscience
07. rhythm
08. playwright
09. embarrass
10. millennium
11. pharaoh
12. liaison
13. supersede
14. ecstasy
15. Caribbean
16. harass
17. maintenance
18. pronunciation
19. occurred
20. recommend

03:00

SYNONYM DOMINOES

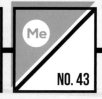

GAME SIGN: Arrange the blocks so that all adjacent words are synonyms.

WHAT YOU NEED: A pen, twelve pieces of paper, scissors and some tape.

PREPARATION: Copy the words on each block opposite on to a piece of paper, ensuring you couple each word correctly, keeping them in their pairs, and cut them out. You should have twelve rectangular blocks.

Using the grid formation found on p.219, lay out the correct blocks accordingly and tape the outline of the shape to the floor or tabletop you are using. Once this is done, remove all the blocks bar two correct blocks of your choosing into position to start the player off. Put the remaining blocks face up on the table, and then call the player in.

GAME: The player must place eight blocks inside the perimeter, so that all adjacent words are synonyms. On the off-chance that your player doesn't know what a synonym is – and their teammates can't advise – then you can maybe help them out a bit. But make sure you deploy sufficient levels of derision and disdain first. Crystals don't just grow on trees.

One more hint you might need to deliver. There are twelve blocks and only eight of them will fit inside the perimeter, so there are several red herrings. (Synonyms for which are 'misleading clues' or 'smoke screens'.)

03:00

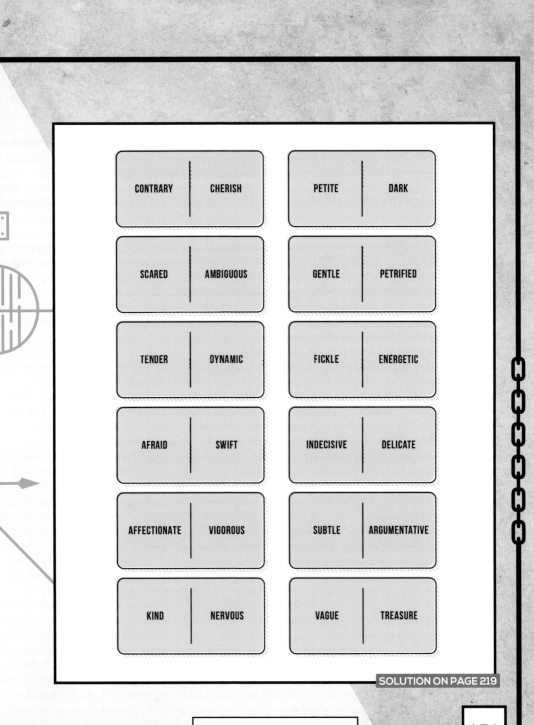

CONTRARY	CHERISH		PETITE	DARK
SCARED	AMBIGUOUS		GENTLE	PETRIFIED
TENDER	DYNAMIC		FICKLE	ENERGETIC
AFRAID	SWIFT		INDECISIVE	DELICATE
AFFECTIONATE	VIGOROUS		SUBTLE	ARGUMENTATIVE
KIND	NERVOUS		VAGUE	TREASURE

SOLUTION ON PAGE 219

MEET YOUR MATCH

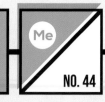

Me

NO. 44

GAME SIGN: Move three matches to create five triangles instead of three.

WHAT YOU NEED: Nine matches and a table.

PREPARATION: Arrange the matches on a table as follows:

GAME: The player must simply move just three matches to create five triangles instead of three. While being shouted at by their team.

MAZE MASTER: Keep an eye on them and make sure that only three matches are moved. If a player is struggling, remind them that they can reset the puzzle to try a different approach.

SOLUTION ON PAGE 219

02:00

ON THE HOLE

GAME SIGN: Hook all the sweets without touching them.

WHAT YOU NEED: A packet of sweets with holes and a knitting needle. (If you don't have a knitting needle to hand, anything long and thin, such as a bamboo skewer, will work fine.)

PREPARATION: For this game you're going to need a packet of sweets. The sweets need to be small and round, and have a hole in the middle. They might even be minty. We refuse to name names.

Spread your holey sweets out on the table and leave a knitting needle next to them.

GAME: The player has two minutes to, very simply, hook each and every sweet on to the knitting needle without touching them. If the player successfully stacks the entire packet of sweets, within the two-minute time limit, they'll win a crystal.

Once finished with the game, why not share out the minty sweets? Obviously, try to target the teammate who has dodgy breath first ... but not whilst reading this last bit out loud.

⧗
02:00

DOMINO EFFECT

Ph

NO. 46

GAME SIGN: Hit the glass with only the twelfth domino.

WHAT YOU NEED: A glass and twelve dominoes.

PREPARATION: All you need for this game is an empty table. At one end place a glass. Then, working back from the glass, line up twelve dominoes so that when you tap the one furthest away they all fall over so the final domino just hits the glass. Mark the table where the first domino in the line should go, then leave the dominoes in a random pile on the table.

GAME: The player needs to hurry to line up the twelve dominoes against the clock so that when they hit the first domino the twelfth hits the glass. This sounds very simple, but under the pressure of a ticking clock will they rush too quickly and not place the dominoes properly, or with butterfingers keep knocking the dominoes over?

This is the sort of game in which teammates love to shout things like 'Do it quicker!', which always seems to help tremendously.

02:00

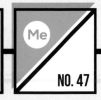
GAME SIGN: Complete the word chain using the items.

WHAT YOU NEED: The picture opposite, paper and pen.

PREPARATION: The contestant will use the illustration opposite to complete the nine-word long word chain, and you'll just need to start them off. On a piece of paper, draw nine boxes in a row, and write the first three items in the first three boxes: 'Dolly', 'Bird' and 'House'. They'll need the pen and paper to complete the chain by writing the remaining six items of the chain correctly.

You can actually make two word chains from this bunch of toys, so effectively there's two games to be had. The three starting words for the chain for Game 2 are 'Turtle', 'Dove' and 'Tale', forming 'turtledove' and 'dovetail'.

GAME: When the time starts, the player will first need to establish the connections between the adjacent pairs of toys as they've been written on the paper, so let them discuss it with their team. However, if they struggle guide them toward "dollybird" and then "birdhouse" - it's just compound words.

Once they've got the gist of what they're looking for, the player should study the picture of the toys. They need to complete the complete the chain by filling in the six blanks, selecting from the toys in the picture. When they complete the chain, they win a crystal!

03:00

SOLUTION ON PAGE 219

LET THE GAMES BEGIN!

ARE WE NEARLY THERE YET?

Me

NO. 48

GAME SIGN: Correctly label the eleven cities on the map.

PROPS: A scanner (or photocopier), a printer, paper, pen, eleven pins and some sticky labels (or post-it notes).

PREPARATION: Firstly, scan and print a copy of the map opposite or hunt out a map of Britain online and add on eleven marker points in the correct places as shown in the illustration opposite.

Next, place a pin in each of the following locations on the map: Edinburgh, Leicester, Birmingham, Bristol, Canterbury, Norwich, Leeds, Glasgow, Liverpool, Swansea, Cardiff.

And finally, write out the names of these eleven cities on to the sticky labels and place them next to the map in the centre of the room.

GAME: The player must simply label all eleven cities on the map next to the correct pin. The team can of course help (or hinder) with their suggestions. When the player has finished marking up the map, you should reveal how many are in the correct position.

MAZE MASTER: Do not reveal the names of the cities that are correctly or incorrectly placed, only the number that are right. Part of the challenge (and fun of watching) is seeing the player and their team bicker about which ones might be in the wrong place.

02:30

THE ORIGINAL MAZE MASTER

The man, the myth, the Maze Master. Richard O'Brien, or 'Reckless Rick' as he would sometimes describe himself, was the original guide to the weird and wonderful world of the maze. His wit, eccentricity, boundless energy and propensity for random harmonica playing ensured he would still be adored by fans of the show long after he left the maze on a Harley Davidson with Mumsey. We were thrilled to be able to ask him how he came to be involved in the show …

▶ **How did you first get involved in the show, and was it even**
The Crystal Maze when you joined?
I was asked by Chatsworth Television to play the role of games
master during a two day test run of a new type of adventure game
show called _The Keys to Fort Boyard,_ a French series filmed in a
real sea fort. Channel 4 viewed this test product and committed to
airing it as part of that year's autumn programming. Unfortunately,
it was at this point that the show's French connection declared that
the fort would not be ready. This placed Chatsworth in an awkward
position and so CEO Malcolm Heyworth flew to France and the two
parties came up with _The Crystal Maze,_ a similar concept but, in my
opinion, far more entertaining.

▶ **Malcolm said that they had no idea you were talking directly into**
a camera until they were editing and realised you were up to such
hilarious mischief. What inspired you to play around like that,
and did you ever imagine it would become such a fan favourite?
There were five cameras, three of which were shooting the
contestant attempting to win a crystal, and two outside the game
waiting for its conclusion. One of the cameramen said to me, 'What
are we supposed to do, Richard, shoot the back of their heads?' The
team were watching their elected player and so I said, 'Come here,'
and looked into the lens and started talking about Mumsey and
kept gabbling until I saw his shoulders start to shake with laughter.
After that it became a nice silly diversion but, as Malcolm has said,
the control room was watching the game, not us, and when they
came to edit the series, there was this lovely nonsense going on.

▶ **Who chose your magnificent outfits and did you provide your**
own leopard-print jacket?!
I bought the first three drape jackets and the designers of the
competitors' jumpsuits made the last one.

▶ **Considering how disposable television is, why do you think the show was so hugely popular at the time (the most watched show on Channel 4 when it aired), and has stayed in people's memories for twenty-six years?**
It was very cleverly shot. The viewers saw more than the player and therefore became slightly frustrated, and that frustration made them become more engaged.

▶ **What were your favourite moments in the maze?**
Our arrival into new zones was always fun, especially Medieval, as the table was always set with something different and that would bring another bit of silliness to the proceedings.

▶ **Did you have a favourite game?**
There was a wooden ball-bearing maze hanging on ropes from each corner that I admired as it had such simple elegance.

▶ **When you think back to your time on the show what first springs to mind?**
I have only fond memories of sharing long cold days with Malcolm, David and the crew. There was never any unhappiness at any time. Not one solitary negative person, and the food was excellent.

▶ **If you ever had to explain what *The Crystal Maze* was to someone who hadn't seen it, what would you say?**
Gosh, I would most likely babble but get there in the end. Don't make me do it in writing.

▶ **What advice would you give a team preparing to tackle the Crystal Maze?**
The same thing that I told all the contestants, which was when you go into the room you shout out very clearly, and concisely, what you see. This has two benefits: one, that one of the team will pick up on that info and come up with some good advice; the other is

even more useful, as by thinking out loud, it will possibly enable the player to twig earlier.

▶ **What was your favourite zone and why?**
Aztec, as it provided us with the illusion of warmth.

▶ **What tips would you give anyone hoping to take on the role of Maze Master?**
Have lunch with the producer and the director.

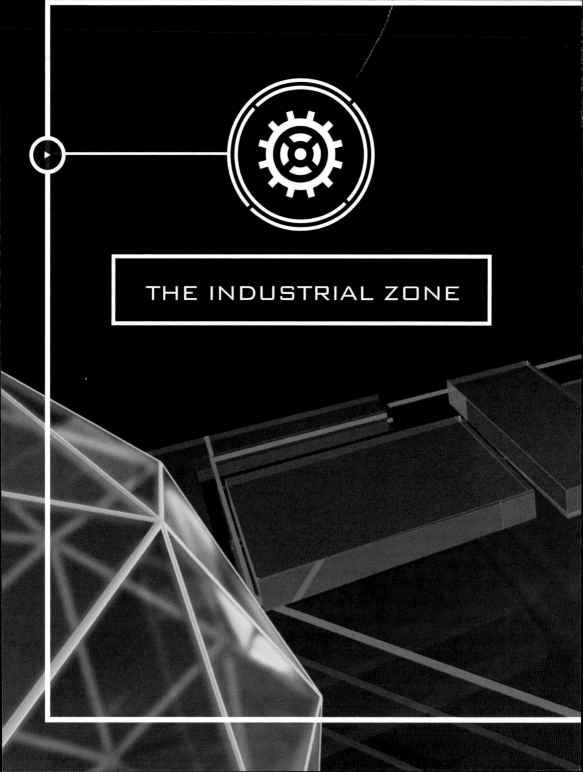

THE INDUSTRIAL ZONE

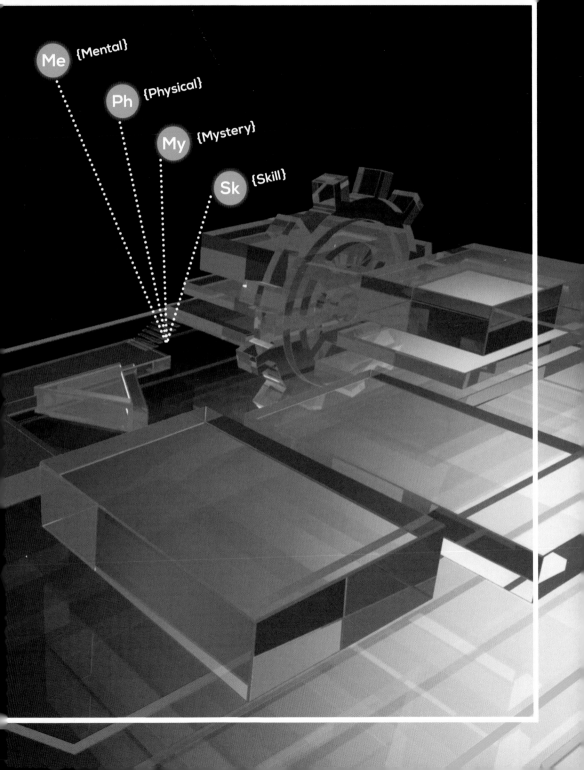

Me {Mental}

Ph {Physical}

My {Mystery}

Sk {Skill}

You have now arrived at your third zone. It's time to tackle the mechanical marvels of Industrial.

The posthumous publication of economic historian Arnold Toynbee's lectures in 1884 is generally accepted as having brought the idea of the Industrial Revolution into popular usage in Britain. According to Toynbee, at its core was 'the substitution of competition for the medieval regulations which had previously controlled the production and distribution of wealth'. It would, of course, be stretching the point to suggest that the kind of competition Toynbee was thinking of at the time was one in which a team of enthusiastic but broadly incompetent goons entered rooms with the express purpose of completing arbitrary tasks against the clock in an effort to redistribute wealth by nabbing time crystals. So, naturally, we won't suggest that. Our commitment to historical accuracy is paramount. (As we all know, they loved wet logs in Aztec times.)

And so to the mechanical marvels that await you in the Industrial zone. Ahead are the tricky trials that will really get your cogs whirring and yank your chains. This could be the zone to turn the screw ... and may even cause someone to blow a gasket.

We're all out of Industrial-based puns now. Crack on.

SET THE CLOCKS

GAME SIGN: Set all the clocks to the correct time.

WHAT YOU NEED: Six clocks that can be manually altered.

PREPARATION: Place the six clocks around the room so everyone can see the faces. Set them all to noon. Write time-based commands between each of the six clocks (five in total). You can make this game as difficult or easy as you like by choosing how much or little time the player must change between each clock. For example, '+8hrs' is easier than '-7hrs 52 seconds'.

Once you've placed the time-based commands between all the clocks set the first clock to the time you want to begin the game. The diagram opposite is an example of how it could look.

GAME: This game is based on the Clocks game in the series. In the show, a player enters a room with multiple clocks on the wall. Between the first and second clock is a sign that asks the player to add or remove time to the next clock face. The team can help (or hinder) in this game by shouting out suggestions. Only when the player sets the last clock to the correct time can the crystal be released.

This version works just the same way, but instead of a cuckoo popping out to reveal the crystal at the moment of victory you can just begrudgingly hand it over.

⏳
03:00

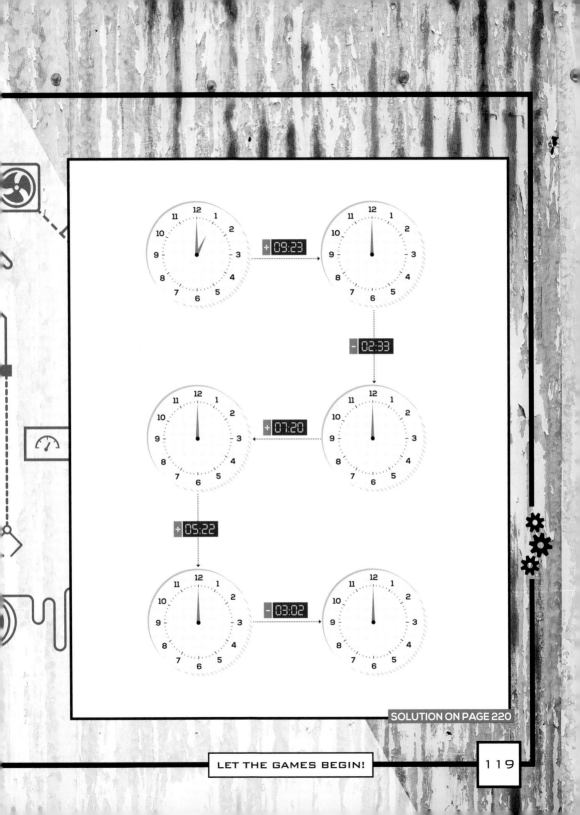

SOLUTION ON PAGE 220

LET THE GAMES BEGIN!

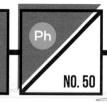

CHUCK BUCKETS

Ph

NO. 50

WHAT YOU NEED: Five buckets and five balls (preferably ping-pong or tennis balls).

PREPARATION: Place the five buckets around the room. The more space available, and the more willing you are to break various precious household objects (WE ARE NOT LIABLE!), the more ambitious you can be with this game.

Finally, place all the balls near the door and set an oche line. What's an 'oche line'? Ask a friend who plays darts (they'll probably be the large one with tattoos and a mullet).

GAME: A player must throw a single ball into each of the five buckets in turn before the time runs out. If a player misses a bucket at any time, they must collect all the balls and start again from the first bucket.

This game is very simple, but with the clock counting down the pressure increases as a player gets closer to hitting five throws in a row. Remind them of this constantly – they'll love that.

⏳

03:00

LET THE GAMES BEGIN!

GAME SIGN: Put all the beermats into the shoebox using the vacuum. **WARNING:** do not touch the floor or drop the beermats.

WHAT YOU NEED: A hand-held vacuum cleaner, scissors, five beermats or coasters, a shoebox and three or four sturdy stools or chairs.

PREPARATION: Firstly, make sure the vacuum is charged (players will look for any excuse to complain). Cut a slot (big enough to post the beermats through) in the lid of the shoebox. Place the crystal inside the shoebox and put the box on one of the stools/chairs next to the door. Position the stools/chairs around the room so that you can step/jump from one to another to get across the room without touching the floor. Lastly, spread the beermats around the floor near the stools/chairs.

GAME: The player is handed the vacuum and must use it to pick up the beermats to post them into the shoebox. The player cannot touch the beermats – and cannot touch the floor at all once the game begins. They must move from chair to chair, reaching down with the vacuum to lift one beermat at a time and take it to the shoebox. The player has three lives. If they touch a beermat or the floor, they lose a life – and if they lose all three lives, its an ALIS.

If the player successfully posts all the beermats without losing all their lives, they can open it to collect the crystal. Then, obviously, smugly swagger out of the room to applause from the team.

ALIS 02:30

ACCESS CODES

GAME SIGN: Shout out the correct answers to the maths puzzle to enter AND exit each square.

WHAT YOU NEED: String or tape.

PREPARATION: Come up with six of your own math puzzles that you keep to hand for the game. Make these as easy or as hard as you want depending on how difficult a challenge you want to make it, e.g. '5x7=' and 'square route of 111'.

Using the string or tape, divide a room into six large squares on the floor, with the crystal placed inside the last square.

GAME: In the series, a player enters a room with six doors. At each door is a maths puzzle and a numbered keypad. The player has to correctly punch in the answer to each puzzle to reach the crystal. The twist is that the player then needs to remember the numbers to work their way back out. It's maths and memory ... can you imagine a worse combination? In this version of the game, your job as Maze Master is to shout out one of your puzzles as a player steps into a new square. The player must shout out the correct answer before they can step into the next square. Once they reach the crystal to be able to move back they need to give the answers for each square to return to the start.

The team can watch but not assist in this game. The fun of the game is discovering if the player has worked out it's a memory test too ... otherwise it's a lock-in!

03:00 ALIS

ICE TO SEE YOU

GAME SIGN: Identify the frozen items to release the crystal.

WHAT YOU NEED: Five small items, five small plastic tubs and a freezer. NB: These five small items must fit inside the tubs and, crucially, will be able to either survive getting wet and being frozen or of sufficiently low value that if they get wrecked, it doesn't matter.

PREPARATION: Put each of the items in a tub, cover with water and freeze solid. Keep them in the freezer till just before you play, when you should turn them out of their tubs and place them on the table for inspection. You might end up cracking the ice or finding that it's so cloudy that you can't see the item inside at all. As such, it might be worth preparing one or two spare items to make sure that the game doesn't have to be abandoned. Heaven forbid!

GAME: There's been a bit of a technical mishap in the Industrial zone's processing plant and a number of items have tumbled into the freezer ... Challenge your adventurer to identify three out of five mystery frozen items in two mins. Once they've committed to an answer, you could just verbally confirm/deny it – but, if you're playing this game outside, for extra theatrics smash the ice to free the item and reveal its identity.

Other equally ridiculous variations on this basic gameplay include baking the items inside pastry or tempura-ing them and wrapping the items in coloured paper. As you can tell, we don't get out much.

02:00

ROD ONE OUT

GAME SIGN: Retrieve the metal object without crossing the line with your body.

WHAT YOU NEED: A small metal item to which a magnet will stick, something with which to mark a line, sticky tape, around ten to fifteen chopsticks, string and a fridge magnet.

PREPARATION: Place the metal item down around 3–4m away from the door the player will enter from. Then mark the line close to the door beyond which the adventurer may not cross. Pile the rest of the items up on what will be the adventurer's side of the line.

GAME: The player has to retrieve the precious metal item from the 'dangerously contaminated' patch of ground, using only what's in front of them. They need to use the tape to join the chopsticks together to make a long fishing rod, with string stuck/knotted to one end and the magnet dangling at the end of the string. The quicker they build this the better as they'll want to allow time for the fishing-style secondary phase of the game.

The player will probably work out what to do, but feel free to help them out by saying things like: 'Do you need to construct something?', 'What kind of thing could help you reach the metal item?' or 'For crying out loud try a fishing pole!'.

02:30

ROAD TO VICTORY

Ph

NO. 55

GAME SIGN: Roll a car from the start line to the finish line. Hitting an obstacle costs a life.

WHAT YOU NEED: As many loo rolls, kitchen rolls or other obstacles you can find and three small toy cars.

PREPARATION: Create an obstacle course in a kitchen or large room without carpet. Make a start line and finish line at the opposite ends of the room. Between these lines scatter loo rolls or other obstacles around. Make sure that there is a pathway between the start line and finish line ... how much room for error you allow is down to you!

GAME: The player must push and release a small toy car from the start line to cross the finish line without touching the obstacles in between. Each obstacle hit means a life lost and three lives means ... yes, it's an ALIS.

Plus, with three cars they have only three attempts ... which makes this game wheely difficult (sorry).

ALIS 02:00

LET THE GAMES BEGIN!

RED CARDS

My

NO. 56

GAME SIGN: Throw the darts to reveal only the red cards.
WARNING: Hitting a black card resets the game.

WHAT YOU NEED: Playing cards, drawing pins, a dartboard and darts. If you don't have a dartboard at home then this game can be modified by laying the cards on the floor and trying to land an object on them.

PREPARATION: Pick eight cards from the deck. Three should be red and five should be black. Shuffle them, then without letting anyone else see them pin them face down to the dartboard.

GAME: The principle of this game is very similar to the Crystal Maze game we call Lights Off. It's all about remembering where the 'hazards' are and then avoiding them.

The player needs to aim their darts at the playing cards. Each time they hit a card it can be turned over. The aim is to turn over all five black cards. However, if they hit a red card all the cards must be turned back over and they must start from the beginning again! We found with Lights Off that a helpful tactic is to have the teammates remember where the 'hazards' are (in this case the position of the red card). Whether or not the player will listen to them is, as we also found, an entirely different matter.

NOTE: If you're worried about getting holes all over your playing cards, then darts aren't the only thing you can throw. You can experiment with throwing peanuts, grapes or popcorn. But please, no throwing tantrums. Show some decorum.

03:00

GAME SIGN: Turn the tins upside down using only one finger.

WHAT YOU NEED: Ten tin cans.

PREPARATION: For this next game, you're going to need to raid your kitchen cupboard. You need tin cans, and you need quite a lot, and luckily it doesn't matter what's in them.

In fact, this might be the perfect time to finally find a use for the mystery tins lurking, long forgotten, at the back of the cupboard. Full English breakfast in a tin? Ideal. Canned eel in jelly? Excellent. That tin of dog food, inexplicably hiding at the back when no one's had a dog since 1983? Yup, get it out.

You'll need about ten, depending on how tricky you want to make this game. Lay them out on a small-ish table, such as a coffee table.

GAME: When the time starts, the chosen player must use just one finger to turn every tin upside down. If they manage to turn every tin on its head within two minutes, they'll have earned themselves a crystal.

⧗
02:00

SQUARE UP

Me

NO. 58

GAME SIGN: Memorise the sequence and replicate it to unlock the crystal.

WHAT YOU NEED: A piece of paper and felt-tip pens in black, green, blue and yellow.

PREPARATION: Opposite is a grid of sixty-four squares, with some squares coloured in; six are green, six blue and six yellow.

Before the game begins, the Maze Master should take the sheet of paper and, using the black pen, draw an empty grid of 8 x 8 squares identical to the diagram without the colours. Four coloured markers should be placed beside the grid.

GAME: When the game starts, give the player this book so they can view the grid. The player will have three minutes to memorise it and then colour in the squares in the correct shade from memory.

The player can spend as much of the three minutes as they wish memorising the pattern, but once they've shut the book and handed it to the Maze Master, they cannot reopen it.

The player must receive no help from their teammates. The Maze Master cannot assist them either, aside from telling them how much time has passed or how long they have remaining. They win their crystal only if they've recreated the colour pattern perfectly within the time limit.

⧖
03:00

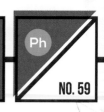

GAME SIGN: Match ten pairs of socks to win the crystal. One push-up = one second of light.

WHAT YOU NEED: Fifteen pairs of socks, a light switch and a laundry basket.

PREPARATION: Lay out the thirty socks in no particular order. Using socks that vary in colour is essential.

GAME: Play the game in a room that is dark unless the light is turned on. At the start of the game, the light should be on for five seconds so the sign can be read. Then the Maze Master must turn the lights off.

The aim of the game is to match ten pairs of socks and drop them in the basket. However, socks can only be matched when they can be seen, so the player must first power the light. For every push-up, the player earns one second of light. The Maze Master must calculate how many seconds to keep the light on for; you may want a torch or to touch the player's back to count the reps. The light should only be on once the player has stopped doing push-ups, so that they have a chance to match the socks.

Every time the lights go out, the player must return to doing push-ups, in order to turn the lights back on.

If the game is completed successfully, not only does the team win a crystal, but the player has done their work out for the day and you also have some laundry chores completed. Winner.

⧖
02:00

LET THE GAMES BEGIN!

PAN-DEMONIUM

Sk

NO. 60

GAME SIGN: Bounce the balls to knock the pans to the ground – but don't cross the line.

WHAT YOU NEED: A selection of cardboard boxes/books/plastic lunchboxes, etc., three kitchen pans, string, five tennis balls and a small bowl.

PREPARATION: Use the boxes etc. to create three stacks and pop a pan on top of each a distance from the door. Then use the string to mark a line across the room. Finally, place the balls in the bowl just by the door. As the game involves bouncing balls, you'd be advised to clear out anything precious/shatter-able (this game is really not one to play in front of your collection of priceless Ming vases).

GAME: The player has to bounce the balls at the stack to try to knock the pans off the top of the stacks but cannot go further than the line to do so. If a ball bounces back across the line, the player can bounce it again – but cannot reach further than the line to grab a ball. However, as they start with five balls, even if none bounce back, they can have two unsuccessful bounces before needing a 'hit' with every ball.

NOTE: The player must bounce each ball before it hits a stack; if they throw directly at a stack, they should be warned and reminded of the 'it's got to bounce' rule – and if they do it twice, it's a lock-in.

ALIS 02:00

RUBBER RIDDLE

Sk

NO. 61

WHAT YOU NEED: Sticky tape, letters, six to eight loo roll and kitchen roll tubes and twenty rubber bands.

PREPARATION: Tape the individual letters of a six- to eight-letter word of your choice (e.g. CAPTAIN) to the base of each of the rolls. Set the tubes around a room at various distances and levels.

Create a marker near the door that the player will not be allowed to cross. Place the twenty rubber bands next to the marker.

GAME: The player must use their hands to ping rubber bands at the loo roll tubes from behind the marker. Once a tube is toppled it may be retrieved. The player must correctly solve the anagram to win a crystal.

{2–3 MINUTES
depending on word length and course distance}

02:00

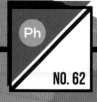

GAME SIGN: Throw one ball from the marker into a bucket.

WHAT YOU NEED: A bucket, a marker, three soft balls and a bedsheet.

PREPARATION: Play this game in the biggest space available – the garden is ideal. The Maze Master should place a bucket on the ground and then take about three or four large strides away from it before laying down a marker. Put the three balls next to the marker. The player should not be present when the bucket and marker are positioned.

Then find two teammates to help in this game. This pair must hold up the bedsheet, so pick your loftiest participants and ask them to suspend the sheet halfway between the bucket and the marker. The idea is to block the player's view, so that they cannot see the bucket from the marker.

GAME: The player should start the game standing on the marker with the three balls beside them. To win a crystal, all they need to do is throw a ball in the bucket. The player has three balls and therefore three attempts to land a ball in the bucket.

When their time starts, they are free to run around the game area. They may dash back and forth from their marker to the other side of the sheet to gauge the distance and location of the bucket as much as they like. However, they may only throw a ball from the marker.

⌛ 03:00

YOU WIN SUM, YOU LOSE SUM

Sk

NO. 63

GAME SIGN: Bounce the ball off two walls into a bucket – twice in a row.

WHAT YOU NEED: Twenty plastic cups, pen and paper, sticky tape, four saucepans, an envelope and some ping-pong balls.

PREPARATION: Fix the plastic cups to a table or the floor in any formation you see fit. Write the numbers one to twenty on a piece of paper and tape one to each cup in a random order. The four saucepans should then be labelled with +, −, x and ÷.

Before the game begins, write a random number between one and a hundred and put it in an envelope in the room.

GAME: The object of the game is for the player to land balls into the cups and saucepans so that they total the chosen number. Starting with zero, the player should throw balls into the cups and saucepans to raise and lower their total, with the Maze Master each time announcing their running total, until they arrive at the chosen number.

For example, if the chosen number were 25, they could throw a ball into the '10' cup, then the 'x' saucepan, then the '2' cup, then the '+' saucepan and finally the '5' cup (totalling 25). The player can throw as many balls as they like into the same cup, as long as they fit, but each number must be separated by a mathematical symbol in order to count.

03:00

DOUBLE TROUBLE

GAME SIGN: Throw the ball into the bucket off two walls twice in a row.

WHAT YOU NEED: A bucket, a bouncy ball and a place marker.

PREPARATION: Find a room that has two adjacent clear walls and doesn't have any fragile valuables in it (there's nothing that spoils the fun of a game more than an angry mum kicking off when her set of porcelain hedgehogs have been knocked over).

Set a bucket down on the floor and place a marker on the floor where you want the player to stand. To make sure that you've set this game up properly and that it's playable (not too easy or too hard) practise throwing the ball so it bounces off two walls and lands in the bucket. Use trial and error to move the bucket and marker around until you're happy it's a doable (but tricky) challenge.

GAME: The player must pick up the ball and throw it so it bounces off the two adjacent walls before landing in the bucket. This in itself is going to be a frustrating challenge. What makes it doubly hard is that as soon as they land a ball in the bucket they have to do it again in the next turn to release the crystal. If they miss with their second effort they have to start again. Only two in a row counts. Simple in theory. Swear-inducing in practice.

02:00

GAME SIGN: Solve two of the three riddles.

TIME: The only time limit here is caused by the seemingly unstoppable march of history. You must be finished with all industrial games before the rise of computers, automation and global capitalism lead to the decline of industry as we know it. (Or you could say 'three minutes'. It's up to you, really.)

PREPARATION: This is another test of your commitment to the mission of recreating the Crystal Maze in a domestic setting. You could decorate everything in corrugated steel, tinfoil and scaffolding poles. Or you could put on a pair of dungarees, rub grease on your face and play the part of a mechanic who's killing time by asking riddles until the parts he needs arrive on the delivery van from Nuneaton. See how you feel.

GAME: Challenge your player to answer two out of three riddles correctly to earn a crystal. There are some example riddles opposite, but you will definitely impress your friends and family more by coming up with your own ... especially if you don't use Wikipedia to look anything up.

EXAMPLE RIDDLES:

1. Geoff the inventor has created a tetchy robot that has generated a number but won't say what number he's thought of ... The only clue the robot's giving is that if Geoff gives him a number from one to ten, the robot will multiply it by the number it's generated and will tell Geoff either the first or second digit of the resulting number. When Geoff said 'eight', the robot said the second digit was 'eight' and when Geoff said 'four', the robot said the first digit was 'four' – so what number has the robot generated?

2. There's another oil crisis on and so there are power cuts across the land. Susie the factory owner can only be sure of power for half a day twice a week. If it takes two days for the factory to make a luxury limousine, how many cars can Susie safely agree to deliver in half a year?

3. Rupa the architect has been asked to make Cathy the millionaire a tower with windows she can look out of at different times of day. At 6 a.m. she likes to look east to see the sunrise. At 11 a.m. she likes to gaze south-west at the handsome policeman on patrol. At 1.30 p.m. she likes to peek north at the factory's fumes blowing in the wind. And at 7 p.m. she likes to peer to the east, to see the last light of the day playing on the brutalist tower blocks. What's the smallest number of sides Rupa could give the tower to give Cathy windows facing everything she wants to see?

SOLUTIONS ON PAGE 220

SPILL THE BEANS

GAME SIGN: Roll the tin to the highlighted area. If the tin rolls off the table, you lose a life.

WHAT YOU NEED: A table, a length of string or tape and a tin of baked beans.

PREPARATION: Clear a long table for this game. Using the string, mark out a distance along the length of the table that is approximately the length of a tin of beans and however much wiggle room you want to allow either side (the bigger the section you allow the easier the game will be, so why not try the game yourself to help decide?).

GAME: The object of this game is for the player to roll a tin of beans from one end of the table to the other, so that it reaches and stops within the marked-out section ... without it falling off the table.

The player should stand at the far end of the table with the tin on its side horizontally flush with the end of the table. The player must use only one finger to roll the tin gently towards the other end. To win the crystal, the player must guide the tin to the designated area. If the tin does not go far enough, the player may pick it up and make another attempt. They may make as many attempts as they wish.

However, this game is an ALIS. If the tin falls off the table, the player loses a life. If they lose three lives, they are locked in the kitchen for the rest of the day, with nothing to eat but cold beans.

ALIS 03:00

GAME SIGN: Roll the car down the ramp so it passes completely through the gap between the two cereal boxes.

WHAT YOU NEED: A long strip of cardboard, a stack of books, two large cereal boxes and a toy car.

PREPARATION: You're going to start by building a ramp for your toy car. Take the long strip of cardboard (timber will also do), and prop it against the stack of books. Place the ramp at the end of a long table or on a flat, smooth floor. Angle your ramp so if you place your car at the top, it runs down the ramp and along the tabletop (or floor). Don't tape the ramp down – the game requires the player to work out how best to angle it.

Now take your two boxes and place them at the other end of the table, taped down on their long edge. They should be positioned side by side so that they are very close together – approximately one and a half car-widths apart is about right.

GAME: The player has until the time runs out to roll the car down the ramp so that it continues along the table and through the passageway created by the boxes. The player can angle the ramp however they see fit, raise or lower the stack of books, or just hold the end of the ramp. The car needs to roll all the way through the gap to earn the crystal.

02:00

SHOE CLUES

GAME SIGN: Follow the clues in the shoes to find the crystal.

WHAT YOU NEED: As many pairs of shoes as you can find, lots of small pieces of paper and a pen.

PREPARATION: Get out everyone's shoes and place them all over the house. They can stay in pairs or be separated, depending on how easy or hard you want to make the game. Put whatever you're using as your crystal inside one of the shoes. Working BACK from the shoe with the crystal, leave a trail of clues on small pieces of paper in some of the shoes, e.g. 'Size 7. Black as night. Made for walking' would go in the preceding pair of shoes to lead the contestant to a pair of black boots or 'Smells like old cheese – has a real kick' would lead the contestant to football boots. Have fun with the clues you create!

Designate a start position with the first clue in the room.

GAME: Starting from the first clue, the player must locate various shoes to find the clue that will eventually lead to the crystal within the time allotted.

MAZE MASTER: Blind luck could scupper this game, so be careful to set the course accordingly. Translation: Don't be a plonker and put the crystal in the first pair of shoes near the start position.

03:00

LET THE GAMES BEGIN!

WORD SHAPES

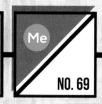

GAME SIGN: Place the shapes on the grid to spell four four-letter words without overlapping.

WHAT YOU NEED: Paper, pen and scissors.

PREPARATION: Photocopy the grids opposite or take a large piece of paper and draw a 4 x 4 grid on to it. Then copy the coloured shapes (or photocopy them too), so that they are sized in proportion to the letter grids. You will need two of each shape. Maze Master – attention to detail is everything, so don't forget to cut the middle out of each shape too, so the player can still see the letters once they've placed a shape on the grid!

GAME: The player must place four of the coloured shapes so that each one lassoes a four-letter word. The shapes are all different, so the words might be in a straight line, around a corner, in an S-shape, an N-shape, a U-shape or a Z-shape. The words can be spelt forwards or backwards, and the shapes can be placed any way round. The options are endless. That's why getting the right shapes earns you a crystal.

None of the shapes may overlap. So, to clarify, that's four shapes, which you can use twice in some of the cases, each lassoing four individual letters, giving you four four-letter words.

We've started you off with a few letter grids opposite, but it's easy to make up your own, providing you know a lot of four-letter words. (Not that kind of four-letter word! Show some respect!)

03:00

J	I	V	E
A	N	X	R
B	O	N	Y
L	E	L	Y

L	I	O	M
L	K	N	A
A	B	T	Z
T	E	L	E

N	E	G	I
P	R	D	F
O	S	T	T
B	A	B	Y

L	K	I	S
A	T	E	S
Z	R	U	E
Y	L	A	C

SOLUTIONS ON PAGE 220

CONNECT THE PAIRS

Sk

NO. 70

WHAT YOU NEED: Twelve pieces of paper, pens (red and blue) and six lengths of string.

PREPARATION: On each piece of paper write the contents of one box as in the illustration opposite, with the blue boxes written in blue pen and the red boxes written in red. Scatter the paper around the room with the red lot on one side and the blue on the other. They should be as far apart as the pieces of string will allow. Finally, connect the red 'B + C' to the blue '5' using a piece of string. Lay the remaining pieces of string in a pile on the floor.

GAME: The object of the game is to connect the pairs, attaching each red piece of paper to its blue counterpart using a piece of string. To start, the player should establish the connection between the pair given to them.

NOTE: Each letter represents its position in the alphabet; A=1 and B=2. So, the B+C equates to 2+3 which is why it's therefore connected to 5. Let the player work the connection out themselves. The player's teammates can help, but do feel free to throw in some helpful hints if they're really struggling. Or not, if they've been really ungrateful about all the effort you've gone to organising the whole thing.

03:00

148

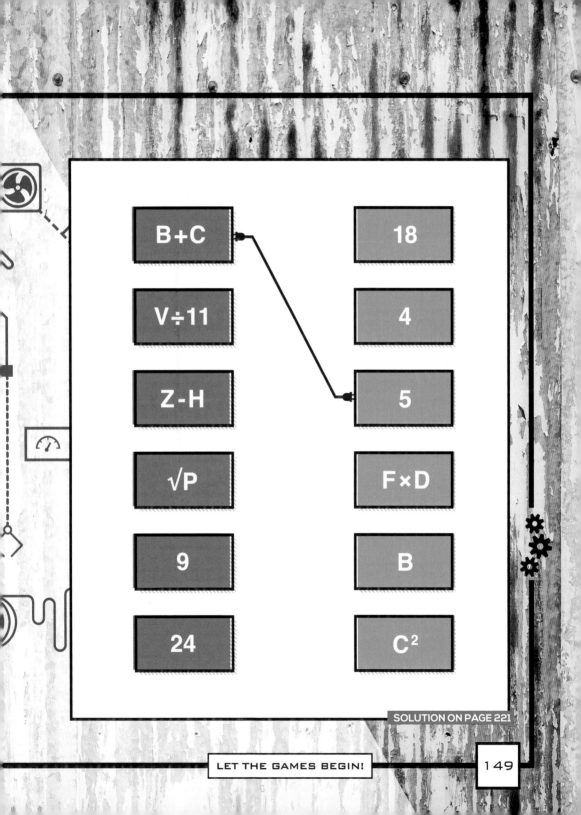

B+C	18
V÷11	4
Z-H	5
√P	F×D
9	B
24	C²

SOLUTION ON PAGE 221

GAME OF PHONES

My

NO. 71

WHAT YOU NEED: Felt-tip pens, twelve large pieces of paper and two mobile phones.

PREPARATION: Write the following colours on each bit of paper: black, white, red, orange, yellow, green, blue, purple, pink, gold, silver and brown. Scatter these pieces of paper across the floor. Next, write a list of questions to which the answer is one of these colours. These can be as simple or cryptic as you choose e.g. 'this is the colour of an emerald gemstone' (green). You'll need about six of these questions. Finally, place the chosen player's mobile phone in the room.

GAME: This is a play-at-home version of the game we call Phone Booth in the series. As soon as the player enters the room, call their phone. Wait for the player to answer and then ask them your first question, the answer to which is one of the twelve colours. To progress in the game, the player should stand on the colour they think the answer is. If they answer a question correctly, call them again and ask them the next question. Continue until they reach the final clue, and then call them once more to announce they have won a crystal.

MAZE MASTER: Make sure you've got your phone with the chosen player's phone number on speed dial, and keep your list of questions to hand.

03:00

LOST AND SOUND

GAME SIGN: Wear the safety helmet and listen out for further instructions!

PROPS: Lots of stackable household clutter, three tennis balls, a rattle or some rice in a water bottle, a bell, a whistle, a spoon, an empty can and a bucket.

PREPARATION: Place the crystal at the far end of the room and then between the crystal and the door create three stacks of household clutter, each with a ball balanced on top. Set the rattle, bell, whistle, spoon and can out on the table outside the door of the room.

GAME: The player must get to the crystal and out of the room again without knocking the balls off the stacks. When a ball hits the floor they lose a life – and if they lose three lives, they are locked in. Sounds easy? Well, it might be if the player didn't have to wear the safety helmet (a bucket on their head). They must rely on their team to direct them, but the team can't call out directions; instead they have to give commands via these signals:

Rattle = walk forward / Bell-ring = stop
Whistle = turn left / Spoon hits empty can = turn right

Once the player has the bucket on their head, they can hear an 'audio key' (i.e. each sound effect and what it means) twice before going into the room and starting the clock, but as soon as they step inside the team cannot say anything. Maze Master, just enjoy the chaos that ensues ...

03:00 ALIS

▶ IN STITCHES

NO. 73

GAME SIGN: Thread five needles.

WHAT YOU NEED: Five threads (preferably different colours) and five needles.

PREPARATION: On a table lay down five threads with a needle next to each. How hard was that? Obviously, we expect that you'll make out that all these games have taken ages to set up ...

GAME: The player merely has to put each of the five threads through the eye of a needle against the clock to win the crystal. Now this sounds very simple, but if there's one thing we've learned in the maze it's that some people completely collapse when it comes to a ticking clock. This task requires steady hands and concentration, so a team shouting at them to do it quicker should go down swimmingly.

⏳
02:00

MIRROR MIRROR

GAME SIGN: Hold the cards arrow side up facing you and use the mirror to identify all ten words.

WHAT YOU NEED: A marker or thick pen, multiple pieces of card and a large mirror or mirrored dressing table.

PREPARATION: Write ten words on separate pieces of card. On the back of each card, draw an 'up' arrow pointing to what would be the bottom of the word. Lay the ten cards word side down on a table in front of the mirror.

GAME: The player must hold up each card with the arrow pointing up towards them, so the word written on the front will now appear backwards and upside down in the mirror. The player has one minute to decipher the ten words on the ten cards to win a crystal. They may not move on to the next word until they have deciphered the one they are holding up. The Maze Master will call correct or incorrect for each attempt.

MAZE MASTER: As your players get better at this, start writing down harder and longer words. If you suspect the player is slightly vain, stick to mostly two- and three-letter words as most of the time they will be transfixed by their own image in the mirror. For the experts, try writing the words in French, Italian or Polish. For the savant in the family, use Sumerian Cuneiform script.

01:00

LET THE GAMES BEGIN!

153

GUTTER CHAOS

Sk

NO. 75

GAME SIGN: Use the guttering to take the radioactive sphere to the toxic bucket. Don't let it contaminate you or the rest of the room.

WHAT YOU NEED: A bucket, a cushion, a 50cm length of guttering/drainpipe that's been cut in half, a golf ball (ideally a bright colour) and furniture/books/boxes/etc.

PREPARATION: Position the bucket by the door of the room. Place the cushion on the floor at the far end of the room, with the guttering on top of it and the golf ball in the middle of it. Then lay out the other objects across the room. You might make a wall of books or boxes or cover a strip of the floor with cushions. You want to make it tricky for the player to cross from one side of the room to the other in less than 30–45 seconds.

GAME: The player has to cross the room, pick up the guttering with the ball inside it and then make their way back to drop the ball into the bucket. However, they are not allowed to touch the ball or let it roll on to the floor. This means the guttering has to be kept horizontal, with the ball in the middle, which is not easy with all those pesky obstacles. If the player does touch the ball or lets it drop into anything but the bucket, then it's an ALIS.

ALIS 02:00

REMEMBER SUM CARDS

GAME SIGN: Correctly identify the sums to collect the crystal, then recall all the cards to exit.

WHAT YOU NEED: Pen, paper and playing cards.

PREPARATION: Write each of the following five symbols on a separate piece of paper: +, –, +, – and x. Choose six numbered cards. Try to select a mixture of numbers and suits. Lay the cards face down with the pieces of paper in a row as follows below, placing the crystal after the sixth card:

Card 1, +, Card 2, –, Card 3, +, Card 4, –, Card 5, x, Card 6

GAME: This game combines maths skills with razor-sharp recall. When the time starts, the player can turn over the first card.

MAZE MASTER: You should guide the player to spend some time committing the card to memory. When they're ready, they should turn the card back face down and then take a look at the next card. They need to add this numeric value of this card to the value of the previous card to be able to turn over the next one, and so on until they reach the crystal. Once they've placed each card back face down it cannot be turned over again.

The player needs to work their way through the sums, adding, subtracting and multiplying the cards' values as instructed. When they've got the final total they can collect the crystal. However, they then need to recall every card, including the suit! If they don't make it all the way back to the first card, they're locked in. Harsh but fair.

02:30 ALIS

COIN A WORD

Sk

NO. 77

GAME SIGN: Slide a coin into the goal to collect a letter. Collect enough letters to form a word.

WHAT YOU NEED: Twelve coins, a bowl, a piece of paper cut into thirty-six pieces and a pen.

PREPARATION: Use two of the coins to make goalposts at one end of a table. At the opposite end of the table place the remaining ten coins in a pile. Next, on the thirty-six pieces of paper write every letter of the alphabet. Every vowel should be written three times, to make fifteen vowels and twenty-one consonants. Fold up all the pieces of paper so the letters are concealed, and place them in the bowl.

GAME: The aim of this game is for the player to make a word out of the letters they pull from the bowl. The word must be three letters or more and can be formed by arranging the letters they select in any order. However, the player may not draw a letter from the bowl until they've used their skill first. The player has ten chances to slide a coin across the table into the goal. For each goal scored, a letter can be drawn.

MAZE MASTER: Make sure they know to be careful with their coins! Not only could they run out of chances, but if they lose all of their coins before the time is up they are locked in!

ALIS 02:00

▶ MASTERMINDS OF THE ORIGINAL MAZE

On 15 February 1990 the first series of *The Crystal Maze* transmitted on Channel 4. The visionaries behind the series were the producer and MD of Chatsworth Television Malcolm Heyworth, the series director David G. Croft, and designer James Dillon. The story behind how such an audacious and creatively ambitious show came about is a fascinating one, so we asked Malcolm and David to share some of their memories from the original series.

▶ *The Crystal Maze* almost happened by accident as you'd originally sold the idea of *Fort Boyard* to Channel 4. How did it all come about?

MALCOLM: I bought the rights to a new format called *Fort Boyard* at MIPCOM (an international television conference) in April 1989. I had just had a big hit on Channel 4 with *Treasure Hunt* so the broadcaster fairly quickly agreed to fund a pilot for *Fort Boyard*, which we shot at Elstree Studios with the French producer and creator Jacques Antoine (who also created *Treasure Hunt*). It became quickly apparent to us and Channel 4 that we needed to make considerable changes to the format for a UK/Channel 4 audience. This would not be possible on the *Fort Boyard* set in La Rochelle as every country making its own series at La Rochelle would have to strictly follow the French format. Channel 4 were insistent that we make our own version in the UK, hence the creation of *The Crystal Maze*. The rest, as the saying goes, is history!

▶ **How did you come up with the idea for *The Crystal Maze*, with four unique time zones and the now iconic crystal dome?**
DAVID: Once Malcolm had made it clear to the French that Chatsworth would not make *Fort Boyard* under the then circumstances – being required to be the first to shoot on an untested French set at sea in the middle of November – we agreed to make our own version. On a visit to Paris we were driven to a warehouse in which stood a full-sized crystal dome, which the French had built but were unsure what to do with. Jacques Antoine showed us a rough sketch of a set that was a dome in the middle of what looked like four other sets. I recall we used that image as an inspiration, putting the dome at the heart of the game with a team of six players (which we kept from *Fort Boyard*) aiming to travel there. We replaced keys with crystals but I can't recall why! Why the time zones? Because we wanted the show to be like nothing before.

▶ **At what point did Richard O'Brien join the project and whose idea was it for him to host? What attracted you to him?**
DAVID: Malcolm had cast Richard for the *Fort Boyard* pilot that we shot in a studio. It was an inspired choice by Malcolm given that Richard had never done anything like this before.
MALCOLM: Channel 4's remit at the time was to be distinctly different and they actively encouraged producers to do the same. That's why I suggested Richard O'Brien for the pilot.

▸ **It was such an ambitious and inventive show on a huge scale. What challenges did you face building the maze the first time around?**
DAVID: First off, finding a venue. We wanted the set to be complete and not split into smaller sections. So many big spaces have pillars supporting the roof and we didn't want that. We wanted the set to feel completely real, giving the contestants a unique fantasy world experience. The next challenge was finding a designer who could cope with the breadth and scale of the show.
MALCOLM: We produced the first series on the H Stage at Shepperton. It was too expensive putting the set up and down for each series, so Channel 4 suggested we find somewhere permanent to house the complete set for each series. Eventually I came across a hangar at North Weald Airfield, which I hired for five years – also very expensive!

▸ **You created nearly 300 games over the six series – a huge creative endeavour. What were your principles behind the games?**
DAVID: Malcolm always wanted an X factor in every game. He wanted the player and the audience to always think they knew what the narrative of the game was, but then we would spring a surprise. We had budget constraints on the cost of every game and almost as important was that the games had to fit into a 3.6m by 3.6m cell. We rejected many ideas because they simply wouldn't fit.
MALCOLM: I only cared about how the viewer related to the game: would they understand it, was there enough jeopardy and would it make compelling television? Was the last twenty seconds dramatically tense? Would the game end in a lock-in?

▸ **Richard's asides to camera were a huge fan favourite and a happy accident. How did you first discover his off-the-cuff moments straight to camera?**
DAVID: Amazingly enough it wasn't until Malcolm and I were in the edit of the first show of series one. When shooting the games our eyes were always glued to the game cameras as we had to see how the contestant was getting on, so we never paid attention to the

cameras outside the cells. Richard's asides were a revelation. The big contribution Malcolm and I made was to realise that this stuff was great for the show and to use it. I am very proud of the fact we broke a major TV convention here: we cut away from the gameplay and switched the focus. This helped establish the role of Richard, and later Ed Tudor-Pole.

▶ **For the fourth series you introduced a new zone, Ocean, to replace Industrial. Why was that, and what was the thinking behind the new zone? What others did you consider?**
   DAVID: Channel 4 offered us the money to refresh the set with a new zone. We debated long and hard, but for me Industrial was visually the dullest at the time so it was clear which zone had to go. I recall we seriously debated having a Wild West zone but finally the sunken liner seemed to offer more gameplay scope and we thought the idea was very bold.

▶ **When Richard left the show at the end of the fourth series you chose Ed Tudor-Pole to replace him. How did you come up with Ed and were there other people in the frame to replace Richard at the time?**
   DAVID: I was sitting in my office leafing through *Spotlight* when I saw a picture of Ed. A lightbulb went on in my head and I went to see Malcolm, who had never heard of him. I remembered Ed from the punk band Tenpole Tudor. I also spoke to Neil Innes from the Bonzo Dog Band as he was a sort of hero of mine and I thought he would be brilliant. We went to see Seamus Cassidy, the Channel 4 commissioning editor, with a list of names including Ed's, and we agreed on three. Each was asked to turn up in an appropriate costume. Ed was by far the best on the day and we loved his costume so we hired him. We didn't want anyone with a presenting background because, as was clear with Richard, it added to their mystery for the audience.

> **We seriously debated having a Wild West zone.**

MALCOLM: David is right: I had never heard of Ed Tudor-Pole or Tenpole Tudor. Our musical tastes were very different!

▶ **You made two further series with Ed. What was it like working with him and how was it different from Richard?**
DAVID: We needed Ed to feel different and he worked extremely hard on defining his personality. Where Richard was cool and in control, Ed was zanier and came across as slightly mad. He was just as hard-working as Richard and he totally believed in what we were doing. He had such a tough gig following Richard and I think he did a brilliant job.
MALCOLM: We wanted Ed to be himself and not in any way copy Richard – which he didn't. Ed had a very difficult job following Richard, but I think he succeeded very well.

▶ **What were your favourite memories when you think back to the original series?**
DAVID: Oh, so many! The camaraderie of the cast and crew was tremendous. Working with Malcolm, who gave me so much creative freedom – he cared deeply about the show and backed his team to the hilt. Then there was the feeling that we were making something very different for UK television.
MALCOLM: Yes, I agree with David, but the main memory I have sustains today: that we made a groundbreaking piece of television that became so iconic that a new generation of producers are making a series twenty-six years later.

▶ **Do you have a favourite zone, and which games do you remember enjoying most?**
DAVID: Medieval. Any automatic lock-in game.
MALCOLM: Aztec and the river. It was so different in look. I enjoyed any physical games.

▶ **In 2015 the team at Little Lion Entertainment came up with the idea of a live experience. What was it like helping them recreate the maze in a way for people to play?**

MALCOLM: They got in touch with me and I had many conversations with Tom Maguire and his team. I said that if this is going to work for you, and punters are going to pay £50 to play the maze, then the players' expectations must be fully realised. I said that there must be a strong wow factor when they have finished playing, and that it must accurately reflect people's memories of the show and they don't feel ripped off. To his credit, Tom Maguire did all that and the event has been great success, to the extent that they have now opened another one in Manchester.

> There was the feeling that we were making something very different.

▶ **Why do you think *The Crystal Maze* has remained so popular and did you ever think it would still be so cherished over two decades later?**

MALCOLM: We had the money to make it to a very high standard. When I occasionally see an episode today it still looks a very high quality of production, particularly the games. That was actually twenty-six years ago.

DAVID: I think when the final series was over Malcolm and I realised we had made a show that had entered the consciousness of the audience and was a bit of TV history, and I'm so proud to have played such a role across all the series. Importantly the games were brilliant and allowed the audience at home to get fully involved; had we failed to do that the series would not have worked. It appeals to people's sense of a fantasy world. The presenters weren't traditional presenters but rather characters. Finally, it was made with such good spirit.

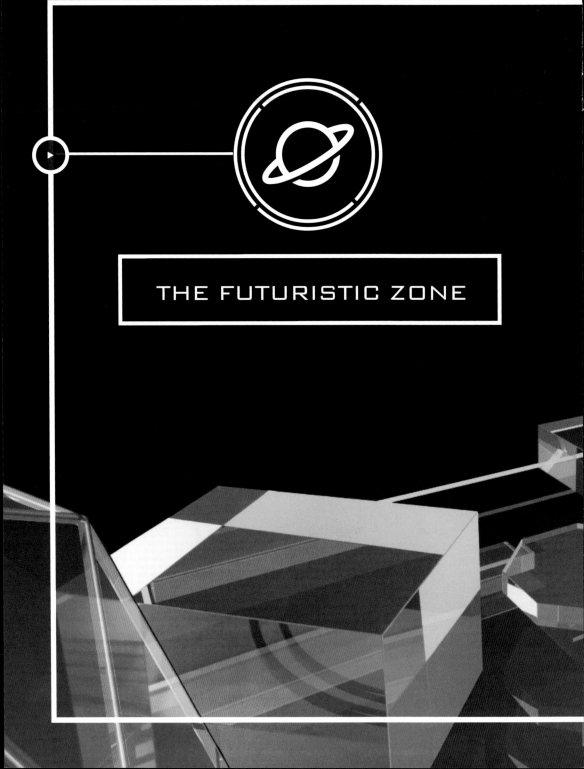

THE FUTURISTIC ZONE

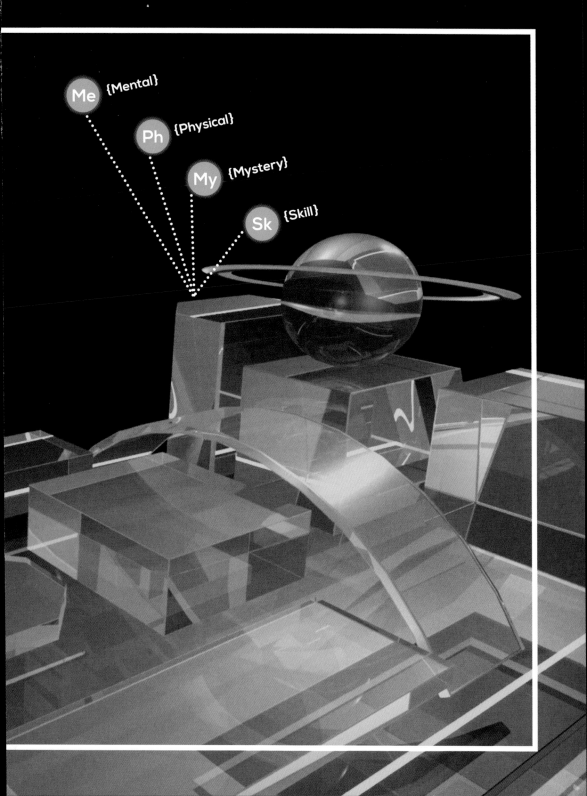

You have been transported onboard the spaceship *Crystal Voyager* in your fourth and final zone, the Futuristic zone.

1.2365

2.3

1.0260

0.236

What does the future hold? Making predictions about the future is, famously, a mug's game. Hollywood producer Darryl F. Zanuck apparently claimed back in 1946 that television wouldn't last because 'people will soon get tired of staring at a plywood box every night'. While it's easy to mock him now, how could he have possibly predicted the majestic sight of Richard O'Brien running about in a leopard-print jacket to the wonderment of kids in the 90s?

If we can learn anything valuable from *The Crystal Maze* (and we definitely can) it's that we should always avoid the safe and boring path, and should instead embrace the possibility of looking like a total plum in the pursuit of fun and victory. Although you may well struggle to recreate a futuristic spaceship that is remotely convincing (even if you use a trolley full of tinfoil to cover all the walls and dress your vacuum cleaner up as a droid), we implore you to try anyway – if something's not worth doing, it's worth not doing well.

Now buckle up for some intergalactic game-based shenanigans. The future awaits you …

INVISIBLE LASER MAZE

Ph

NO. 78

GAME SIGN: Reach the crystal and return to the start without touching the string. Touch the string three times and it's an ALIS.

WHAT YOU NEED: A ball of string, some tape (any kind will do), and something that will work as a blindfold. This game assumes you don't have sophisticated laser technology lying around the house.

PREPARATION: To emulate the physical challenge of navigating through a secret laser maze this game requires a little bit of preparation. Find a room with a clear space on the floor (or if you're feeling especially mean, a room full of obstacles). Using your string and tape at various heights and angles, clearly mark out a route that requires a variety of twists and turns from the doorway to reach a small object, and for the player to reverse and make their way back out of the room ... all in under three minutes.

GAME: When you are ready to start the game, blindfold the chosen player and keep the door open as they enter so the rest of the team can shout instructions. Every time the player touches the string on the floor they lose a life. Lose three lives and it's a lock-in (and probably a tantrum).

ALIS 03:00

LET THE GAMES BEGIN!

GAME SIGN: Learn the number sequence. Clear the number sequence. Repeat the number sequence.

WHAT YOU NEED: A calculator or portable device with a calculator app.

PREPARATION: Type a thirteen-digit number into a calculator or portable device. Jot it down so you can refer to it during the game without revealing it to the team.

GAME: It's a simple yet fiendish memory challenge. The player must try to memorise a thirteen-digit number. They can only attempt to recall the number once they have cleared the screen. This means they have to judge how long they spend memorising the sequence before giving themselves time to attempt it ... and there is no second chance to see the sequence again.

MAZE MASTER: You have the correct sequence to hand so you can verify if they've got it right. The team can watch, but they can't assist.

The players can continue attempting the sequence until you count them down from ten seconds (which will probably be really annoying if they're in the middle of shouting out the sequence).

02:00

HIGH FIVE

NO. 80

GAME SIGN: Correctly identify five from ten. (The rest of this sign depends on what content you want to put into the game.)

WHAT YOU NEED: Pens and ten pieces of paper. Or printed pictures if you want to be more fancy pants about it.

PREPARATION: For this game you create your own statement, then choose five items/people/animals that correctly match that statement and five that don't. You then either write the names of all ten on to ten pieces of paper or print pictures of each to place in the room. Here's an example to get you started: Animals that can run faster than 10 mph.

5 animals that can: **lion, ostrich, elephant, dog, bearded dragon.**
5 animals that can't: **spider, chicken, slug, mouse, sloth.**

GAME: When the player enters the room, as Maze Master you should advise them to make their selection of five. Only when a player has committed to their choice can you reveal how many are correct. DO NOT REVEAL WHICH ONES. The fun of this game is the players doubting themselves, putting correct answers back in the pile and generally making a hash of it.

NOTE: The trick to this game is making a couple of the correct and incorrect answers easy, but making a few really hard so the player and their team (who may well be shouting hysterically) will get flustered.

02:00

BUMPY SCRUMPY LOO ROLL RACE

Sk

NO. 81

GAME SIGN: Complete the course without knocking over any obstacles.

WHAT YOU NEED: As many empty loo rolls or kitchen rolls as you can save, an equal number of apples or tennis balls, a piece of paper, a red marker pen and a remote-control car.

PREPARATION: Set the cardboard rolls vertically on a flat floor surface to create an obstacle forest, placing the apples on top of each roll (or tennis balls if you don't want to eat slightly bruised apples later on).

Create a start and finish line by placing a red 'X' on a piece of paper at each end of the room.

GAME: The player must pick up the remote control and steer the car from from start to finish and back to win a crystal.

MAZE MASTER: You need to inform the player that they have three lives. Yes, this is an ALIS. Each apple or ball the remote-control car knocks over loses a life. If three fall, they are locked in!

ALIS 02:00

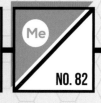
GAME SIGN: Build a tower so all four sides add up to the same number.

WHAT YOU NEED: Four regular playing dice.

PREPARATION: The dice should be jumbled up and placed down randomly prior to game play.

GAME: This is a great mind-boggler, requiring nothing more than four humble dice. In the time allocated, the player must stack all four dice to form a tower, whereby all four sides add up to the same number.

Hopefully you can get hold of some dice by raiding your long-forgotten board games. Or check the basement to see if your mum is secretly running an illegal casino at the weekends.

02:00

JARHEAD'S RIDDLES – AKA 'JARHEADACHES'

My

NO. 83

GAME SIGN: Solve two of the three riddles.

TIME: There's no time limit on this one – other than the fact that you are all busy people, with lives that need living. So, you know, just encourage people not to be ultra-ditherers.

PREPARATION: It all depends how far you want to go. You might want to be Jarhead by popping your head over the back of the sofa and putting on a silly voice. Then again, you may fancy trying to design your own mind-controlled laboratory and build a contraption to create the illusion of your head being suspended in a jar of liquid. Do you have time to do this? If so, what is wrong with you?

GAME: Take on the character of Jarhead and challenge your adventurer to answer two of three riddles to win a crystal. Here are a few ... but can you do better? For instance, why not devise your own personal versions about things and people that you and your team know about? That way the player will be doubly embarrassed when they get any wrong.

EXAMPLE RIDDLES:

1. I am named after a famous Norse god.
I turn up once a week, like it or not.
Making thunder was among his powers.
All I do is last for twenty-four hours.
What am I?

--:--

2. I lay eggs but I do not have feathers.
My skin is used for fancy shoe leathers.
I do not have limbs but I do have bones.
I was a fun game on old mobile phones.
What am I?

3. I'm quite small but I'm bigger than a flea.
Buddy Holly's band was named after me.
Some of me have long tails and some have short.
I'm an insect but I'm also a sport.
What am I?

4. I am wet and hot and brown.
I refresh when I'm drunk down.
People in Britain enjoy me every day,
But I'm made from leaves grown very far away.
What am I?

5. I'm roughly round and most of me is white.
I've evolved to be sensitive to light.
This is so easy, can't you see?
You're only reading this because of me.
What am I?

6. I stand tall in London town.
A bloke once tried to blow me up.
People inside me like to exchange views.
I like to ring at the start of the news.
What am I?

SOLUTIONS ON PAGE 221

FAN FAIR

Ph

NO. 84

GAME SIGN: Blow twenty rolled-up tissues across the line.

WHAT YOU NEED: Two electric fans, box of tissues and stopwatch or timepiece with a second hand.

PREPARATION: Test how far the fans can blow a tissue and set a start and finish line. Place one fan on the start line (to be used by the player) and the other just behind the finish (to be controlled by the Maze Master).

GAME: The player must successfully blow twenty tissues across the finish line – one at a time – in the time allotted. The Maze Master must (prior to the start of play) determine a pattern they will turn their own fan on and off with (which will obviously hinder the player's own fan and efforts). This pattern must be consistent and have at least five-second gaps built in so the player can time their turns.

This game is an ideal use of household resources as there are about only two to three days a year in the UK when you actually need a fan. The rest of the time the weather is miserable and the fans collect 362 days' worth of dust.

02:00

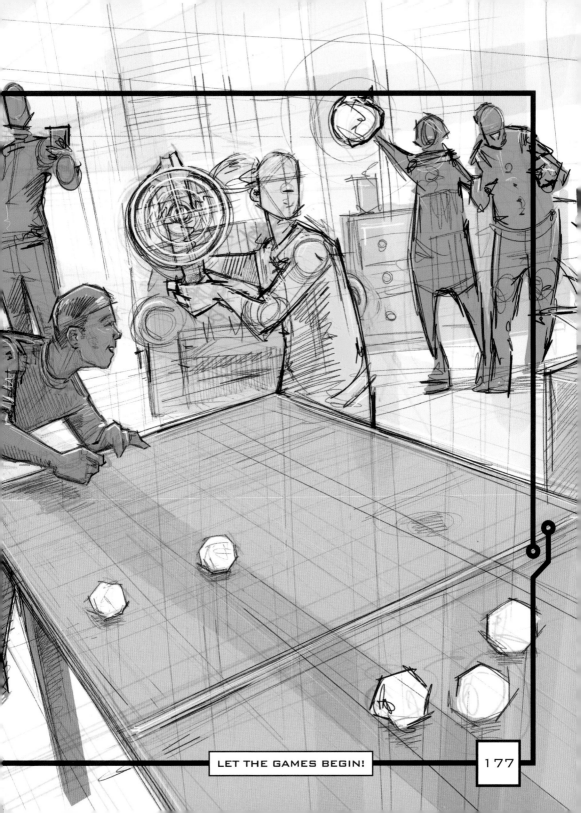

TWELVE ANGRY COINS

NO. 85

WHAT YOU NEED: Twelve coins of different denominations and one cup.

PREPARATION: Put six of the coins under the cup. The rest of the coins should be laid on a surface heads side up. The wider the variety of coins, the harder the challenge will be.

GAME: This game combines memory, skill and a little splash of pure undiluted frustration.

When the time starts, the player must lift the cup and memorise the combination of coins lying flat on the table underneath. The player can spend as long as they see fit on this portion of the game; it is totally up to them how much of their time they use. When the player returns the cup, the memorising time is over, and they must not take another look.

The next task is to toss each of the six coins that are outside the cup and currently heads side up so that they land tails side up on the table. They can do this repeatedly until they are successful. Only when all of the coins are successfully turned can the player attempt to recall the coins under the cup – and they only have one chance to guess. As Maze Master you can then lift the cup to see if they are correct. Or mock them. It's up to you.

03:00

CODE WORD

NO. 86

GAME SIGN: Crack the code to find the crystal.

WHAT YOU NEED: Pen, paper and a plant pot.

PREPARATION: Write the following clue on a piece of paper.

CRYSTAL = DSZTUBM

Then write a letter containing the line below. It's fun if you make the letter look like you're a spy from the future trying to save the galaxy – but a simple handwritten note will also do.

UIF DSZTUBM JT JO UIF QMBOU QPU.

Finally, take your makeshift crystal and hide it in a plant pot.

GAME: The player gets just one clue: if they can crack the code, then the letter will lead them to the crystal. It's as simple as that. The player should be given the clue and the letter at the same time.

A top tip for making this game look a bit more impressive is to bulk-buy tinfoil and cover the entire room from floor to ceiling in it to present the illusion of a futuristic spaceship. Hours of work, for less than three minutes. And will people thank you for it? Welcome to our world.

02:00

GAME SIGN: Find the crystal by decoding the letters.

WHAT YOU NEED: Pen and paper and envelopes.

PREPARATION: Write or print out three letters (see examples below and opposite) and put in envelopes. The letters are very short and each has a coded clue in them.

Here are three examples that presume that you're playing in the kitchen, but you can obviously write your own to fit wherever you want to play.

GAME: The adventurer is handed the first cryptic letter and has three minutes from opening it to crack its code to find the next letter, and so on, till they are led to the crystal. The team may try to help.

LETTER 1:

> *The First Letter. Understand nothing. Do everything.*
> *Read this highly explanatory material unsparingly.*
> *Genius system!*

MAZE MASTER: The clue to understanding it is right there. Read the first letter of each word – it spells out 'U N D E R T H E M U G S' – and that's exactly where the second letter is hidden …

03:00

LETTER 2:

The Second Letter. Pick another. Stop there before offending or riling adventurers again. Mental!

NOTE: Again, the clue is right there. Read the second letter of each word – they spell out 'I N T H E F R I D G E', which is where the final letter is.

LETTER 3:

The Third Letter. Think 'dinner'.
Eat other pies, though never the candy.

NOTE: They've either got it by now or they're just shouting and wandering aimlessly around the kitchen. The third letters spell out 'I N T H E O V E N', which is where the crystal is to be found.

ONE RINGTONE TO RULE THEM ALL

GAME SIGN: Find the phone and answer it to learn the crystal's location.

WHAT YOU NEED: A working mobile phone.

PREPARATION: Hide the mobile phone somewhere in the house and hide the crystal elsewhere, in a much trickier, more squirrelled-away location (e.g. under the boxes in the cupboard under the stairs, or in amongst the ready-to-be-washed clothes at the bottom of the laundry basket – that kind of annoying-to-find spot).

If the phone's settings can be tweaked so as to stop a call going to answerphone (i.e. and allow it to keep ringing), then do this before hiding it. Also, why not create or choose an especially space-age set of sounds as a ringtone so as to make the game that bit more futuristic? Some music by Kraftwerk would be ideal, for instance!

GAME: Have a friend/associate call the mobile phone to make it ring. The player then has to race around, listening out for the phone and trying to answer it. If they find it and answer it, your friend/associate should adopt a fun robot voice as they tell the player the location of the crystal. The player then has to try to get to the crystal before the time runs out.

02:30

STACK 'EM HIGH

Sk

NO. 89

GAME SIGN: Make four stacks of eight marshmallows within the playing area.

WHAT YOU NEED: Thirty-two large marshmallows (for now) and graham crackers* and squares of chocolate (for later).

PREPARATION: Place the marshmallows on a table surface – delineate a 30cm-size (large plate) playing area.

GAME: The player needs to make a 2 x 2 tower of marshmallows, eight marshmallows tall (without eating any). If the tower tumbles, they must start again.

When the game is done you can treat yourself and the team to some homemade s'mores!

S'MORES RECIPE: Heat your marshmallow over an open flame until it begins to brown and melt. Break the graham cracker in half. Sandwich the chocolate and the hot marshmallow between the crackers – the chocolate will melt. Allow the molten goo to cool before eating.

*What's a graham cracker? Ask an American to explain. You may substitute two digestive biscuits if you can't find the real deal (although we've been told by our resident American that that's apparently not normally acceptable).

02:00

FLYBY

Ph

NO. 90

GAME SIGN: Create five paper planes to fly over the finish line.

WHAT YOU NEED: Multiple sheets of paper in different stocks and sizes.

PREPARATION: Create a start and finish line.

GAME: The player must build and fly five paper aeroplanes to win a crystal. Take-off must be from behind the start line and the landing must be after the finish line.

Each plane must float over the line ... throwing a wadded-up piece of paper is cheating.

This is a great opportunity for the player to impress their friends and family with their speed and engineering prowess. We also think that making paper planes could be the next big thing with hipsters and soon in east London they'll be doing that instead of learning the ukulele and growing silly beards.

02:00

LET THE GAMES BEGIN!

SOUP-ER POWERS

NO. 91

GAME SIGN: Identify the foods contained in each bowl by taste.

WHAT YOU NEED: Various foods of your choosing (that can be mulched in a food mixer), e.g. lemons, pickled herrings, bananas, chilli peppers, etc., a food mixer, three bowls, three spoons and a glass of water.

PREPARATION: Take two very different tasting food items items and blend them in a mixer until it is a thick liquid like a soup (hence the title ...). Pour the mix into one of the bowls and repeat this process with the next two food items, making sure to clean the mixer in between each one to ensure the different flavours don't 'contaminate' each other.

GAME: Here, in the future, normal meals are a thing of the past. Some people have their food in the form of special pills, some just breathe in special nutritious gases – and some have everything as soup.

Show the player taking on this game the three bowls of soup and tell them that each one contains two types of food. They have two minutes to correctly identify the two ingredients in each bowl and to win the crystal they have to do this for at least two of the three bowls. They can drink some of the water to cleanse their palate between soups.

02:00

SWEET MEMORIES

GAME SIGN: Arrange the sweets in the same order on the second tray.

WHAT YOU NEED: Thirteen coloured sweets and a plate or tray.

PREPARATION: To set up this game, you need to start by deciding on two locations as far apart as possible. Perhaps the kitchen and upstairs bedroom will work, or the front room and bottom of the garden.

Next, you need a pack of multicoloured sweets. Give them a really good shake and then spill thirteen of them out on to the table at your first location. Try not to eat any just yet. Line the sweets up as close as you can to the order in which they naturally fell. Write the colour order down, or take a picture, as you'll need to be able to reference this later on.

Next, position a plate or tray in your second location.

GAME: All the player needs to do to win their crystal, is reassemble the line of sweets in exactly the same colour order as was on the table in the first location. They can carry as many or as few as they choose at a time, but once they take the initial line apart, they'll need to remember it or rely on their teammates for help. It's a tricky one, this ... it'll take a real smartie to crack it.

02:00

GAME SIGN: Follow the clues to find the crystal.

WHAT YOU NEED: This game needs to be played in a home complete with all the expected mod cons, such as a clock, a phone and salt! You will also need a pen and paper to write down clues.

PREPARATION: Preparing this game is almost as fun as playing it. Almost. First, write down the following clues on separate pieces of paper.

Clue 1: NaCl

Clue 2: There's a clue that we must tell.
Find the means to give us a bell.

Clue 3: Sometimes measured by the sun, but sometimes measured by the sand. The next clue measures it with its hands.

Clue 4: The end of start, the start of tree. You can't find me in milk, but you can find milk in me.

Clue 5: I'm in the frame but you just see through me every time.

Clue 6: You have won the crystal.

(This depends on the size of your house. Take the full three minutes if you're a castle owner.)

02:00

Then hide the clues around the house as follows ...

Clue 1 is to be given to the player when the timer starts.
Clue 2 is to be hidden where you keep your salt.
Clue 3 is to be hidden under the telephone.
Clue 4 is to be hidden behind the clock.
Clue 5 is to be hidden where you keep your tea.
Clue 6 is to be hidden on the windowsill.

GAME: Since the beginning of time, or at least the beginning of the Crystal Maze, there has always been the classic Murder Mystery-type game. In these games, contestants enter a room to find a skeleton clutching a clue. The clues are then followed to find the crystal. Or the clues are completely bungled with hilarious consequences – depending on the contestant.

We have come up with a crystal hunt that any household should be able to take part in, but feel free to make up your own clues and make your own mischievous murder mystery mayhem.

QUICK FLICK

GAME SIGN: Flick the card to leave the coin in the glass.

WHAT YOU NEED: A glass, some card and a 1p coin.

PREPARATION: Have you ever seen the trick where the magician pulls a tablecloth out from underneath a beautifully set table in a single swipe without smashing a single piece of crockery? Well, here is the Crystal Maze version ...

Assuming you don't have a table, tablecloth and inordinate amounts of fine china your mum's willing to risk, here's our budget version. You'll need a glass with a piece of card placed on top of it. Balance your penny in the centre of the card.

GAME: The player must remove the card in one flick, so that the penny lands perfectly in the glass. Sounds easy, right? The player will have as many attempts as they need, but it's harder than it looks.

Here's a little tip ... it's all in the speed and direction in which you flick the card.

⏳
02:00

LETTER GET MOVING

NO. 95

WHAT YOU NEED: Something to use as a blindfold and a flat surface.

PREPARATION: Place the blindfold in the centre of the room. This game will involve the player wandering around the room blindfolded, so it might be an idea to clear away any breakables, small children or pets.

GAME: When the time begins, the player should enter the room and put on the blindfold as instructed. They should then be given a letter of the alphabet (chosen randomly by the Maze Master, but crucially on the basis that there are numerous items in the room that begin with that letter). All the player must do is locate three items beginning with that chosen letter and then place those items on the table.

The player is blindfolded so it's down to their teammates to guide them around the room, and into other rooms if required, to lead them to items beginning with that letter. The item can be anything, so long as it can be physically placed on to the table. If three items beginning with the chosen letter are on the table within three minutes, the player wins the crystal.

03:00

HEAD HOCKEY

Sk

NO. 96

GAME SIGN: Knock over the bottles using only the balloon hat.

WHAT YOU NEED: One pair of clean tights, ten balloons and ten empty plastic bottles.

PREPARATION: No one can predict the future. Least of all future fashions. But just try imagining a world where style has advanced to a place where hipsters wear legwear as hats. Welcome to the future!

For this next game, you will need a pair of ladies' tights. Next, blow up ten balloons and stuff as many as you can into each leg of the tights – you should be able to squeeze four or five into each side. Lastly, position the plastic bottles around a large room; they shouldn't be too close to each other. Also, make sure the room is clear of any breakables as this game could get a little chaotic.

GAME: The player should pull the gusset of the tights over their face. Trust us, it's a strong look. The balloon-filled legs should stick up in a V, like a pair of horns. The player should still be able to breathe, but depending on the denier, you might want to cut them a little breathing hole around the nose area (health and safety first).

The player has two minutes to knock over at least eight of the bottles using only their nylon-covered balloon horns. Success will deliver a well-earned crystal, but it will have minimal impact on the post-game levels of dignity.

⏳
02:00

HAT TRICK

GAME SIGN: Remove the items from the hat in the correct order: (list the items you've put in the hat in the order you want them removed).

WHAT YOU NEED: Twenty small items that will fit inside a hat, pen, paper, a large woolly hat, an old pair of dark tights (preferably clean), tape, scissors and nail varnish.

PREPARATION: Put the small items – perhaps a paperclip, a rubber band, a 10p coin, a dice, a pen lid, a rubber ball and a folded piece of paper with 'crystal' written on it – into the hat. Half of these will be the items the player is looking for; the remainder will be red herrings. We encourage you to make your red herrings deliberately misleading – a 2p that feels like a 10p, a piece of paper with 'no crystal' written on it and so on.

Then place the hat upside down and stretch the tights around the opening, pulling them taut. Tie the tights firmly or tape them to the underside of the hat. Then cut a small hole in the top where the opening is: big enough for the player's hand, but small enough that they cannot see the items inside. Paint some nail varnish around the hole so that the tights don't ladder.

GAME: The player has two minutes to find and remove the items in the listed order from the hat to win a crystal. The player must replace a wrongly pulled item before continuing.

As Maze Master you need to verify the items are removed in the correct order.

02:00

PANNING FOR CRYSTALS

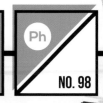

Ph

NO. 98

GAME SIGN: Carry the ping-pong ball through the obstacles on the back of the saucepan and deposit it in the bucket. **WARNING:** Avoid the floor!

WHAT YOU NEED: A ping-pong ball, a saucepan and some soft items to use as obstacles.

PREPARATION: For this game, the player will carry a ping-pong ball on the back of a saucepan through an obstacle course without touching the floor.

Setting this up takes a little preparation and creativity. The Maze Master should create an obstacle course that enables the player to get from a start point to an end point without touching the floor – so they might need to climb over the back of the couch, balance on a line of books, clamber across a row of chairs or use two cushions like big soft roller skates to shuffle along the floor.

GAME: When the player enters the room they should pick up the saucepan with the ping-pong balanced atop and make their way through the course.

Each time the player drops the ball they must start again from the very beginning. If the ball is dropped three times, it's an ALIS. AND ... if the player themselves touches the floor, at any point, they instantly face the dreaded ALIS. Brutal.

ALIS 03:00

LET THE GAMES BEGIN!

COLOURED BLOCKS

Me

NO. 99

GAME SIGN 1: Stack the blocks in a three-by-three formation so that both sides follow the rules.

WHAT YOU NEED: Paper, coloured felt-tip pens, scissors and glue or tape.

PREPARATION: If you've already made blocks for the Four Symbols game, these can be repurposed (though you need nine blocks for this game). All you'll need to do is paint over the symbols using the colours on each face as per the diagrams below. Otherwise, refer to instructions for block assembly, and this is much the same – in a nutshell, use the below diagrams to make nine cubes. If you are resourceful, you might be able to find something cubic at home (such as a child's building block) that you can simply pop coloured stickers on. Don't say we don't give you options.

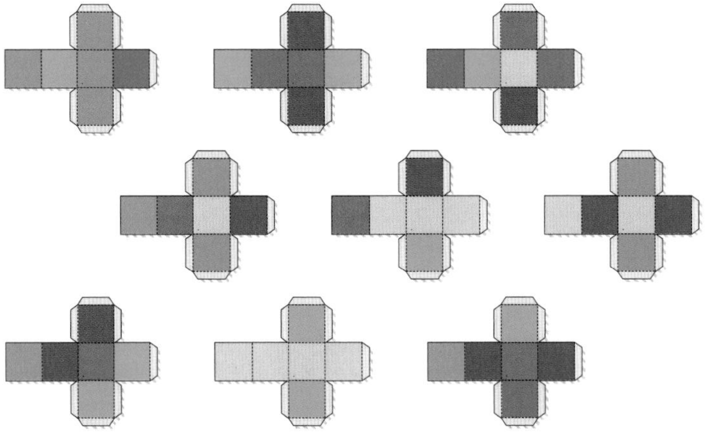

03:00

196

GAME SIGN 2: The Rules:
  1. Only red blocks may appear in the right-hand column.
  2. There must be a yellow block in the centre.
  3. No green blocks may be adjacent to any purple blocks.

GAME: This is the impossible Coloured Blocks game that featured in the show. We say impossible, but we're sticking with it because it's fun to play and fun to watch other people fail miserably.

The object of the game is to stack the nine blocks into a three by three formation so that they follow the rules on both sides.

MAZE MASTER: Ensure your player understands that the pattern of blocks doesn't have to be identical on either side, they just need follow the same rules on both sides.

NOTE: Since you've gone to all the trouble of making nine blocks, here are two more sets of rules that these blocks will work with, which will give you three full plays of this game.

GAME SIGN 2 (for version 2): The Rules:
  1. There should never be two blocks of the same colour next to each other.
  2. The bottom row must contain two blue blocks.
  3. There should be more red blocks than yellow blocks.

GAME SIGN 2 (for version 3): The Rules:
  1. There must be two purple blocks in the middle row.
  2. There must be two yellow blocks in the central column.
  3. No red blocks may be adjacent to any blue blocks.

HOLE IN ONE

NO. 100

GAME SIGN: Pass the pencil through the DVDs – without touching them – to knock the crystal off its perch.

WHAT YOU NEED: Three DVDs or CDs, some sticky tack, a kitchen roll tube and a pencil.

PREPARATION: To set up this game you'll need a trio of DVDs or CDs. (This isn't an excuse to judge your host's movie or music collection – any three will do.) Place each one upright on a table, held in position with a hefty wodge of sticky tack, or wedge them in between something.

The three DVDs should be parallel, approximately three finger-widths apart. Test you've got them straight by kneeling and checking you can see through all three. Finally, place the kitchen-roll tube at the end, directly in the middle, and balance the crystal atop the kitchen-roll tube. Make sure the distance between the first DVD and the tube is no longer than the length of the pencil.

GAME: The player has two minutes to thread the pencil through the holes in the middle of the three DVDs without touching the sides. Their goal is to get it all the way through and then knock down the kitchen roll tube at the end and to free the crystal. If the crystal falls off its perch, you're on to a winner.

Now this is an ALIS. If the player touches the edge of the DVD with their pencil, they lose a life. Three lives gone and it's a lock-in.

ALIS 02:00

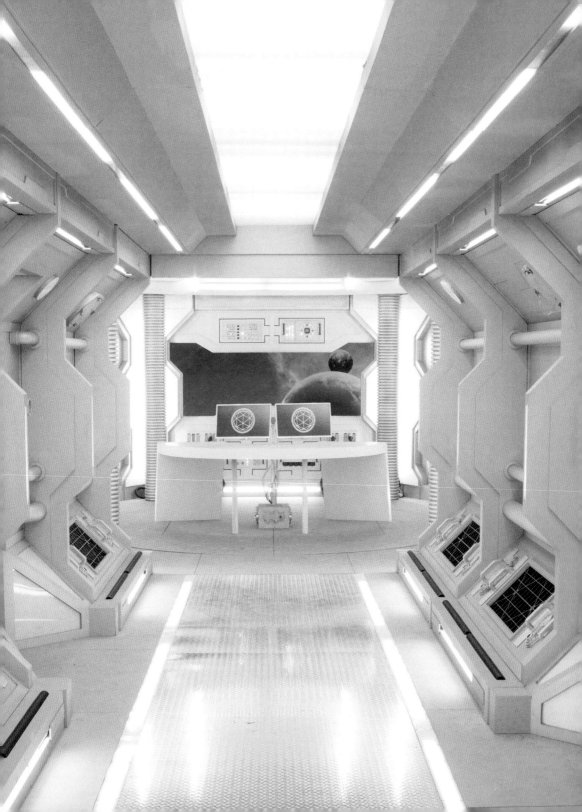

THE WIZARD BEHIND A WORLD OF WONDER

James Dillon designed and built the original maze back in 1990. He returned to reimagine it all for a new generation for the latest series and talked to us about how the two worlds compare.

▸ **How did you first come to be involved in the original series?**
At the time I was working with David [G. Croft] on an emerging-talent show called *First Exposure* for London Weekend Television. David asked me to come along and meet Malcolm [Heyworth] at Chatsworth TV as they had a project they were developing for Channel 4. It was a UK studio-based version of *The Keys to Fort Boyard*. Chatsworth had already shot a pilot but Channel 4 weren't happy with the result. Three weeks after that meeting we went to see Seamus Cassidy, the commissioner at Channel 4, and presented him with our idea in the form of a concept studio plan, which we had called *The Crystal Maze*. After that it was straight on to the drawing board to get the sets drawn and built.

▸ **How did the idea for the four zones and dome come about?**
It came out of discussions we had about ways to make the show more interesting and exciting. We decided that we could make

it a journey and not be stuck in any one place and that opened up the design possibilities for both the look of the sets and the games within those sets, which could then also be themed. The dome concept came from another game show that *The Keys to Fort Boyard*'s creators were looking at. In the end we decided to build our own version of that structure and called it the Crystal Dome.

▶ **How did you approach designing each zone and what were the biggest challenges in bringing them to life?**

The prep time for getting everything designed and built was incredibly short for such a large show. There were only about thirteen weeks between our first meeting to discuss the show and the first studio record. I started creating the Medieval zone first as it was closest in spirit to *The Keys to Fort Boyard*. I wanted it to feel very atmospheric and dungeon-like. It needed to look moody and scary and would be lit with flames, candles and shafts of cold light through ivy-covered barred windows.

After Medieval I moved on to designing the Industrial zone. The zone needed to be a steel and concrete installation that was a visual contrast to the others and have as many pipes, chains and metal walkways as possible.

Aztec was probably the most complicated set to design and build. I imagined it to have the appearance of a lost temple somewhere in the Andes, which was overgrown and abandoned and only accessible via the Crystal Maze's secret tunnels. The bright exterior and sunny feel of the Aztec zone provided important visual contrast with the more dark and gloomy spaces of Medieval and Industrial.

Futuristic was the zone I designed last. The look I was after was an abandoned space station orbiting the Earth. I included TV monitors with electronic motors, hydraulic lifts, ripped and broken electronic circuit boards and fluorescent lighting. CO_2 extinguishers sent jets of smoke into the set and complemented the futuristic sliding doors that open into the games rooms (in reality there was a man behind the set pulling them open and shut). All these years later we're using the same method. Sometimes hand-a-matic just works best.

▶ **Did you ever think the show might return, and how did you feel when you realised you might be involved in the return of a new series?**
Over the years many people had suggested that it would be great if *The Crystal Maze* were to return. The impact of the Stand Up To Cancer special made everything feasible and it was very exciting to be asked to come in and meet the new producers to talk through all the pros and cons of doing a full-scale new version of *The Crystal Maze.*

▶ **What were the biggest challenges this time around and how was it different from the original?**
The first big challenge was getting the right space. We needed a minimum of 2787 sq m and Channel 4's commitment to regional productions meant we needed a location outside London. The Bottle Yard Studios in Bristol proved to be the answer. They have a great combination of space, workshops, storage, offices and on-site facilities and local skill base. We had to rethink how the zones would fit into the new studio though. Fortunately, I had kept a lot of my original drawings and eventually located them in dusty tubes in a box at the back of the attic. That meant that with a few alterations we were able to start building quite quickly and efficiently once we got the go-ahead.

Another challenge was seeing if Dave Green of Scenechange, who was the original construction manager, would be willing to come back on board to recreate the sets. Fortunately he was, and he and his team set about building the Medieval, Industrial and Aztec zones. In the meantime I started to create mood boards, visuals and concepts for the new Futuristic zone.

An important difference is that the new series is filmed in high definition, using twice as many cameras as in the original, and the cameras' aspect ratios have changed from 4:3 to 16:9. This makes everything look bigger, more detailed and more cinematic than before.

▸ **How did the idea for the new dome come about?**
From the outset the dome was something we felt could be improved upon. The original glazing panels were made of Perspex and dust from the studio would get sucked in and deposited on the internal surface because the airflow from the fans created a lot of static.

I approached Solardome, the company that had built the original dome, and they agreed to engineer a new one for us. Solardome suggested we use toughened glass, which would be easier to keep pristine. Due to the weight of the new glass panels we decided to make the new dome a three-frequency pattern, with more and smaller facets. The result is a more rounded shape, which better mirrors the design of the game crystals.

▸ **What are your favourite parts of the new maze?**
I particularly enjoyed having the chance to design a whole new look for the Futuristic zone. We have incorporated a large revolve into the floor of the main control room that turns and gives moving perspectives of the set. I also like the matter transporter room, which makes for efficient transitions to anywhere in the maze.

Aztec's sunny skies and flora and fauna means it's always a favourite. This time round the large water game room there has swimming pool-standard filters and heaters so it's ideal for a quick dip in the morning before filming begins. Afterwards it's possible to take a shower in the new waterfall feature in the Aztec transition. Very relaxing after a hard day's shoot!

The Aztec Temple just before 7257kg of sand arrived.

Up go the walls of the Medieval zone.

Finishing touches to the Medieval zone include over two hundred candles and twenty-five torches.

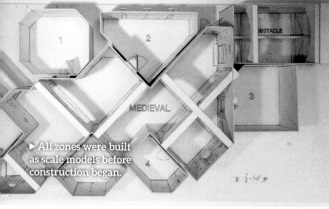

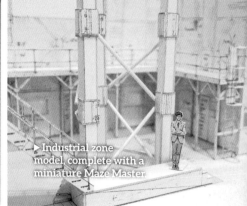

All zones were built as scale models before construction began.

Industrial zone model, complete with a miniature Maze Master.

▶ Constructing an Industrial world. One of the blue pillars is actually part of the structure of the studio, the other two are for dressing ... can you tell which?

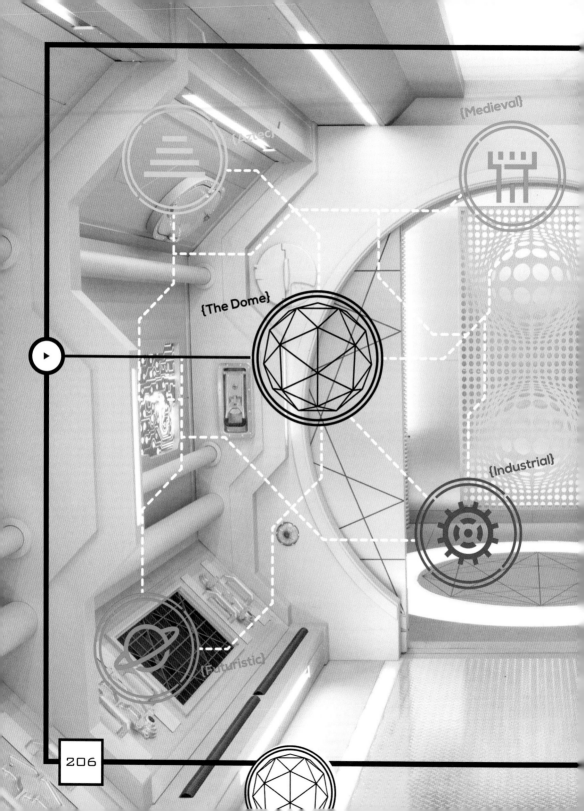

{Medieval}

{The Dome}

{Industrial}

{Futuristic}

ADVENTURERS, YOUR TIME IN THE MAZE IS ALMOST COMPLETE.

You have ventured through the Aztec, Medieval, Futuristic and Industrial zones. You have tackled the physical, skill, mystery and mental challenges that awaited you within.

Some of you succeeded in your endeavours. Some of you failed. Some of you took photos of those failures and quickly posted them on social media. That's just how you roll.

Regardless, you now stand with the precious crystals you have collected on your epic journey through the maze.

The only thing that remains to be said is ...

TO THE DOME!

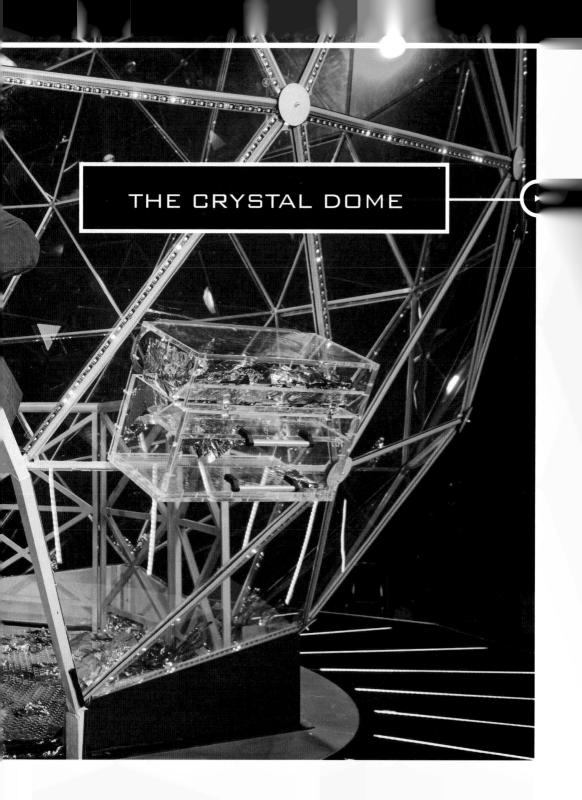

THE CRYSTAL DOME

WILL YOU START THE FANS PLEASE!

In the series, the geodesic dome is an architectural work of wonder, a visually spectacular feat of engineering. The dome itself is 4.5m tall and made of 156 individual panes of triangular-cut glass, all housed within a one-of-a-kind steel frame that is finished with intelligent LED lighting to bring it to life.

You probably don't have one of these to hand. We also assume you don't have access to one of those highly questionable glass conservatories that were all the rage in the 90s, so you're going to need to come on a free-thinking journey with us to create your own dome-inspired end game.

When we first pondered how to recreate the experience at home we of course toyed with the idea of hairdryers in a tent. That's a given. The reality is that the amount of wind and finely tuned physics-based tinkering involved in creating the perfect environment for gold and silver tokens to form a consistent whirlwind is, ultimately, rather a lot of faff. A hairdryer isn't going to cut it. Two hairdryers? You're fooling yourself, my friend.

So, we took the spirit of the dome (a frantic, physical, fun-packed finale in a confined space) and came up with something that will hopefully end your team's adventure in the maze with a bang. Literally.

THE CRYSTAL DOME

WHAT YOU NEED: A lot of balloons, a pump (or some help with blowing up the balloons), some pins, a stopwatch and a whistle.

PREPARATION: Find a small room and remove as much furniture as you can so the space is as empty as possible. Next, blow up enough balloons to fill the room from floor to ceiling, leaving only enough room for the five adventurers to squeeze inside. If you can source gold and silver balloons, that's perfect. If not, if you can source two colours, then assign them gold/silver status. If you can't even manage that (have you never heard of Amazon?), then simply write 'G' for gold and 'S' for silver on the balloons as you put them in the room. You want a ratio of around three gold for every two silver balloons.

GAME: This is the climax of the Crystal Maze adventure. Maze Master, make the most of this moment! How have the team done? What have they learned on their adventures? What would they do differently? Was it really necessary to leave Uncle Keith locked in that long? Isn't it time to let him out?

Next, count up the team's crystals – each is worth five seconds of time in the dome – and explain the rules as officiously as possible ...

In a moment, you are about to invite the team to enter 'the dome'. Once inside, the team will have their allotted number of seconds to burst as many gold balloons as possible. Any silver balloons they burst will be deducted from their total. The team will start bursting on your first whistle. They must stop bursting on your second whistle.

Depending on how many balloons you have blown up, allocate three tiers of prize:

- Zero to not very many gold balloons means they leave with nothing.

- Not very many balloons to a few more balloons – they win a 'middling prize'. This can be anything of your choosing. However, if you want to stay true to the show, then do please ensure it's underwhelming.

- A few more balloons to lots of balloons – they win a 'top prize'. Again, this can be anything you like. It should obviously be better than the middling prize, but only slightly.

Once the team have finished popping, ask them to leave the room while you count up their burst balloons. Perhaps put on some mood music while they wait nervously for the results. Or if you're really terrible at counting, let them watch an episode of *The Crystal Maze* on All4.

Once you're ready, gather the team together for the result. Using all the hammy conventions of television presenting do please drag this bit out. Begin by revealing the gold tally, then, first counting to ten in your head to milk your time as Maze Master to the very end, reveal the silver total with your most unnecessarily dramatic of deliveries.

Commiserate or celebrate with the team. No. Wait. Only celebrate with the team. Together you've recreated the magic, mayhem and mischief of the maze in your very own home. Regardless of the outcome, that's surely worth celebrating, isn't it?

LET THE GAMES BEGIN!

215

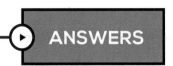
Page 36: THE EIGHTH CUBE
SOLUTION = B

Page 40: CRYSTAL CROSS-THROUGH
There are multiple solutions for this game but the below is just one example.

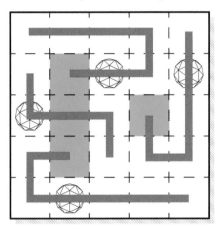

Page 49: SLIDING PLANKS

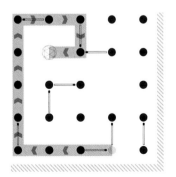

Page 52: AZTEC RIDDLES

1) 765 (3 + 6 + 12 + 24 + 48 + 96 + 192 + 384).
2) 900 (400 green skulls + 50 red (terracotta) skulls = 450 fake skulls, and so there are also 450 real skulls).
3) Nine times (he has all food once for every letter in the word – so as 'sweetcorn' is nine letters long, he has it nine times a week).

Page 62: WORD YOU BELIEVE IT?

In the grid here, HOUSEHOLDERS takes you from the arrow to Key #1, STEGOSAURUS gets you to Key #2, SURFING leads you to the box, and GINGERBREAD gets you to the out arrow.

Page 76: ROMAN NUMERALS

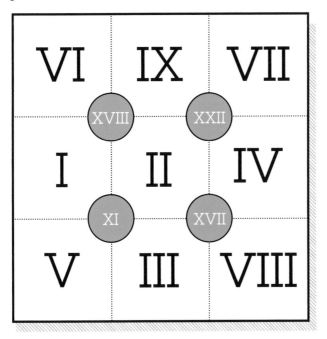

Page 90: ANAGRAM MAZE

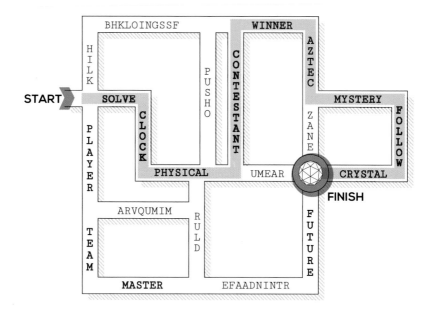

Page 96: THE KNIGHT'S RIDDLES

1) 5 (a cygnet is a baby swan so you count cygnet and swan as one. And obviously plums, marrows, crust and roses aren't birds).

2) Tristram the Trustworthy is far and away the cheapest option. His 2400 groats for 8 ships = just 300 groats for 1 ship, while Reginald the Reliable's 7800 groats for 13 ships = 600 groats for 1 ship, and Penelope the Prudent's 1300 for 2 ships = 650 groats for 1 ship.

3) 1/125 (each arrow has a one-in-five (1/5) chance of hitting the bull's-eye and to multiply fractions you multiply the ones on top – the numerators – in this case 1 x 1 x 1 = 1 and put that over the multiplication of the bottom ones – the denominators – in this case, 5 x 5 x 5 = 125).

Page 100: SYNONYM DOMINOES

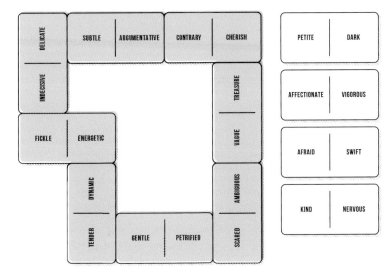

PETITE	DARK	
AFFECTIONATE	VIGOROUS	
AFRAID	SWIFT	
KIND	NERVOUS	

Page 102: MEET YOUR MATCH

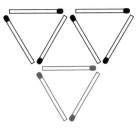

Page 106: CHAIN OF FOOLS

GAME 1

DOLLY	BIRD	HOUSE	PLANT	POT	SHOT	GUN	DOG	EAR

GAME 2

TURTLE	DOVE	TAIL	LIGHT	HOUSE	FLY	PAPER	BOY	COT

Page 118: SET THE CLOCKS

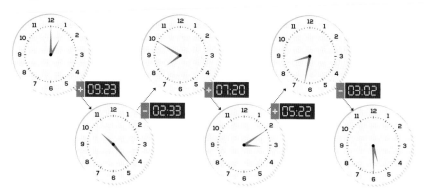

Page 140: INDUSTRIAL RIDDLES

1) 11 (11 x 8 = 88, 11 x 4 = 44).

2) 13 (2 x ½ day of power = one day of power a week, and two days to make a car means two weeks to be sure to have enough power to make one. This means it's an average of one car every two weeks. There are 26 weeks in half a year, and so 13 fortnights).

3) Three – it could be a triangular tower with a north side, an east side (which she looks out of twice), and (on the hypotenuse) a south-west side.

Page 146: WORD SHAPES

J	I	V	E
A	N	X	R
B	O	N	Y
L	E	L	Y

L	I	O	M
L	K	N	A
A	B	T	Z
T	E	L	E

N	E	G	I
P	R	D	F
O	S	T	T
B	A	B	Y

L	K	I	S
A	T	E	S
Z	R	U	E
Y	L	A	C

Page 148: CONNECT THE PAIRS

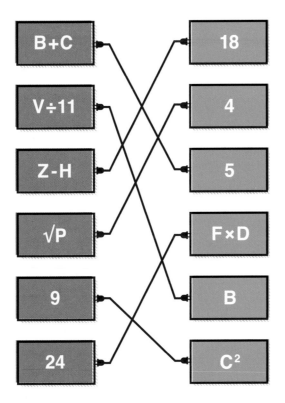

Page 174: JARHEAD RIDDLES

1) Thursday – which is named after Thor
2) A snake
3) A cricket
4) Tea
5) An eye
6) The Houses of Parliament and Big Ben

ACKNOWLEDGEMENTS

First and foremost, thank you to Malcolm Heyworth, David G. Croft, James Dillon and Richard O'Brien. Together you created a show that defined a generation and inspired so many of us to try to think as ambitiously and mischievously as you.

Thank you to Ed Tudor-Pole, Stephen Merchant and Richard Ayoade, the uniquely talented and magnificent maze masters who have each introduced new audiences to this remarkable world of adventure.

A massive thank you to everyone at Channel 4, who have supported us every step of the way in trying to start the fans again. Especially to Tom Beck, who always matched our passion and commitment and calmly managed my various meltdowns along the way.

Thank you to the gang at Little Lion, who are the masters of their own magnificent mazes. We're here because of your audacious ideas and your remarkable dedication, skill and talent in realising them.

Thank you to Sarah, Grace and the team at Headline for believing in this crazy idea for a book. Thank you also for not flinching when you discovered that it involved a disproportionate amount of string, sticky tape and ping-pong balls.

Thank you to the incredible team at Fizz and RDF, who made this all possible. Peter, Tammy, Sam, Jane ... there's 137 supremely talented production team and crew who all worked wonders. And, of course, to our dear leader who inspires us to care (perhaps too much?) about all we do – Jim Allen, you are the most belligerent and brilliant man I know.

Thank you to Anna, Chris, Meral and Toby. What an adventure we've been on together this past year. It's been so much fun making it last that little bit longer by working on this book with you. I'm sure you'll all agree my games were the best ones ...?

Thank you to Ellis and Eva, two people who remind me how important being silly is every day. Never lose that mischief please. Lastly, a much needed thank you to Claire for, well, everything. Being able to share all these adventures with you is the best bit. Also, sorry, I may still be going on about *The Crystal Maze* for some time yet.

Neale Simpson

PICTURE CREDITS